Discovering Food and Nutrition

Sixth Edition

Helen Kowtaluk

Glencoe McGraw-Hill

New York, New York   Columbus, Ohio   Woodland Hills, California   Peoria, Illinois

Brand Name Disclaimer:

Publisher does not necessarily recommend or endorse any particular company or brand name product that may be discussed or pictured in this text. Brand name products are used because they are readily available, likely to be known to the reader, and their use may aid in the understanding of the text. Publisher recognizes other brand name or generic products may be substituted and work as well or better than those featured in the text.

Glencoe/McGraw-Hill

A Division of The McGraw·Hill Companies

Copyright © 2001 by Glencoe/McGraw-Hill. Previous copyrights 1997, 1995, 1992, 1982, 1978 by Helen Kowtaluk. All rights reserved. Except as permitted under the United States Copyright Act, no part of this publication may be reproduced or distributed in any form or by any means, or stored in a database or retrieval system, without prior written permission of the publisher.

Send all inquiries to:

Glencoe/McGraw-Hill
3008 W. Willow Knolls Drive
Peoria, Illinois 61614-1083

ISBN 0-02-647265-1

Printed in the United States of America

3 4 5 6 7 8 9 10   003   06 05 04 03 02 01

NUTRITION CONSULTANT

Elizabeth Shipley Moses, M.S., RD
Falls Church, Virginia

RECIPE CONSULTANT

Mary Sutkus
Florissant, Missouri

TECHNICAL REVIEWER

Linda S. Eck, RD, FADA
Bernville, Pennsylvania

EDUCATIONAL CONSULTANTS AND REVIEWERS

Ann L. Branch, M.Ed.
Family and Consumer Sciences
   Teacher
Jefferson Senior High School
Alexandria, Minnesota

Gloria Casher
Family and Consumer Sciences
   Teacher
Blackburn Middle School
Jackson, Mississippi

Vikki Jackson
Family and Consumer Sciences
   Teacher
Kathleen Middle School
Lakeland, Florida

Wanda Renfroe
Family and Consumer Sciences
   Teacher
Upson-Lee Middle School
Thomaston, Georgia

Patricia A. Sánchez
Consumer and Family Studies Teacher
Preston Junior High School
Fort Collins, Colorado

Susan Takahashi
Former Consumer and Family Studies
   Teacher
Rocky Mountain High School
Fort Collins, Colorado

Connie Woody
Family and Consumer Sciences
   Teacher
Fred J. Carnage Middle School
Raleigh, North Carolina

CONTENTS

UNIT THREE DEVELOPING SKILLS

UNIT FOUR GOOD WORK HABITS

UNIT FIVE MEALTIME

UNIT SIX   LEARNING ABOUT FOODS

UNIT SEVEN CREATIVE COMBINATIONS

UNIT EIGHT BAKING

SPECIAL FEATURES

How to

Highlighted Topics

CHAPTER 1

THE ADVENTURE OF FOOD

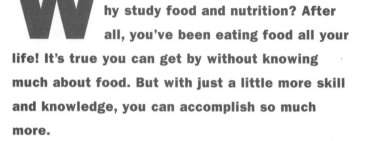

Discover...

★ *what you can gain from the study of food and nutrition.*

★ *how to set and reach goals.*

Key Terms
short-term goal
long-term goal
self-confidence

Why study food and nutrition? After all, you've been eating food all your life! It's true you can get by without knowing much about food. But with just a little more skill and knowledge, you can accomplish so much more.

FOOD FOR THOUGHT

What skills might you need to prepare food for a birthday party? To plan nutritious on-the-go meals?

WHAT CAN YOU GAIN FROM THIS COURSE?

You're about to start on a great adventure—the study of food and nutrition. What do you think you'll learn along the way?

LEARNING ABOUT NUTRITION

For one thing, you'll learn how to choose nutritious, flavorful snacks and meals. Your body needs a variety of foods to keep you healthy and active. Eating a variety of nutritious food every day can help you look and feel your best.

LEARNING TO PREPARE FOOD

What's your favorite food? Pizza? A burger? Stir-fried chicken? You can learn not just how to make these dishes yourself, but how to give them a special flavor all your own. That's the fun part of cooking.

Once you learn basic food preparation skills, you can use them all your life. You'll be able to:

◆ Cook for yourself.

◆ Plan and prepare meals for your family.

◆ Entertain friends.

◆ Contribute to community service.

◆ Perhaps even find a rewarding career in the food industry.

Preparing food can be fun—and so is sharing it with family and friends.

DEVELOPING SKILLS FOR LIFE

As you learn to choose and prepare food, you'll also practice other useful skills. Some of these are:

◆ Using basic math.

◆ Reading, writing, speaking, and listening.

◆ Working with others as a team.

◆ Making decisions.

◆ Planning and organizing your work.

◆ Thinking critically and asking questions.

As you work through this course, think about the skills you're developing.

SETTING AND REACHING GOALS

One way to get the most out of this course is to set goals. A goal is like a target you aim at. Setting goals helps you see what you want to accomplish.

LONG-TERM AND SHORT-TERM GOALS

Working toward a goal is like climbing a staircase. You don't get to the top in one jump. Instead, you take one step at a time. Suppose one of your goals is to learn how to prepare meals for your family. You might start with these steps:

◆ Learn how to read a recipe.

◆ Learn more about the types of food you'll be preparing.

◆ Practice your skills in the kitchen.

The small steps you take along the way are called **short-term goals.** A short-term goal is a task that can be accomplished in the near future. It helps you move toward your **long-term goal**, or what you want to accomplish further in the future.

Why are short-term goals important? Every step you take, no matter how small, proves that you can be successful. As a result, you gain self-confidence. **Self-confidence** means your belief in your ability to succeed. This book will help you learn one step at a time.

Goals are reached one step at a time.

Try It!

Setting Personal Goals

Think about what you most want to learn from this course. (Look at the Table of Contents for ideas.) Write down your specific goals.

★ In what ways might writing down your goals help you?

★ What steps can you take to move toward your goals?

STICK WITH IT

Learning any new skill takes time and practice. Don't be discouraged if the foods you make don't look like the pictures you see in magazines and cookbooks. Keep in mind that you're just learning.

One way to measure your progress is to ask yourself:

◆ Am I giving my best effort?

◆ Am I getting closer to my goal?

◆ Have I learned from my mistakes?

If the answers are "yes," you can be proud of yourself.

Success! Preparing food is an accomplishment to be proud of. The results are tasty, too!

Understanding Key Ideas

1. Explain why choosing nutritious snacks and meals is important.
2. How can food preparation skills help you throughout your life? Give three examples of other skills you'll practice as you learn about food.
3. What is the difference between a short-term goal and a long-term goal? How are the two related?
4. Explain what self-confidence is. Give an example of when you have felt self-confident.

Applying Knowledge and Skills

◆ **Communication:** Develop a brochure to tell other students about the benefits of taking this course. You may use a computer or other available resources.

◆ **Identifying Goals:** Describe one long-term goal you have for learning about food and nutrition. What short-term goals will help you reach your long-term goal? Illustrate your goals on paper in the form of a staircase of goals.

Exploring Further

◆ **Teamwork:** Assume that you are the team leader for your foods lab group. Your job is to give advice to the other students on how to be a good team member. What five teamwork strategies might you suggest to them?

The Adventure of Food 13

MANAGING YOUR RESOURCES

A resource is something you can use to help you meet your goals. Using resources wisely to meet your goals is called *management*. In this book, you'll discover how to manage your resources as part of good nutrition and food preparation.

Discover...

★ types of resources.

★ how to use your resources wisely.

★ steps in making good decisions.

Key Terms
resource
management
evaluate

FOOD FOR THOUGHT

Think about how you prepare and eat food every day. What resources do you use? How well do you manage those resources?

WHAT ARE YOUR RESOURCES?

You have many different resources:

Personal resources include your time, energy, knowledge, skills, and imagination. Although you can't always see or touch them, personal resources can help you accomplish a great deal.

Material resources include possessions such as tools, money, and food. Food can be one of the most important resources in helping you stay healthy. Well-prepared, flavorful food also brings enjoyment.

Social resources come from other people. Your family and friends provide love, companionship, and support. They also have skills and knowledge that you can draw on. Communities offer resources, too, such as hospitals, libraries, parks, and restaurants. What others can you think of?

Natural resources are materials provided by nature. Life depends on natural resources—clean air to breathe, water to drink, and soil to grow food. Natural resources also help provide many conveniences. For example, fuel is used to run cars, appliances, and heating systems.

USING RESOURCES WISELY

Resources can be very helpful, but they must be used wisely. Different situations call for different ways to manage resources.

INCREASING RESOURCES

You can increase the supply of some resources—especially personal resources. You can add to your knowledge and skills by reading a book or taking a class. Eating right and staying healthy can give you more energy to get things done.

CONSERVING RESOURCES

Some resources can't easily be increased. Conserving means using resources carefully instead of wasting them. For instance, you may have only a certain amount of money for the week. To make it last, you spend it on what's most important to you.

Conservation is especially important for natural resources. Many of them can't be renewed— once they are used up, they're gone forever. Chapter 23 discusses ways to conserve natural resources.

Cleaning up a park is a way to share in the care of a community resource.

SUBSTITUTING RESOURCES

Another way to manage resources is to substitute one for another. Suppose you don't have time to prepare the lunch you had planned. What other resources could you substitute for time? You could:

◆ Eat at a restaurant (using money and a community resource).

◆ Ask a friend or family member to help you prepare the meal.

◆ Use your imagination and the food you have on hand to plan a quicker meal.

MAKING DECISIONS

As part of managing resources, you'll often have to make decisions. You can make decisions with more confidence if you follow these steps:

1. **Identify the decision.** Unless you know exactly what you're trying to do, it's hard to decide how to do it. For example: "I'm always running out of money for snacks. How can I keep that from happening?"

2. **Consider your resources.** Since money is in short supply, what other resources could help you?

3. **Think of options.** You might come up with these ideas:

   • Cut back on other expenses.
   • Make snacks at home and bring them to school.

4. **Compare the options.** What are the good and bad points of each? How will other people be affected? You may need to discuss your ideas with them. For instance, if you're thinking of bringing snacks from home, talk to the family members who do the food shopping.

5. **Choose the best plan.** You might decide to add nutritious snacks to your family's weekly shopping list.

6. **Put your plan into action.** Many people are good at planning, but never carry out their plans. Take responsibility for making the snacks and packing them.

7. **Evaluate the results.** To **evaluate** means to judge how well you reached your goal. When you've carried out your plan, ask yourself whether you're happy with the results. How can you improve the plan?

CHAPTER 2 REVIEW

Understanding Key Ideas

1. How is management related to resources?
2. What type of resource is food? What goals can it help you reach?
3. Why is it important to conserve natural resources?
4. What is the first step in the decision-making process? What is the last step?

Applying Knowledge and Skills

◆ **Using Resources:** Describe how you can use one of your personal resources in food preparation.

◆ **Making Decisions:** Identify a specific convenience food item, such as a frozen pizza or a cake mix. Then find a recipe for a similar homemade version. Use the decision-making process to decide which you'd rather prepare and eat. (You may need to research some information, such as the cost of each option.) Explain what you thought about at each step of the process.

Exploring Further

◆ **Research:** Using the library or the Internet, learn about ways you can conserve natural resources at home. Report to the class.

◆ **Writing a Story:** Jeremy and Kendra have been given $10 by their parents for food on Friday evening. Write a story showing how Jeremy and Kendra use good management in this situation.

CHAPTER 3

WHAT ABOUT CAREERS?

Today is a starting point for your future. Have you thought about the kind of career you want? A *career* is the work you choose to do for a long period or in a specific field.

FOOD FOR THOUGHT

Your career should involve something you enjoy. Think about your interests and hobbies. Could you base a career on any of them?

PREPARING FOR THE WORLD OF WORK

You may not be able to decide now on the kind of career you want. But you can work on becoming the kind of person who will have a successful career. No matter what kind of career you choose, all employers look for certain abilities. You can start now to develop these abilities. They're the foundation for a successful career.

Be responsible. Good employees take responsibility for their actions. When they are given an assignment, they follow through on it. When they make a mistake—as everyone does at times—they admit it and learn from it.

Be willing to learn. The learning process will continue throughout your lifetime. No matter where you work, you'll need to keep up to date on new information, products, methods, systems, and technology.

Develop good communication skills. These skills are essential in many situations—such as listening to customers, discussing ideas with coworkers, reading directions, and writing reports.

Know basic math skills. Most jobs require at least basic math. Even if you use a calculator or computer, basic math principles help you understand what to do.

Gain computer skills. Computers are used in a wide variety of jobs. For instance, the servers in many restaurants use computers to send customers' food orders to the kitchen.

Develop thinking skills. Every job requires that you think clearly and make good decisions. Workers who can find creative solutions to problems are more likely to be successful.

Learn teamwork. In most jobs, people work together to achieve a specific goal. Employers are impressed with people who work well on a team.

Learn to manage resources. Good workers manage their time and accomplish tasks on schedule. Some jobs also involve managing money, materials, or other workers.

WHERE TO START?

How can you develop all these skills and qualities? You have many opportunities right now. You can...

◆ Make a commitment to your school studies.

◆ Spend time reading and learning on your own.

◆ Look for ways to practice communication skills, teamwork, management, and responsibility at home.

What skills would be useful in this workplace situation?

◆ Take part in school clubs or committees.

◆ Volunteer to help the community. You might clean up litter or read to the elderly, for example.

CHOOSING A CAREER

Working is a way to earn income, but it can also provide personal satisfaction and enjoyment. The key is to find a career that fits you— your talents and abilities, interests, personality, family life, and goals. A guidance counselor can help you find information about types of work that might suit you. You might also talk to people in different fields. Ask them what their job is like and how they prepared for it.

Within each career area there are different job levels. Many people start with an **entry-level job**, one that doesn't require experience or a college degree. With more training and education, you can move up to higher-paying jobs. You might even start your own business someday.

CAREERS IN THE FOOD INDUSTRY

If you're interested in food and nutrition, why not consider turning that interest into a career? Many jobs related to food and nutrition are available. Here's just a small sampling.

NUTRITION

Dietitians help people develop healthful eating habits. They teach individuals and families how to choose nutritious food and stay within their budget. They also evaluate food service systems in hospitals and nursing homes.

TEACHING

Perhaps teaching is for you. Food and nutrition teachers instruct students in nutrition principles, food preparation, and good consumer practices.

COMMUNICATION

If you like to work with words and pictures, you might enjoy writing about food, arranging and photographing food, or helping to create advertisements. These are just some of the ways you can combine an interest in food and nutrition with other interests and abilities.

RESEARCH

Some food specialists work as researchers. They may develop new products, test new chemicals to be added to food, or make new discoveries about nutrition. Researchers can work for government, colleges or universities, or private industry.

FOOD PRODUCTION

The food you eat begins with farming and fishing. Some farms grow grains, vegetables, or fruits. Others raise cattle, hogs, or poultry. There are even fish farms. Related career areas, such as farm equipment and animal health, provide other job opportunities.

FOOD PROCESSING

After food is grown, it's processed—made ready for sale. Food processors employ thousands of people with many opportunities for advancement. One important job is inspecting food for quality before it's packaged, canned, or frozen.

FOOD DISTRIBUTION AND MARKETING

After food is processed, it's stored in warehouses. From there it's sent to supermarkets and other stores. Along the way, many workers help transport and store the food.

Food marketing careers involve selling food. At supermarkets, you can find many entry-level jobs such as stocking shelves, working a cash register, or assisting customers with their bags.

Your goal might be to become a supermarket manager. The manager directs and coordinates all the activities of the supermarket.

FOOD SERVICE

Today many meals are purchased and eaten away from home. Those meals are provided by workers in the food service industry.

When you go to a restaurant, most of the workers you see are part of the customer service staff. They are responsible for bringing the food from the kitchen to the customer. They may wait on tables, take orders at a counter, or serve food in a cafeteria.

Many other people work behind the scenes. For example, managers and their assistants may plan menus, keep track of costs, order supplies, and supervise workers.

Of course, many jobs involve actually preparing food. If this interests you, you might start as a fast-food cook or a kitchen helper. With experience and training, you can move up to jobs that call for more skill and creativity. The most highly trained food service cooks are called chefs. Chefs prepare special dishes, develop original recipes, and manage the kitchen. Some chefs own their own restaurants.

Not all food service takes place in restaurants. Many food service workers are employed by hospitals, schools, and nursing homes. Others help supply food to vending machines, airlines, and company cafeterias. Caterers plan and prepare food for banquets and parties.

Understanding Key Ideas

1. Identify three skills that can lead to success in any career. Why is each important?
2. How can you develop career skills at school, at home, and in your community?
3. What resources can help you choose a career?
4. What types of workers helped make it possible for you to eat your most recent meal? Identify at least four jobs, each in a different career area.

Applying Knowledge and Skills

◆ **Analyze Your Strengths:** Select a favorite career from this chapter. Why does it interest you? Describe qualities and abilities you have that would make you successful.

◆ **Restaurant Manager:** Imagine you're opening a new restaurant. Identify three positions for which you'd need to hire workers. For each position, explain which of the personal qualities and skills described in this chapter would be most important and why.

Exploring Further

◆ **Ad Analysis:** Check the classified ads in a local newspaper. What types of food-related jobs are available? Use charts or graphs to classify them in different ways, such as entry-level or advanced.

◆ **Career Research:** Learn more about a food-related career and write a report about it. Include job description, education and training requirements, salary information, and job outlook.

WELLNESS—YOUR GOAL FOR LIFE

Discover...

★ *the meaning of wellness.*

★ *healthy habits that lead to wellness.*

Key Terms
wellness
nutrients
aerobic
stress

Many people today are emphasizing wellness. *Wellness* means taking steps toward your own good health—physical, emotional, and mental.

FOOD FOR THOUGHT

In what ways do you practice wellness? What additional steps can you take to improve your health?

CHOOSE NUTRITIOUS FOOD

One way to increase your health and wellness is to choose food carefully. Food provides the body with nutrients. **Nutrients** are chemicals in food that the body needs to work properly. When you choose nutritious foods, you give your body the nutrients it needs. This helps you to:

◆ Look and feel your best.

◆ Have energy to last throughout the day.

◆ Handle the stress of everyday living.

As you read further in this book, you'll discover how to choose nutritious food for good health.

ACCEPT YOUR OWN BODY SHAPE

People come in all sorts of shapes and sizes—tall, short, stocky, thin. Some have narrow shoulders and big hips. Others have a large waistline and narrow hips. Part of wellness is realizing that there's nothing wrong with any of these shapes.

Does that surprise you? Chances are, you're used to thinking that a tall, slim body is the "ideal" shape. Advertisements, movies, and fashions all promote it. The truth is, very few people in the world will ever look like a fashion model or a superstar athlete—and that's okay. People of all shapes and sizes can be happy and healthy.

In fact, trying to achieve an "ideal" body shape isn't a good idea. Why? You were born with a tendency toward a certain body shape—one that's all your own. You can change your body to some degree, but you can't change its shape completely. Trying to achieve an impossible body can make you feel discouraged. It may also lead to poor eating and activity habits that can endanger your health.

Why feel bad about not looking like someone else? Be glad you're you!

Perhaps someday, the notion that there's an "ideal" body shape will disappear. Meanwhile, accept the body you have. Work on keeping it healthy and fit, but base your goals on what's right for you.

Remember, it's the total person that counts. Whatever your shape and size, you have something worthwhile to offer the world.

STAY PHYSICALLY ACTIVE

People of all ages and abilities benefit from being active. Physical activity:

◆ Firms and tones your muscles, including the heart.

◆ Helps build strong bones.

◆ Reduces the risk of many health problems.

◆ Can help you sleep better at night and feel more alert during the day.

◆ Helps improve physical abilities such as strength, speed, and balance.

◆ Can even improve your mood and the way you feel about yourself.

To be active, just look for ways to get moving. Dancing is an example of physical activity. So is walking the dog, climbing the stairs at school, and raking leaves. You might enjoy playing a sport or going to an exercise class with your friends.

For the most benefit, aim for at least 30 minutes of moderate physical activity on most or all days. "Moderate" physical activity means a medium amount of effort. Brisk walking is an example. You can add up shorter sessions of activity to reach your goal of 30 minutes. If you choose more vigorous activities, such as running, 15 to 20 minutes a day, three days a week, can be enough.

If you're already active, keep it up! If you're not, increase your activity gradually. Give your body time to get used to it. Always use the proper safety equipment, such as a helmet when you ride a bike.

Different types of physical activity benefit you in different ways. Make sure your wellness plan includes physical activities that help improve:

Strength. When you force your muscles to work hard at pushing or pulling, they become stronger. Ways to build strength include push-ups, chin-ups, and using strength-building machines.

Flexibility. Gentle stretching helps make your muscles and joints more flexible. Stretching muscles correctly helps prevent injury from other activities.

Endurance. Endurance is your ability to continue a physical activity for a long time. Activities such as brisk walking, climbing stairs, dancing, and biking build endurance in two ways. First, they train your muscles to work longer before tiring. Second, they are **aerobic** (uh-ROE-bik) activities. This means they help the body use and take in more oxygen than it normally does. As a result, the heart and lungs work more efficiently.

When you make physical activity a habit, it will benefit you now and for the rest of your life. Best of all, it's fun!

GET PLENTY OF SLEEP

Sleep is essential to good health. When you sleep, your body gets rid of waste products that your muscles have collected during the day. It mends and builds new cells. It also builds up a fresh supply of energy for the next day's activities.

Teens often need more sleep than others because their bodies are growing and changing. If you're getting enough sleep, you wake up easily in the morning and feel alert all day.

LEARN TO HANDLE STRESS

Have you ever felt nervous or tense before a test, during a competition, or when meeting someone new? If so, you were feeling stress. **Stress** is emotional and physical tension. It's caused by events in your life and the way you react to them.

Stress is not necessarily bad. It can give you the energy to face a challenge and do your best. However, if stress gets out of control, it can affect your body and your health. For example, being angry or upset can make it hard to sleep and to digest food.

Stress can't be avoided—it's part of life. The secret is to learn to react positively to stressful situations. Here are some suggestions:

Give yourself a break. Take time out every day for rest and recreation. Visit with a friend, go to a movie, or spend time on a hobby.

A relaxing hobby can be a great way to reduce stress. How do you handle the stress in your life?

Accept what you can't control. Instead of becoming angry when you have to wait in line, relax and accept the situation. Do something constructive while you wait.

Look on the bright side. Look for the good in people and situations. Develop a sense of humor—laughter helps relieve tension.

Give of yourself. Help someone or work for a cause. It will not only benefit others, but take your mind off your own problems and give you a sense of accomplishment.

Keep physically fit. Good health makes you feel good and helps you to cope with life situations more easily.

Work off your tensions. Any kind of physical activity—such as skating, taking a walk, or cleaning out your closet—can help.

Break large tasks into small steps. Handle just one step at a time. You'll get more done with less tension.

Talk things over. The more you worry about a problem, the bigger it gets. Talking it over with someone you trust can bring it back down to size.

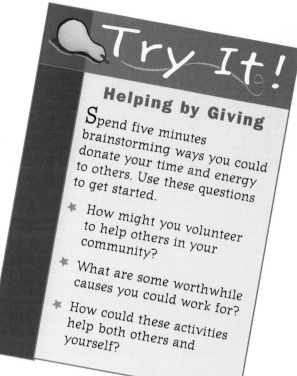

Try It!

Helping by Giving

Spend five minutes brainstorming ways you could donate your time and energy to others. Use these questions to get started.

* How might you volunteer to help others in your community?

* What are some worthwhile causes you could work for?

* How could these activities help both others and yourself?

AVOID HARMFUL SUBSTANCES

One of the major responsibilities of your wellness program is to avoid using harmful substances. These include:

Tobacco. Using tobacco increases the risk of developing a serious disease later in life. Smoking has been linked to cancer, heart disease, lung disease, and other health problems. Chewing tobacco has been linked to cancer of the mouth.

Alcohol. Alcohol is a drug that can affect your judgment and reactions. Heavy use can cause liver damage and death. Drinking and driving is a major cause of auto accidents. Innocent victims are often injured or killed.

Other drugs. Drugs such as marijuana and cocaine can damage your health permanently and even lead to death.

Misused medicines. What about over-the-counter medicines or drugs a physician prescribes? These can be helpful if taken according to directions. If used incorrectly, they can be dangerous.

Other harmful substances. Almost any substance may be harmful if used for something other than its intended purpose. For example, inhaling spray from aerosol cans is dangerous and can be fatal.

Alcohol and other harmful substances claim many victims each year. How can these tragedies be avoided?

Alcohol, tobacco, and other drugs won't make you popular or solve your problems for you. They can only create more problems—not just for the user, but for society. Drugs interfere with work and school and can tear families apart. Many drugs are illegal.

When it comes to harmful substances, you have the power to choose. No one can force you to take them. You have the power to say "NO" to drugs.

YOUR PERSONAL WELLNESS PROGRAM

Right now is a good time to put a wellness plan into action. It's easier to develop good habits while you're young than to try to change them when you're older.

Before you begin, you may want to discuss your ideas with a health professional. He or she can give you advice about nutrition, physical activity, and other parts of your plan.

Remember, you can make choices that lead to wellness. It's never too early to begin planning for good health for the rest of your life!

You can't control every aspect of your health. But practicing wellness can help you live a long, healthy life.

CHAPTER 4 REVIEW

Understanding Key Ideas

1. What does the term *wellness* mean?
2. What are six basic wellness habits that can improve health?
3. Why can it be harmful to try to look like a movie star or professional athlete?
4. How can physical activity improve your mental and emotional health?
5. What problems can be caused by alcohol use?

Applying Knowledge and Skills

◆ **Physical Activity Plan:** Make a weekly plan showing how you can fit in 30 minutes of moderate physical activity each day.

◆ **Stress Tips:** Give three examples of stressful situations that many teens face. What suggestions for handling stress would be particularly useful in those situations? Why?

Exploring Further

◆ **Advertising Evaluation:** Develop a collage showing positive and negative effects advertising has on teens' wellness habits.

MEET THE NUTRIENTS

Discover...

★ how nutrients work together in the body.

★ what each type of nutrient does for you.

★ how to get the nutrients you need.

Key Terms
carbohydrates
fiber
cholesterol
proteins
amino acids
osteoporosis

Food provides nutrients—chemicals the body needs to work properly. But what are the different nutrients? What foods are they found in? What does your body do with them? This chapter will help you find out.

FOOD FOR THOUGHT

How many nutrients can you name? Do you know what each one does?

NUTRIENT TEAMWORK

Think of a football or soccer team. Each player has a specific job to do as part of the teamwork. If one of the players is missing or doesn't do the job, the team can't play well.

Nutrients also work as teams. Each nutrient has certain jobs to do in the body. One nutrient can't work a miracle. But if a nutrient is missing, it can keep the rest of the team from working well.

The nutrients can be grouped into six basic types. These are the six members of the nutrient team:

◆ Carbohydrates

◆ Water

◆ Proteins

◆ Vitamins

◆ Fats

◆ Minerals

HOW THE BODY USES NUTRIENTS

The body uses nutrients for three main purposes:

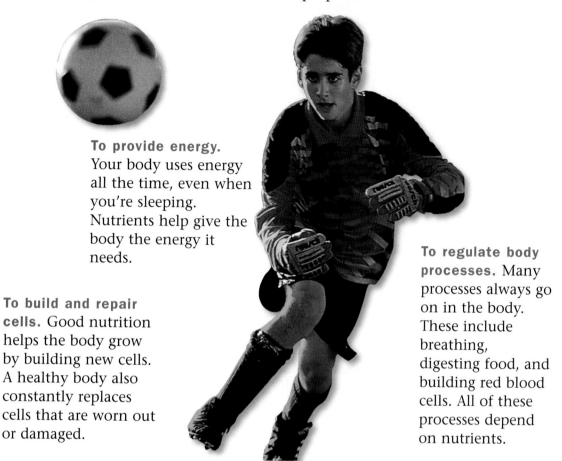

To provide energy. Your body uses energy all the time, even when you're sleeping. Nutrients help give the body the energy it needs.

To build and repair cells. Good nutrition helps the body grow by building new cells. A healthy body also constantly replaces cells that are worn out or damaged.

To regulate body processes. Many processes always go on in the body. These include breathing, digesting food, and building red blood cells. All of these processes depend on nutrients.

When you eat, your body breaks down food into liquid through the process known as digestion. As food is digested, nutrients are absorbed into the blood. The blood carries the nutrients to where they're needed in the body. Now take a closer look at where each type of nutrient comes from and what jobs it performs in your body.

CARBOHYDRATES

Carbohydrates (car-bo-HIGH-drates) are nutrients made of carbon, hydrogen, and oxygen. They come mostly from plant foods, such as grains, dry beans and peas, vegetables, and fruits.

What do carbohydrates do for you?

◆ They're your body's main source of energy.

◆ If you don't eat enough carbohydrates, your body uses proteins and fats for energy. Then the proteins and fats can't do their regular jobs.

TYPES OF CARBOHYDRATES

Carbohydrates can be divided into two groups:

Complex carbohydrates are starches. For good health, eat plenty of foods high in complex carbohydrates:

Carbohydrates give your body the energy it needs for all your activities.

◆ Dry beans, dry peas, and lentils.

◆ Starchy vegetables, such as potatoes, corn, and green peas.

◆ Rice, grits, pasta, oatmeal, and cornmeal.

◆ Breads and cereals.

These foods supply not only carbohydrates but also other nutrients, such as proteins, vitamins, and minerals.

Simple carbohydrates are sugars. They're a natural part of some foods, such as fruits, vegetables, and milk. Sugars can be removed from their natural sources, then added to other foods to sweeten them. Candy, soft drinks, cookies, jams, and jellies are examples of foods high in added sugar. For good health, limit the amount of food with added sugars.

FIBER

Grains, dry beans and peas, vegetables, and fruits contain fiber. **Fiber** refers to plant materials that your body can't digest completely. Fiber is needed for a healthy digestive system. It may also help reduce the risk of cancer and heart disease.

How much fiber do you need? If you are under age 18, just add 5 to your age. For example, if you're 13 years old, 13 + 5 = 18 grams of fiber each day.

FATS

Fats perform several useful jobs in the body:

◆ They supply chemicals called essential fatty acids. You need these for healthy skin, healthy cells, and other bodily functions.

◆ Fats transport certain vitamins.

◆ Fats keep food in your stomach longer so you don't feel hungry as quickly.

◆ Your body stores fat as a reserve supply of energy. This stored fat also insulates you from heat and cold and cushions vital organs. Your body makes this fat from any extra amounts of carbohydrates, proteins, and fats that you eat.

Some foods contain hidden fats.

What foods contain fats? Butter, margarine, and oils are all fats. Fats are also hidden in many foods, such as meat, fish, poultry, eggs, dairy products, nuts and seeds, baked goods, and fried foods.

Try It!

Finding Hidden Fats

Test foods for hidden fats. Use a large sheet of brown paper. Rub several foods hard against it. Label the spot for each food and let dry. See which foods leave an oily-looking spot behind. Some foods you might try are sliced apples, carrots, avocados, cheddar cheese, flour, sugar, several kinds of bread and crackers, and nuts.

★ Which foods contain fat?

★ How can you use what you have learned about these foods?

CHOLESTEROL

Cholesterol is a fat-like substance that helps the body carry out its many processes. Your body makes all the cholesterol it needs. It may also get cholesterol from food. Cholesterol is found only in foods from animal sources: meat, poultry, fish, egg yolks, and dairy products. It's not found in any foods from plant sources.

High levels of cholesterol in the bloodstream are linked with heart disease. For this reason, health experts advise eating less cholesterol in foods.

SATURATED AND UNSATURATED FATS

The level of cholesterol in the blood is also affected by the types and amounts of fat that are eaten.

Saturated fats are usually solid at room temperature. They tend to raise the amount of cholesterol in the blood. Saturated fats are present in all animal foods and in the tropical oils: coconut, palm and palm kernel. Of all the animal meats, fish tends to have the least amount of saturated fat.

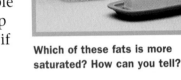

Unsaturated fats are usually liquid at room temperature. They're found mainly in vegetable oils, except the tropical oils. They tend to help lower the amount of cholesterol in the blood if they're eaten instead of saturated fat.

Which of these fats is more saturated? How can you tell?

Hydrogenated oil is oil that has been turned into a more solid fat. In the process, it becomes more saturated. Margarine is made from hydrogenated oil.

Most people eat much more fat than the small amount they need. Health experts advise people to eat less fat of any kind. The fat that's eaten should be mainly unsaturated.

PROTEINS

Proteins (PRO-teens) are substances that the body uses to build new cells and repair injured ones. They're necessary for growth and to help you fight off disease.

Proteins are made up of **amino acids.** So far, 22 amino acids have been discovered. Of these, the body can make 13. The other 9 are called essential amino acids because the body must get them from food.

You can think of amino acids as building blocks. They combine in different ways to make different kinds of protein. Depending on the amino acids they contain, foods are said to provide *complete protein* or *incomplete protein*. To learn more about these two types of protein, see the next page.

Like members of a sports team, nutrients work together. How do amino acids work together in your body?

Complete and Incomplete Proteins

Proteins in food are either incomplete or complete, depending on the kind of amino acids they contain. Think of the building blocks below as amino acids.

Complete proteins contain all the essential amino acids in the right amounts. Foods from animal sources, such as meat, poultry, fish, eggs, and dairy products, provide complete proteins.

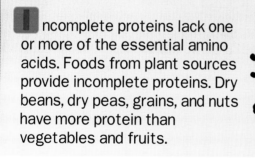

Incomplete proteins lack one or more of the essential amino acids. Foods from plant sources provide incomplete proteins. Dry beans, dry peas, grains, and nuts have more protein than vegetables and fruits.

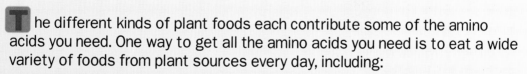

The different kinds of plant foods each contribute some of the amino acids you need. One way to get all the amino acids you need is to eat a wide variety of foods from plant sources every day, including:

- Cooked dry beans, peas, or lentils.
- Assorted grain products, vegetables, and fruits.
- Smaller amounts of nuts and seeds.

WATER

Water is essential for life. It's a part of all the cells in your body. The human body can live a long time without other nutrients, but only a few days without water.

Health experts recommend drinking 4 to 6 glasses of water a day. This doesn't include beverages that contain water, such as fruit juice. The water you drink will replace the amount that you lose every day through breathing, perspiration, and waste.

VITAMINS

Vitamins are chemical mixtures found in many types of foods. Vitamins themselves don't provide energy or become part of the body. Instead, think of vitamins as being helpers to the other nutrients. Without vitamins, your body can't work properly.

There are two basic types of vitamins: fat-soluble and water-soluble.

Fat-soluble vitamins can mix only with fat. Your body stores any extra fat-soluble vitamins you eat in the liver. If the amount stored gets very high, it can harm your body. The fat-soluble vitamins are vitamins A, D, E, and K.

FAT-SOLUBLE VITAMINS

Vitamins and What They Do	Some Food Sources
Vitamin A Helps bones, teeth, skin, and hair stay healthy Needed for good night vision	• Dairy products • Egg yolk • Liver • Yellow-orange and dark green fruits and vegetables (These contain beta carotene, which the body turns into vitamin A)
Vitamin D Helps build strong bones and teeth	• Salmon • Fortified milk • Egg yolk
Vitamin E Helps form red blood cells Helps protect cells from damage by oxygen	• Whole grain breads and cereals • Dark green, leafy vegetables • Dry beans and peas • Nuts and seeds • Vegetable oils
Vitamin K Needed for normal blood clotting	• Dark green, leafy vegetables • Cauliflower • Cabbage • Egg yolks

Water-soluble vitamins can mix only with water. Most can't be stored by the body, so be sure you eat foods containing these vitamins every day. The water-soluble vitamins include the B vitamins and vitamin C.

WATER-SOLUBLE VITAMINS	
Vitamins and What They Do	**Some Food Sources**
Vitamin C Helps build and maintain a healthy body Helps fight infection and heal wounds	• Many fruits and vegetables
B vitamins (Thiamin, riboflavin, niacin, B_6, B_{12}, folate, pantothenic acid, and biotin) Help the body get energy from carbohydrates Help keep nerves and muscles healthy	• Grain products • Dry beans and peas • Dark green, leafy vegetables • Dairy products • Meat, poultry, fish • Eggs

MINERALS

Your body uses minerals for many processes. The minerals also become a part of the human body—cells, fluid, muscles, and bones.

Minerals are a good illustration of nutrient teamwork. For example, calcium and phosphorus work together, along with vitamins D and A, to help build strong bones and teeth.

Building healthy habits now can help your bones stay strong when you're older.

MINERALS

Minerals and What They Do	Some Food Sources
Calcium Helps build strong bones and teeth Helps your heart, muscles, and nerves work properly	• Dairy products • Calcium-fortified orange juice • Canned fish eaten with the bones • Tofu (soybean curd) • Dark green, leafy vegetables
Phosphorus Helps build strong bones and teeth Helps your body get energy from food	• Meat, poultry, fish • Dry beans and peas • Dairy products • Grain products • Eggs
Iron Helps red blood cells carry oxygen	• Meat, fish, shellfish • Egg yolk • Dark green, leafy vegetables • Dry beans and peas • Grain products • Dried fruits
Potassium Helps keep the water balance in your body Needed for a normal heartbeat	• Fruits and vegetables • Dry beans and peas • Meat, poultry, fish • Dairy products
Sodium Helps keep the water balance in your body	• Many foods • Salt
Zinc Helps the body make proteins Helps heal wounds	• Meat, poultry, fish • Dry beans and peas • Whole grains • Dairy products • Eggs

Some of the other minerals you need:

Copper	Iodine (EYE-uh-dine)
Magnesium (mag-NEE-zee-um)	Manganese (MANG-guh-neez)
Selenium (suh-LEE-nee-um)	Chromium (KROH-me-yum)

Building Strong Bones for Life

Your body is constantly removing and replacing the calcium stored in your bones. Before age 30 to 35, more calcium is added to the bones than is removed. The bones keep getting stronger and heavier.

After age 30 to 35, more calcium is taken away from the bones than is put back in. The bones begin to lose strength. If too much calcium is lost, the result is a condition called **osteoporosis** (AH-stee-oh-pour-OH-sis). The bones become so weak that they break very easily.

To help prevent osteoporosis, start building strong bones now!

- Choose plenty of foods rich in calcium, such as dairy products.

- Eat right to get the other bone-building nutrients you need. These include vitamin D, vitamin A, and phosphorus.

- Get plenty of exercise. Activities that make your body "carry its own weight," such as walking, strengthen your bones.

GETTING THE RIGHT AMOUNTS

The body needs a certain amount of each nutrient. Your nutrient needs depend on your age, how active you are, and whether you're male or female.

Researchers have developed lists showing how much of each nutrient people need. However, you don't need to memorize these lists or measure all the nutrients you get. If you eat a wide variety of nutritious foods each day, you should get all the nutrients your body needs. You'll learn more in later chapters.

What happens if you don't get enough of a nutrient? You can come up a little short once in a while without harm. However, if the shortage continues over a long period, your body can't work properly. You may develop poor health.

What if you get too much of a nutrient? That depends on the nutrient.

- The body gets rid of some extra vitamins and minerals as waste.

- Extra amounts of carbohydrates, proteins, or fats are turned into body fat.

Do these people all have the same nutrient needs? Why or why not?

- Getting too much of some nutrients can have harmful effects. Too much vitamin C, for instance, can cause diarrhea. Some vitamins and minerals build up in the body and can create health problems. A diet too high in fat increases your risk of certain diseases.

DO YOU NEED SUPPLEMENTS?

Many known nutrients are available as supplements. They are sold in the form of pills, powders, and liquids.

Health professionals may recommend supplements for specific reasons. For example, people who are allergic to milk may need to take a calcium supplement. Most people, however, don't need supplements.

If you're wondering about supplements, ask your physician or a registered dietitian for advice. Deciding on your own to take supplements isn't a good idea:

- You could harm your health rather than help it. High doses of some nutrients can be dangerous.

- Taking supplements that you don't need can be a waste of money. The body may just get rid of the extra amounts of nutrients.

Remember, eating a wide variety of nutritious food is your best source of nutrients. Supplements contain only known nutrients. Food contains *all* the nutrients—those people know about, and those that haven't been discovered yet.

NEW DISCOVERIES

It's taken decades to discover the known nutrients (over 40 of them). Researchers aren't finished yet. They're still looking for other nutrients and for new facts about known ones.

For example, beta carotene (BAY-tuh CARE-oh-teen) is found in yellow-orange and dark green fruits and vegetables. It's not a vitamin, but your body can use it to make vitamin A. At first, scientists thought that was its only function in the body. However, recent research suggests that beta carotene may help prevent some forms of cancer. More research is being done to find out.

Beta carotene is just one example of a phytochemical (FIE-toe-KEM-ih-kuhl). Phytochemicals are natural chemicals found in most fruits and vegetables. Evidence suggests that many different phytochemicals may possibly help prevent diseases. Perhaps one day some of these chemicals will be added to the list of nutrients.

Researchers are studying how the natural chemicals in plants may help protect against diseases such as cancer.

CHAPTER 5 REVIEW

Understanding Key Ideas

1. Is any nutrient more important than the others? Explain.
2. Which nutrient is your body's main source of energy?
3. Why do you need to eat some fats?
4. Where does your body get amino acids? What does it do with them?
5. What's the best way for most people to get the nutrients they need?

Applying Knowledge and Skills

◆ **Meal Analysis:** Write down the foods in a favorite meal. Based on what you've read in this chapter, what nutrients does each food provide? Are any nutrients missing? If so, what foods could fill the gap?

◆ **Bone Builders:** Make a list of foods and activities that help build strong bones. Use the information to design a brochure, poster, or web page aimed at teens.

Exploring Further

◆ **Critical Thinking:** Why do some people who don't need supplements take them anyway? Are their reasons valid? Explain your opinion.

◆ **Nutrient Research:** Find an article describing a recent scientific discovery about nutrients. Share it with the class.

ENERGY AND CALORIES

Key Terms
calories
nutrient density
basal metabolic rate

Your body uses energy in many ways. It's the fuel you need to walk and run, to recover from illness, to grow, even to stay alive.
Fueling the body isn't as simple as putting gasoline in a car. Your "fuel mixture"—the mixture of foods you choose to supply your energy needs—can affect your long-term health.

> **FOOD FOR THOUGHT**
>
> What "fuel mixture" are you giving your body? How well does it meet your energy needs?

WHAT ARE CALORIES?

Everyone talks about calories, but do you know what they really are? **Calories** are simply a unit of measure for energy. Just as inches measure length, calories measure energy supplied by food and energy used by the body.

Calories aren't an "ingredient" in food. If someone asks "How many calories are in this?" they really mean "How much energy does this food provide?" Also keep in mind that one calorie is the same amount of energy whether it comes from a hamburger, a slice of cake, a vegetable, or candy.

THE ENERGY IN FOOD

The energy in food comes from just three nutrients: carbohydrates, proteins, and fats. Water, vitamins, minerals, and fiber have no calories.

Fats have more than twice as many calories as the same amount of proteins and carbohydrates, as shown in this chart:

ENERGY FROM NUTRIENTS	
Nutrient	Calories
1 gram pure carbohydrate	4
1 gram pure protein	4
1 gram pure fat	9

Since foods are made up of different types and amounts of nutrients, they supply different amounts of energy. For example, margarine is made up mostly of fats. It's much higher in calories than the same amount of applesauce, which is made up mostly of water.

FINDING CALORIE INFORMATION

How can you find out how many calories of energy a food supplies? The nutrition label on the food package gives you that information. (You can read more about nutrition labels in Chapter 12.) In addition, many recipes tell how many calories there are in a serving.

You can also get the information from calorie charts. A calorie chart lists foods and gives the number of calories for a certain size serving. A sample of a calorie chart appears below.

Pay attention to the serving size. The serving size shown in the label, recipe, or calorie chart may be smaller than the amount you usually eat. If so, remember that your larger serving has more calories.

CALORIE CHART		
Food	Serving Size	Calories
Apple	1 medium	80
Apple pie	1/6 of 9-inch pie	405
Ground beef, lean, broiled	3 oz.	230
Cheeseburger, fast food	1 sandwich (1 bun, 3 oz. meat, 1 slice cheese)	445

BALANCING CARBOHYDRATES, FATS, AND PROTEINS

As you read earlier, the "fuel mixture" you choose affects your long-term health. Why? Because in addition to energy alone, you need the right balance of nutrients.

Health experts say that eating too much fat can increase the risk of certain health problems, such as heart disease and cancer. Yet fat is an important nutrient. What does "too much fat" mean? How much of your food energy should come from fats compared to proteins and carbohydrates? Based on research findings so far, health experts have come up with some guidelines. They say that of all the energy (calories) you take in:

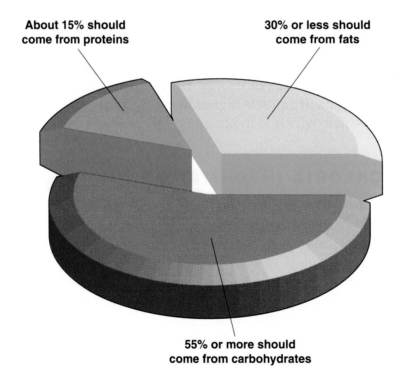

About 15% should come from proteins

30% or less should come from fats

55% or more should come from carbohydrates

These goals apply to food chosen over several days. They don't apply to just one meal or food.

Currently, most people in the United States get too many of their calories from fats and proteins, and not enough from carbohydrates. That may change, however, as people take steps to meet the guidelines.

95 calories
Good source of:
- vitamin C
- folate
- potassium
- thiamin

110 calories
Not a good source of vitamins and minerals

**8 oz.
orange juice**

**8 oz.
orange soda**

Orange juice and orange-flavored soda have about the same number of calories. Orange juice provides vitamins and minerals that the soft drink lacks. Which has a higher nutrient density?

NUTRIENT DENSITY

When it comes to choosing your energy sources, there's another aspect to consider. You need to make sure that along with food energy, you're getting *all* the nutrients you need, including vitamins and minerals. Paying attention to food's nutrient density can help. **Nutrient density** is a way of comparing the amount of energy, or calories, supplied by a food with the nutrients it provides.

Some foods have a low nutrient density. Compared to the number of calories they provide, they are limited in nutrients. Foods with a higher nutrient density are good sources of nutrients such as vitamins and minerals.

Here's an example. A lean hamburger patty and a 2-oz. candy bar each have about 230 calories. The hamburger is high in protein, B vitamins, and iron. The candy bar is not a good source of any nutrients except sugar (simple carbohydrates) and fat. Which has a higher nutrient density? You're right if you said the hamburger.

THE ENERGY YOU USE

Food gives you energy so your body can do its work. But how much energy do you need? The answer is different for every individual. It depends on how much energy you use for basic body processes and for activities.

BASIC BODY PROCESSES

Even when you sleep, your body carries on basic processes—such as breathing, circulating blood, digesting food, and building new cells. It's always using a few calories of energy for these and other processes.

The speed at which your body uses energy for its basic processes is known as the **basal metabolic rate** or BMR. Everyone has a different BMR. It depends on body build, age, and gender. A person with a high BMR uses more calories while at rest than someone with a low BMR.

ACTIVITIES

You also use energy for everyday activities. Getting dressed, walking to class, playing sports, raking leaves—every movement of your body uses energy.

The more strenuous an activity, the more energy you use. Take a look at the chart below to compare the energy used during different activities.

ENERGY USED IN ACTIVITIES	
Sitting or standing quietly	1 to 2 calories per minute*
Light activity: cleaning house, playing baseball	4 calories per minute*
Moderate activity: brisk walking, gardening, cycling, dancing, playing basketball	6 calories per minute*
Strenuous activity: jogging, playing football, swimming	9 to 10 calories per minute*
Very strenuous activity: running fast, racquetball, skiing	12 calories per minute*

*These figures are for someone who weighs 140 pounds. Someone who weighs more would use slightly more calories. Someone who weighs less would use slightly fewer.

ENERGY BALANCE FOR A HEALTHY WEIGHT

You've read about the energy you take in from food and the energy your body uses. The balance between energy taken in and energy used affects your weight. Finding the right energy balance is the key to keeping your weight at a healthy level.

More food than activity. If the food you eat supplies more energy than your body uses, your energy doesn't balance. Your body turns the extra food into fat and stores it as a future source of energy. If you keep on taking in more energy than you need, your body keeps storing fat and you gain weight.

More activity than food. If you use up more energy than you take in by eating, your energy doesn't balance. To get the rest of the energy it needs, your body turns stored fat back into energy. If this keeps up over time, you lose weight.

Food and activity balance. If the food you eat supplies the same amount of energy as you use up, your energy balances. Your weight stays the same.

WEIGHT MANAGEMENT IN THE TEEN YEARS

Some teens become concerned when the scale shows added pounds or their clothes feel tight. Do they need to lose weight? In most cases, the answer is no.

The teen years are a period of rapid growth. It's natural to gain weight during this time. Weight gain and growth in height often come in uneven spurts. A teen may become heavier without growing taller. A few weeks or months later, a sudden growth in height makes up for the added pounds.

Remember, too, that everyone has a unique body shape. It's far better to accept your natural shape than to harm your health by trying to reach an impossible ideal.

Dieting to lose weight during the teen years can be harmful. You need nutritious food to grow into a healthy adult. Cutting back on food could rob you of nutrients and interfere with growth. If you're concerned about your weight, get advice from a physician or registered dietitian.

The teen years *are* a good time to build healthy eating and activity habits. The combination of daily activities and nutritious food choices can help you keep a healthy weight throughout your life.

AN ACTIVE LIFE

Being active is a good habit to develop—and not just to help you manage your weight. People who are active are less likely to have certain health problems. Many people say that living an active life just helps them feel better, both mentally and physically.

How can you become more active? Just look for simple ways to increase your activities during the day. Here are some ideas:

◆ Walk or use a bike instead of riding in a car or bus.

◆ Walk up stairs instead of riding in elevators.

◆ If you're watching your favorite television program, don't just sit. Stand up and stretch, or walk in place.

◆ Choose one or two fun activities to help you get moving. You might pick dancing, roller hockey, gardening—whatever you enjoy. If you start to get bored, switch to something new.

Just be sure to balance the energy you use in activities with energy from healthful, nutrient-dense food choices. Start now for a lifetime of healthy living!

Understanding Key Ideas

1. What does the number of calories in a food tell you?
2. What mixture of energy sources is recommended for your body? Why?
3. Why do some foods have a higher nutrient density than others?
4. What are two basic ways your body uses energy?
5. What does *energy balance* mean? Why does it affect body weight?

Applying Knowledge and Skills

◆ **Calorie Display:** Find out how many calories are in one serving of three different foods. With your classmates, make a display showing the sequence of foods from least to most calories.

◆ **Energy Usage:** Make a list of your physical activities over the last three days. Estimate the amount of energy you used in each.

◆ **Comparing Nutrient Density:** Identify at least six pairs of foods that differ in nutrient density, such as orange juice and orange soda. Explain which food in each pair has a higher nutrient density and why.

Exploring Further

◆ **Math Connection:** If you kept track of how many grams of fat, protein, and carbohydrate you ate over several days, how could you calculate the percentage of food energy from each nutrient? Show what formulas you'd use. Then use your formulas with these amounts: 267 grams fat, 304 grams protein, and 972 grams carbohydrates. What do you conclude?

Energy and Calories   53

CHAPTER 7

THE DIETARY GUIDELINES

Discover...

★ the purpose of food guides.

★ how the Dietary Guidelines for Americans help you select food wisely.

Key Terms
food guides
diet

Nutrition experts study how the food you eat affects your health. Their findings are used to develop *food guides*—simple guidelines to help you make healthy food choices. One of the most commonly used guides is the Dietary Guidelines for Americans.

FOOD FOR THOUGHT

What are the advantages of using guidelines to help you make food choices? Are there any disadvantages?

CHOOSING FOOD FOR HEALTH

What can people do to improve their health? How can they decrease the risk of health problems such as heart disease and cancer? The answers are complex and are still being studied. It appears, however, that food choices play a role.

When you think of the word *diet,* you may think of losing weight or a special medical diet. In food guides, however, **diet** refers to the total balance of foods that you eat over a period of time. The Dietary Guidelines for Americans can help you plan and carry out a healthful diet.

These guidelines are for healthy Americans, ages 2 years and over. They are not for younger children and infants.

Dietary Guidelines for Americans

Aim for Fitness
- Aim for a healthy weight.
- Be physically active each day.

Build a Healthy Base
- Let the Pyramid guide your food choices.
- Choose a variety of grains daily, especially whole grains.
- Choose a variety of fruits and vegetables daily.
- Keep food safe to eat.

Choose Sensibly
- Choose a diet that is low in saturated fat and cholesterol and moderate in total fat.
- Choose beverages and foods to moderate your intake of sugars.
- Choose and prepare foods with less salt.

AIM FOR FITNESS

Health experts have studied how people's weight is related to their health. They believe that weighing too much or too little creates a greater risk of health problems.

As you learned in Chapter 6, food provides energy for your body. Your body uses the energy for all its activities. Reaching and maintaining a healthy weight is a matter of energy balance. Aim for a healthy weight by making wise food choices and staying active.

Being active helps you in other ways. It helps you stay strong and healthy. It can even improve your mood, and it's fun! Look for ways to add physical activity to your daily routines.

How do you stay physically active?

YOUR FOOD CHOICES

For good health, you need a variety of foods in the right amounts. Variety helps you get the nutrients you need. No single food can supply all nutrients in the right amounts.

Variety also makes eating more fun. Think of food as an adventure in eating. Try new foods regularly, and look for different ways to prepare familiar foods. You may discover a delicious taste treat.

You've probably seen the Food Guide Pyramid, a tool to help you make wise food choices. You'll learn more about it in the next chapter.

Variety makes eating more fun—and more nutritious.

WHY GRAIN PRODUCTS, VEGETABLES, AND FRUITS?

Grain products, vegetables, and fruits are high in complex carbohydrates and also low in fat. They are good sources of vitamins, minerals, and fiber. Fruits and vegetables are the only food sources of beta carotene, which may prevent certain diseases. Whole grains are a good source of fiber. Examples include whole wheat bread, brown rice, and oatmeal.

Grains, vegetables, and fruits are inexpensive, nutrient-dense foods.

Here are some ways to add grain products, fruits, and vegetables to your daily food choices. What ideas can you add to the list?

◆ Choose breads and cereals that have a whole grain as one of the first ingredients listed on the label.

◆ Munch on snacks such as graham crackers, toasted whole-wheat pita bread, or air-popped popcorn.

◆ Enjoy fresh fruits and vegetables as snacks and in packed lunches.

◆ Add fresh or leftover cooked vegetables to pizza, pasta sauce, hamburgers, and meat loaf.

KEEPING FOOD SAFE

When food isn't handled and prepared properly, it can cause illness. You'll learn more in Chapter 21. For now, remember these rules for keeping food safe to eat:

◆ Keep hands and surfaces clean when you work with food.

◆ Separate raw, cooked, and ready-to-eat foods while shopping, preparing, or storing.

◆ Cook foods to a safe temperature.

◆ Chill foods that spoil easily.

FATS, CHOLESTEROL, AND YOUR HEALTH

A diet low in saturated fat and cholesterol reduces the risk of heart disease. A diet moderate in total fat can help you stay at a healthy weight throughout your life. Eating too much fat can lead to excess weight, since fat is higher in calories than carbohydrate or protein.

Most people in the United States eat more fat than is recommended. How can you cut down on fats?

◆ Choose low-fat foods, such as low-fat milk, lean meat, and cooked dry beans and peas. (As you study different kinds of foods in this book, you'll learn more about making low-fat choices.)

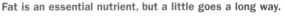

Fat is an essential nutrient, but a little goes a long way.

◆ Read labels. Compare the amount of total fat and saturated fat in foods you buy. (Chapter 12 explains how to find nutrition information on food labels.)

- Choose cooking methods that add little or no fat. For example, baked chicken is lower in fat than fried chicken.

- Use only small amounts of butter, margarine, sour cream, salad dressings, and other fats.

THE SUGAR STORY

A diet that's high in sugar is out of balance. Sugary foods—such as candy, sweetened cereals, soft drinks, cookies, and cakes—often have a low nutrient density. The sugar adds calories without adding vitamins, minerals, complex carbohydrates, or protein. If you fill up on sugary foods, you may not get enough of the nutrients you need. If you eat sugary foods in addition to more nutritious foods, you may get more calories than you need.

To cut down on sugar, use less at the table. Read labels to find the amount of sugar in foods. Try snacking on fruit instead of foods with added sugar.

To cut down on foods high in added sugar, try snacking on fruit.

Try It!

Comparing Sodium Content

At a grocery store, find several brands of canned and dry chicken broth or bouillon. Compare the amount of sodium in each.

★ By how much does the sodium content vary?

★ How might you reduce the sodium in recipes that call for chicken broth?

SODIUM SENSE

Eating too much sodium may be linked to high blood pressure in some people. Most Americans eat more salt and sodium than they need. Processed foods provide most of the sodium. It's also found in table salt.

How can you eat less salt and sodium?

- Try not to salt food when you eat.

- Use as little salt as possible in cooking. With foods such as vegetables, meats, soups, and stews, you can usually omit salt or cut down on the amount. Try flavoring with pepper and herbs instead.

- Limit processed foods such as canned and dried soups, lunch meats, and frozen dinners. When you do use these foods, compare labels. Choose those lower in sodium.

- Use only small amounts of highly salted foods, such as some nuts, mustard, some types of crackers, and pickled foods.

Herbs add flavor without sodium.

CHAPTER 7 REVIEW

Understanding Key Ideas

1. Why have food guides been developed? What are they based on?
2. Name any two of the Dietary Guidelines. Explain how each can benefit you.
3. Explain three ways people can reduce the fat in their diet.

Applying Knowledge and Skills

- **A Personal Plan:** How well do you follow the Dietary Guidelines in your own eating and activity habits? Choose one area in which you feel you could improve. Identify three specific steps you could take to build healthier habits.

- **Sharing Favorite Foods:** Think of a food you enjoy that might be new to some of your classmates. Find or draw a picture of it. Write a description of its color, texture, aroma, and flavor. How do you like it to be prepared and served? Share your description with the class. Which foods described by your classmates would you like to try?

- **Snack Display:** Design a poster or other display showing pictures of tasty snacks, featuring grain products, vegetables, and fruits, that can replace sugary, high-fat snacks.

Exploring Further

- **Seasoning Ideas:** Make a chart showing ways to flavor foods with herbs or spices instead of sugar and salt. Use a cookbook or other resources for ideas.

THE FOOD GUIDE PYRAMID

Discover...

★ *how the Food Guide Pyramid can help you.*

★ *how to count Pyramid servings.*

★ *smart choices from the five food groups.*

Key Term
Pyramid servings

You've probably seen the Food Guide Pyramid before. Did you know you can use it to give your food choices a checkup? With a little Pyramid know-how, you can tally your food choices and see whether they add up to a balanced diet. Even better, the Pyramid can help you plan tomorrow's food choices for good health.

> **FOOD FOR THOUGHT**
>
> How many fruits and vegetables did you eat yesterday? Did you get enough? Read on to find out!

THE FIVE FOOD GROUPS

The Food Guide Pyramid makes healthy eating simple. It organizes foods into five food groups. As long as you eat the recommended number of servings from each group, you're probably getting the right balance of nutrients.

All five food groups are equally important. Each group provides some, but not all, of the nutrients you need. For good health, you need foods from all five groups. Later in this chapter, you'll find highlighted information about each food group.

LOOKING AT THE PYRAMID

The food groups are arranged in the shape of a pyramid. Why? This shape helps you remember how to balance your food choices. The larger the food group section, the more servings you need.

The food group at the base of the pyramid is the Bread, Cereal, Rice, and Pasta Group. It's the largest section because you need more servings from this group than any other.

Now take a look at the smallest section at the top of the pyramid. It's the place for foods that don't fit in any of the food groups—fats, oils, and sweets. Examples include cooking oils, butter, margarine, salad dressings, candy, and soft drinks. These foods have low nutrient density. In other words, they're high in calories but limited in nutrients. Fats, oils, and sweets are placed in the smallest section of the pyramid to remind you to use them in very small amounts.

Food Guide Pyramid

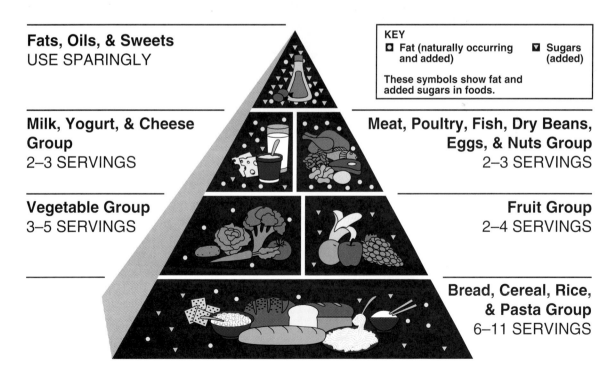

Fats, Oils, & Sweets
USE SPARINGLY

KEY
◻ Fat (naturally occurring and added)
☑ Sugars (added)
These symbols show fat and added sugars in foods.

Milk, Yogurt, & Cheese Group
2–3 SERVINGS

Meat, Poultry, Fish, Dry Beans, Eggs, & Nuts Group
2–3 SERVINGS

Vegetable Group
3–5 SERVINGS

Fruit Group
2–4 SERVINGS

Bread, Cereal, Rice, & Pasta Group
6–11 SERVINGS

Notice the small circles and triangles found throughout the pyramid. These symbols represent fats and added sugars. They show that fats and added sugars are found in some of the foods in each food group.

PYRAMID SERVINGS

For the five food groups, the recommended number of servings is given as a range. The number of servings right for you depends on your age and gender, your physical condition, and how active you are.

Almost everyone should have at least the lowest number of servings in the ranges. Most teen girls need the number of servings in the middle of the range. Teen boys may need the highest number of servings, especially if they're active. All teens need three or more servings from the Milk, Yogurt, and Cheese group.

This meal includes 1 cup of rice and a dinner roll. That counts as three servings from the Bread, Cereal, Rice, and Pasta Group.

COUNTING YOUR SERVINGS

Before you can count how many servings you've eaten, you need to know how much food counts as one serving. The Food Guide Pyramid uses specific amounts of food called **Pyramid servings.** As you read about each food group, look for examples of Pyramid servings in the box labeled "What Is a Serving?"

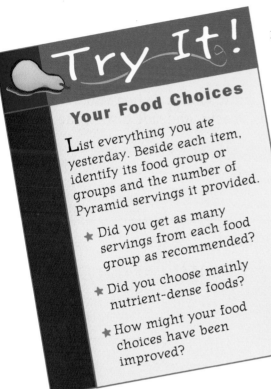
Often, the portions people eat at a meal or snack are larger than Pyramid servings. Keep this in mind when you count your servings. A Pyramid serving of meat, for instance, is 3 ounces—about the size of an audio cassette. If you eat a portion twice that size, it counts as two Pyramid servings, not one.

Some foods, such as pizza or sandwiches, are mixtures. They include foods from several groups. When you add up your servings for the day, think of a food mixture in terms of its separate parts. Estimate how many Pyramid servings from each food group the food provides.

TIPS FOR CHOOSING FOODS

You're responsible for choosing healthful foods in each food group. The following tips can help you make good choices.

◆ Choose a variety of foods from within each group. The foods in a group don't all contain exactly the same kinds or amounts of nutrients. One day your choices from the Vegetable Group might include carrots, lettuce, and broccoli. The next day you might choose spinach, tomatoes, and corn.

◆ Choose mainly nutrient-dense foods that are low in fat (especially saturated fat), cholesterol, sugar, and sodium.

◆ Prepare and serve foods with little or no added fats and sugars.

BREAD GROUP TIPS

◆ Have several servings of whole grain foods every day to be sure you get enough fiber.

◆ Getting 6 to 11 servings a day is easier than it sounds. When you include grain products as breakfast foods, snacks, and side dishes, the servings add up quickly.

Bread, Cereal, Rice, and Pasta Group
Number of Daily Servings — 6 to 11

Foods Included

• Baked products—breads, rolls, bagels, English muffins

• Flat breads—tortillas, pita bread, pizza crust

• Breakfast cereals—ready-to-eat or cooked

• Grain products—rice, pasta, grits, bulgur

• Snacks—pretzels, air-popped popcorn, tortilla chips, crackers

Key Nutrients

Foods in this group are a good source of:

• Carbohydrates

• B vitamins

• Vitamin E

• Minerals

• Fiber

What Is a Serving?

• 1 slice of bread

• ½ cup cooked cereal, rice, or pasta

• 1 ounce ready-to-eat cereal

VEGETABLE GROUP TIPS

For nutrient variety, include these several times a week:

◆ Dark green leafy vegetables (such as spinach, romaine lettuce, broccoli).

◆ Deep yellow vegetables (carrots, sweet potatoes, winter squash).

◆ Starchy vegetables (potatoes, sweet corn, green peas).

◆ Dry beans and peas (kidney beans, baked beans, split peas, lentils).

◆ Other vegetables (tomatoes, green beans, onions, and more).

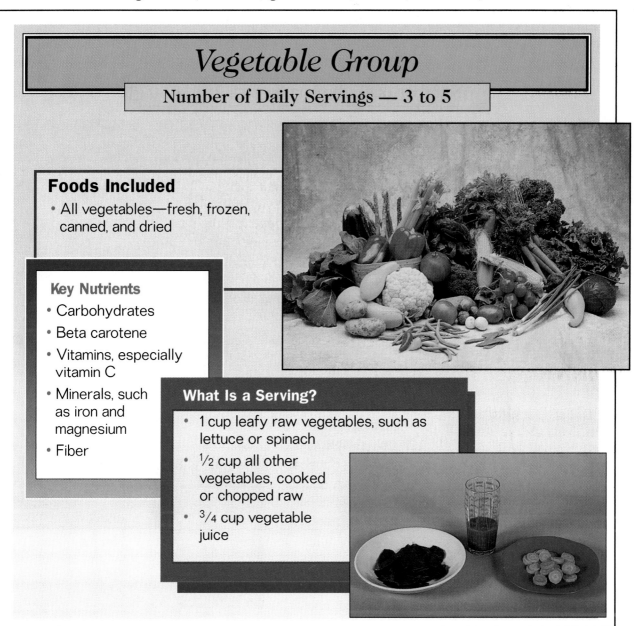

Vegetable Group

Number of Daily Servings — 3 to 5

Foods Included
- All vegetables—fresh, frozen, canned, and dried

Key Nutrients
- Carbohydrates
- Beta carotene
- Vitamins, especially vitamin C
- Minerals, such as iron and magnesium
- Fiber

What Is a Serving?
- 1 cup leafy raw vegetables, such as lettuce or spinach
- 1/2 cup all other vegetables, cooked or chopped raw
- 3/4 cup vegetable juice

FRUIT GROUP TIPS

◆ Eat citrus fruits, melons, and berries regularly. They're rich in vitamin C.

◆ Eat whole fruits often. They have more fiber than fruit juices.

◆ For less sugar, select fruits canned in natural juices instead of heavy syrup. Look for fruit juices and frozen fruits without added sugars.

◆ Count only 100% fruit juice as fruit. Punches, "ades," fruit "drinks," and sodas don't count as fruit juice.

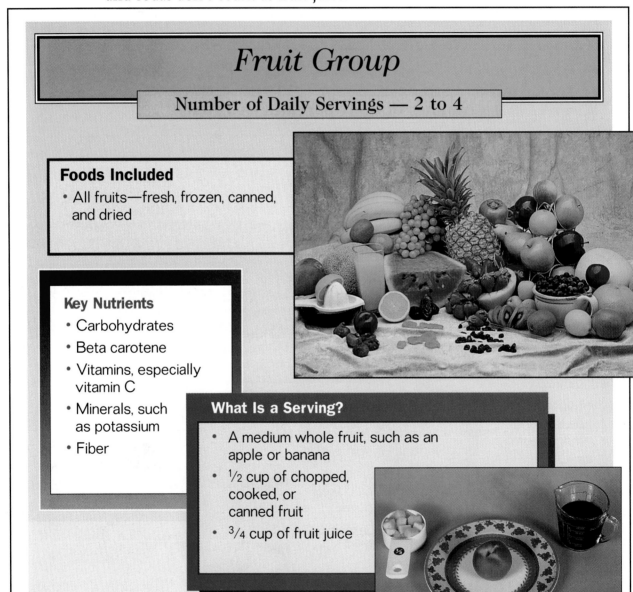

Fruit Group

Number of Daily Servings — 2 to 4

Foods Included
• All fruits—fresh, frozen, canned, and dried

Key Nutrients
• Carbohydrates
• Beta carotene
• Vitamins, especially vitamin C
• Minerals, such as potassium
• Fiber

What Is a Serving?
• A medium whole fruit, such as an apple or banana
• $^1/_2$ cup of chopped, cooked, or canned fruit
• $^3/_4$ cup of fruit juice

MILK GROUP TIPS

◆ For less fat, choose fat-free or low-fat dairy products.

◆ If you don't like to drink milk, have cheese, yogurt, or foods made with milk, such as pudding.

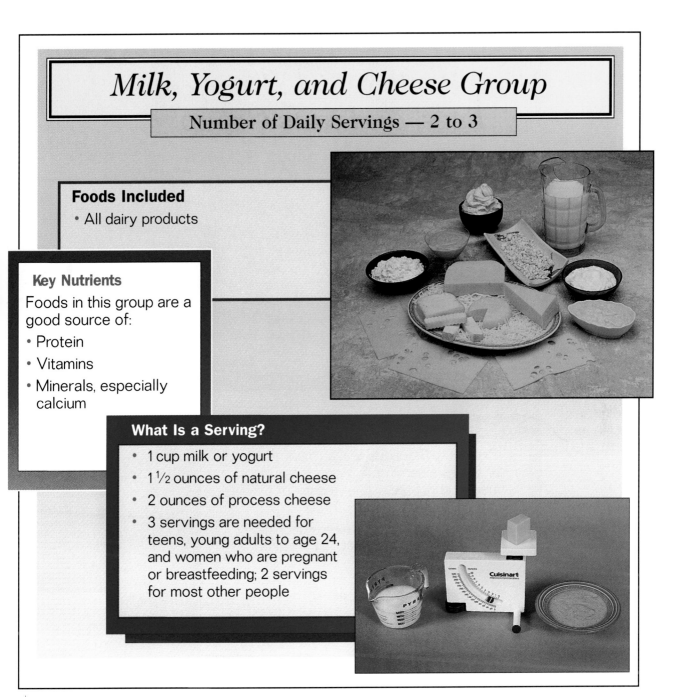

Milk, Yogurt, and Cheese Group
Number of Daily Servings — 2 to 3

Foods Included
- All dairy products

Key Nutrients

Foods in this group are a good source of:
- Protein
- Vitamins
- Minerals, especially calcium

What Is a Serving?
- 1 cup milk or yogurt
- 1 1/2 ounces of natural cheese
- 2 ounces of process cheese
- 3 servings are needed for teens, young adults to age 24, and women who are pregnant or breastfeeding; 2 servings for most other people

MEAT GROUP TIPS

◆ Choose dry beans and peas often. They have little or no fat and are a good source of fiber.

◆ Other choices for less fat are fish, poultry without skin, and lean meat.

◆ Go easy on nuts and seeds. They're high in fat.

Meat, Poultry, Fish, Dry Beans, Eggs, and Nuts Group

Number of Daily Servings — 2 to 3

Foods Included
- All meats, poultry, fish, legumes, eggs, and nuts

Key Nutrients

Foods in this group are a good source of:
- Protein
- B vitamins
- Minerals, such as iron and zinc

What Is a Serving?

Count 2 to 3 ounces of lean meat, poultry, or fish as a serving. A 3-ounce serving of meat is about the size of a deck of playing cards.

The following equal 1 ounce of lean meat.

- ½ cup cooked dry beans
- 1 egg
- 2 Tbsp. peanut butter

The total amount of these servings should equal 5 to 7 ounces of cooked lean meat.

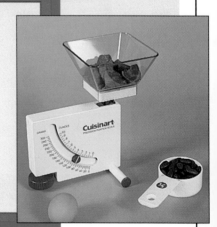

Why are these foods grouped in the tip of the Pyramid?

Understanding Key Ideas

1. Briefly explain what type of information the Food Guide Pyramid gives you. How does this help you plan a healthful diet?
2. What nutrients do foods in the Bread, Cereal, Rice, and Pasta Group provide?
3. Estimate the Pyramid servings provided by a sandwich made with 2 slices of bread, 4 ounces lean turkey, a 1-ounce slice of process cheese, a lettuce leaf, 2 slices of tomato, and mustard.
4. For each food group, give an example of advice for choosing foods.

Applying Knowledge and Skills

◆ **Meal Planning:** Use the Food Guide Pyramid to plan meals and snacks for one day for Marcus, age 14, who is active on the track team.

◆ **Food Group Ideas:** In a small group, brainstorm creative ways to enjoy foods in one of the five food groups.

Exploring Further

◆ **Food Guides Around the World:** Like the U.S., many other countries have food guides to teach people about making healthy food choices. Using the Internet or other resources, learn about at least three of them. How do they compare with the Food Guide Pyramid?

CHAPTER **9**

YOUR DAILY FOOD CHOICES

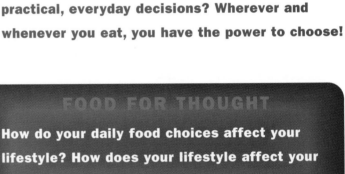

Discover...

* *what affects your food choices.*

* *the difference between food fact and fiction.*

* *strategies for making daily food choices.*

* *facts about vegetarian food choices.*

Key Terms

meal pattern
vegan

In other chapters, you've learned about the nutrients and guidelines for good nutrition. How will you apply that information to make practical, everyday decisions? Wherever and whenever you eat, you have the power to choose!

FOOD FOR THOUGHT

How do your daily food choices affect your lifestyle? How does your lifestyle affect your food choices?

WHAT AFFECTS YOUR FOOD CHOICES?

Why do you choose the foods you eat? You might say it's because you enjoy the flavor. That's just part of the answer. Your food choices are also affected by:

Your lifestyle. The patterns of your daily life influence the food you eat. For example, if you're always on the go, you're more likely to plan quick meals or eat out.

Your priorities and values. Many people today place a high priority on good health. They look for foods low in fat, cholesterol, and sodium.

Your family and culture. Many of your food likes and dislikes begin at home. You may prefer chicken prepared a certain way because that's how you're used to eating it. Does your family have food traditions for holidays or special occasions? Perhaps you have a favorite dish that's part of your cultural heritage.

Your friends. Do you enjoy going out with friends for a snack? When a group gets together, food is usually an important part of the activities. People within a group often eat the same kind of food.

Your culture and family background may influence the foods you like to eat. These foods are from India.

Trends and technology. New developments affect the choices you have. Think of how many different food products are made just for the microwave oven. Before the microwave oven was introduced, none of these products existed.

The media. Have you ever had a craving for a candy bar or a fast-food burger because you saw it on television? Advertisements are everywhere—in newspapers and magazines, on television and radio, on buses and trains, and on the Internet. All of these ads are intended to influence you. News reports, magazine articles, talk shows, and other forms of mass communication also affect your choices.

FOOD FACT AND FICTION

Information about food and health comes to you from many sources. For example:

◆ A friend says you should try the latest herbal extract.

◆ An Internet posting promotes a new supplement guaranteed to "energize" you.

◆ The evening news reports that a certain food is now thought to increase the risk of heart disease. Just a month ago, you read that the same food may help prevent cancer.

It's no wonder many people are confused about nutrition and health. Who and what should you believe?

THINKING CRITICALLY ABOUT CLAIMS

The key is to evaluate whether information is reliable. Use your nutrition knowledge, critical thinking skills, and decision-making ability. Ask yourself questions such as:

Does this fit in with what I already know? Suppose a supplement claims to give you the fiber needed for good health. That may be true. However, you also know that all fruits, vegetables, and whole grain products supply fiber. By eating a variety of these foods every day, you can get all the fiber you need along with other nutrients.

How is this advertisement trying to influence me? The goal of advertising is not to improve your health—it's to sell a product. Learn to recognize the ways that advertisers try to influence you. Most ads appeal to emotions. They may make it seem, for example, that choosing a certain soft drink will make you more popular or a better athlete.

When you read about food and nutrition, consider the source. Some are more reliable than others.

Is it too good to be true? "Miracle" products are usually suspect. They may claim to cure almost any health problem and guarantee fast results. In reality, about the only thing you can count on is losing your money.

What is this news report based on? News reports are often based on the early results of just one study. More studies must be done before researchers can agree on the results and on what they mean for consumers. Not all news reports explain that more work needs to be done. Instead, they may exaggerate the statements made in the study.

Where can I get reliable information? Here are some reliable sources that can help you get the facts:

- ◆ Registered dietitians.
- ◆ Physicians and other health professionals.
- ◆ Food and nutrition teachers.
- ◆ A consumer group or local consumer specialist.
- ◆ Local office of the Food and Drug Administration (FDA).

CHOOSING WHAT TO EAT

As you make food choices, remember two words: "variety" and "moderation." They are keys to healthful eating.

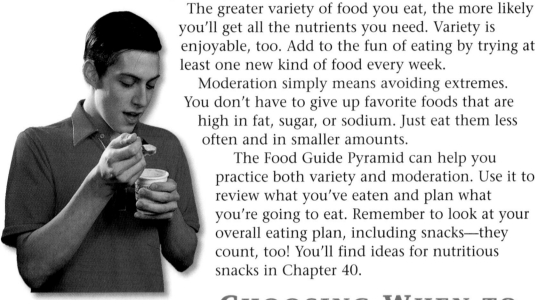

The greater variety of food you eat, the more likely you'll get all the nutrients you need. Variety is enjoyable, too. Add to the fun of eating by trying at least one new kind of food every week.

Moderation simply means avoiding extremes. You don't have to give up favorite foods that are high in fat, sugar, or sodium. Just eat them less often and in smaller amounts.

The Food Guide Pyramid can help you practice both variety and moderation. Use it to review what you've eaten and plan what you're going to eat. Remember to look at your overall eating plan, including snacks—they count, too! You'll find ideas for nutritious snacks in Chapter 40.

Snacks can provide food group servings to help meet your nutrient needs.

CHOOSING WHEN TO EAT

People have different schedules, so they often have different meal patterns. A **meal pattern** refers to how many meals and snacks you eat throughout the day and when you eat them. Some people eat three meals a day and perhaps a snack or two. Others prefer to eat five or six small meals instead of three larger ones. As long as you meet Food Guide Pyramid guidelines for the whole day, any meal pattern can be healthful.

Whatever your meal pattern, make sure you eat at regular intervals. Skipping meals can harm your health. Your body may not get the nutrients it needs. You may feel tired and dragged out. At the next meal, you may be so hungry that you eat more than you really need.

BREAKFAST IS IMPORTANT

Be sure to eat breakfast—it's the most important meal of the day. When you wake up, you haven't had anything to eat for about eight to twelve hours. But your body has to work anyway. It needs a supply of nutrients to get it going and keep it active.

Studies show that students who eat breakfast do much better in school than the breakfast-skippers. They have more energy and interest in their school work and get better grades.

Those who skip breakfast:

◆ Find it hard to concentrate on their work.

◆ Have less interest in what they're doing.

◆ Feel cross and tired.

Why don't breakfast-skippers eat breakfast? Here are two common reasons.

I HATE BREAKFAST!

It may be that you just don't like traditional breakfast foods. Don't skip breakfast—just eat something else. You can have any nutritious food you like for breakfast. Try to eat foods from at least two or three food groups. For example, you might eat a ham and cheese sandwich.

I DON'T HAVE TIME FOR BREAKFAST...I'D RATHER SLEEP!

Everyone needs sleep. But if you sacrifice breakfast for a few more minutes of sleep, you're not helping your body. A nutritious breakfast doesn't have to take much time. You might grab a leftover slice of pizza or some low-fat yogurt with fruit. Prepare as much of the food the night before as possible and refrigerate it. You'll have less to do in the morning.

CHOOSING WHERE TO EAT

Many meals are prepared and eaten at home. Preparing food at home has several advantages:

◆ You can control your food costs better. Eating at home often costs less than eating out. You can buy a food that's on sale and build a low-cost meal around it.

◆ You can control the ingredients that go into the food. This can be especially helpful if you want to cut down on fat, sugar, and salt.

◆ You can more easily control serving sizes. This helps ensure you get just the amount of food you need. It also reduces waste.

What are the benefits of preparing and eating meals as a family?

◆ Eating at home gives you a chance to have a family meal. This is a time when family members can share their experiences and enjoy each other's company. Many families make a special effort to eat together as often as possible. In some families, all members also help prepare the meal.

With busy schedules, it's not always possible to prepare and eat meals at home. The food choices you make when eating out are just as important. Chapter 10 will give you some tips for making healthful choices when you eat out.

IMPROVING YOUR FOOD CHOICES

Do you want to improve your food choices? Begin by taking a look at the food choices you make now. Everyone makes good and poor food choices throughout the day. Give yourself credit for the good choices. Then work at replacing poor choices with better ones.

Try It!

Keeping a Food Record

To get a picture of your current food choices, try keeping a food record for two or three days. Write down all your food choices, including what you ate, when, and where. At the end of that time, review your choices.

★ Did you get enough servings from each of the food groups?

★ How are you doing at following the Dietary Guidelines?

★ What influenced your food choices?

How can you improve your food choices? Use your management and problem-solving skills to make a plan. Decide on one specific change you can make, such as having a snack of fresh fruit each day. When that becomes a habit, decide on another healthful change.

Don't worry if your diet isn't "perfect" every day. You can balance your choices over several days. If you miss a serving from one of the food groups one day, just include an extra serving the next day.

VEGETARIAN FOOD CHOICES

Some people choose a vegetarian eating plan. They don't eat meat, poultry, fish, or shellfish. Although these foods are nutritious, vegetarians choose not to eat them for religious or personal reasons.

What foods do vegetarians eat? That depends on the type of vegetarian:

- **Vegans** (VEE-guhns) eat only foods from plant sources—grain products, dry beans and peas, vegetables, fruits, nuts, and seeds.
- Lacto-vegetarians eat dairy products in addition to plant foods.
- Lacto-ovo vegetarians eat dairy products, eggs, and plant foods.

If vegetarian foods are chosen carefully, they can provide all the nutrients people need. For example, a well-planned vegan eating plan provides:

- Protein from the amino acids in grains, dry beans and peas, and other plant foods. (See page 39 to review incomplete proteins.)
- Calcium from foods such as calcium-fortified soy milk, broccoli, kale, and dry beans.
- Iron from dried fruits, dark green leafy vegetables, and many cereals and breads.

Vegan food choices should include as wide a variety of plant foods as possible every day. Foods made from soy protein can help add variety to the vegan diet. Some, such as soy burgers, resemble meat. Others include soy milk, soy cheese, and tofu (see page 250).

Popular ethnic dishes are often suitable for vegetarians. Examples include bean tacos from Mexico, stir-fried vegetables and rice from Asia, and spicy vegetable stews from the Middle East. These dishes and many others were invented at a time when meat was scarce or expensive in many parts of the world.

If you choose to be a vegetarian, talk to your foods and nutrition teacher or health professional. They can help you make healthful food choices.

Foods such as bean tacos, couscous, and vegetable bean soup give vegetarians a variety of options.

Understanding Key Ideas

1. Why might someone choose microwave popcorn as a snack? Explain at least four factors that might have influenced that food choice.
2. Suppose you see an ad for an herbal tea that promises to make you smarter. Explain your response to this claim.
3. What two things are true about any nutritious meal pattern?
4. What is a vegan? What basic advice should a vegan follow and why?

Applying Knowledge and Skills

◆ **Breakfast Menu:** Imagine you're opening a breakfast buffet restaurant for teens. Design a menu of nutritious foods that will encourage teens to enjoy breakfast as part of their daily routine.

◆ **Vegetarian Meals:** Plan a meal for each of the three types of vegetarians discussed in this chapter. Explain the nutritional value of each.

Exploring Further

◆ **Critical Thinking:** When it comes to your food choices, what are the benefits of advertising? What are the drawbacks? How can you make the best use of advertising?

EATING OUT

 Discover...

* *how to make healthful choices when eating out.*

* *tips for eating take-out foods at home.*

 Key Terms

au gratin
scalloped

Eating restaurant and take-out meals is a popular option. Almost half the average food budget is spent on food prepared outside the home.

Your choice of where to eat out often depends on how much time you have and how much money you can spend. No matter where you eat out, it's important to keep nutrition in mind.

> **FOOD FOR THOUGHT**
>
> **How can your choice of restaurant affect your food choices when you eat out?**

MAKING MENU CHOICES

Choices in restaurants range from nutritious, low-fat foods to those that are high in fat and sugar. It's up to you to make choices that fit into a healthful eating plan. The following guidelines can help you.

FINDING NUTRITION INFORMATION

Making choices is easier if the restaurant provides nutrition information. At fast food restaurants, look for a sign or brochure with a nutrition chart.

Some restaurants have developed menu items especially for the health-conscious customer. You might see a special symbol next to menu items that are low in fat, cholesterol, and sodium. If a restaurant makes a nutrition claim for any item on the menu, it must be able to back up the claim. The information must be available to any customer requesting it.

ADDING VARIETY

As you know, variety is one of the keys to good nutrition. What can you do to increase the variety of nutritious foods in the meals you eat away from home?

Luncheon Creations

♥ **Stir-Fried Vegetables & Chicken**
Broccoli spears, mushroom, peppers & fresh vegetables.
$4.75

♥ **Chicken Breast Sandwich**
Prepared grilled, instead of fried.
$4.25

♥ **Fettuccini**
Fettuccini topped with meat sauce. Served with garlic toast.
$4.25

♥ **Tortellini**
Meat-filled tortellini in marinara sauce. Served with garlic toast.
$4.25

◆ Start by choosing restaurants that offer a wider variety of choices. It's much easier to eat healthfully at a restaurant that offers lean meat sandwiches, baked potatoes, and fresh vegetable salads than at one that serves only fried foods.

◆ Remember the recommended servings from the Food Guide Pyramid. Review the foods you have already eaten that day, or plan to eat, and then make your choices.

Fried Chicken

Baked Chicken

Read the menu or ask the server to find out how foods are prepared. Baked chicken, for example, has less fat than fried.

◆ Look for ways to include whole grain products, fresh vegetables and fruits, and low-fat dairy products in your meal. You might want to bring something from home, such as an apple, to round out your meal.

CUTTING DOWN ON FAT

If you're not careful when you order, you can easily get more fat than you need. Try these suggestions for lowering the fat when you eat out.

◆ Ask for a baked potato instead of fries. Top it with salsa or taco sauce instead of butter or sour cream.

◆ Remember, natural cheese is high in fat. When ordering pizza, for instance, you might ask for less cheese or a low-fat variety.

◆ Pasta dishes can be high or low in fat, depending on the sauce. Tomato sauces, such as marinara, are usually good choices. White sauces made with cream and butter, such as alfredo, are high in fat.

◆ Ask for salad dressings and other high-fat toppings "on the side." That way you can decide how much to use. Sometimes low-fat alternatives are offered.

◆ Look for signal words that tell how the food is prepared. For instance, **au gratin** (oh GRAH-tun) means topped with cheese or buttered bread crumbs. **Scalloped** means baked in a creamy sauce topped with crumbs. More signal words are shown in the chart on the next page.

CONTROLLING PORTION SIZES

Some restaurant portions offer far more food than the average person can or should eat. This can make it harder to get the right number of servings from the Food Guide Pyramid. It can also make it difficult to cut down on fat, sugar, and sodium and to maintain a healthy weight.

How can you eat in moderation when eating out? Try these ideas:

◆ If you know you may be eating large portions in a restaurant that day, eat smaller portions at your other meals.

◆ Choose the small or regular size instead of "super," "giant," or "double."

MENU SIGNAL WORDS

High-Fat Signal Words	Lower-Fat Signal Words
• au gratin	• baked
• breaded	• broiled
• buttered	• poached
• cheesy	• roasted
• creamy	• rotisseried (a type of roasting)
• gravy	• steamed
• scalloped or escalloped	

◆ If the menu has an "Appetizer" section, look in it for smaller portions of foods that can be eaten as your main meal.

◆ Ask the server to pack leftover food so you can take it home. Do this only if you're going straight home after eating so you can refrigerate the food. Otherwise, harmful bacteria could grow rapidly in the food and cause illness when the leftovers are eaten.

◆ If you and a friend agree on the same menu item, order just one serving. Ask for another plate so you can divide and share the food. You may have to pay a small service charge for the extra plate.

◆ At salad bars and all-you-can-eat buffets, be careful of the portions you take. It's easy to eat much more than normal.

"EATING OUT" AT HOME

With today's fast-paced schedules, people often don't have time to prepare food at home. Instead, they may bring home take-out food or have it delivered.

"Eating out" at home gives you the opportunity to balance the meal by combining a variety of foods. Suppose your family has ordered a pizza for dinner. Perhaps a family member on the way home from work can pick up a salad from the supermarket salad bar and some fresh fruit for dessert.

Even though the food you eat has been prepared outside the home, take a few extra minutes to create a more relaxing, home-cooked atmosphere. You and your family will enjoy the meal and each other's company that much more. Here are some tips for serving the meal:

- Mix the salad fixings in a bowl so people can help themselves.

- Don't put the take-out cartons on the table. If possible, put a serving on each person's plate. Keep the rest of the food warm or cold, as needed.

- When the meal is over, refrigerate leftovers. Perhaps they could be tomorrow's breakfast.

How can you make a take-out meal more enjoyable?

Food Safety Warning

It takes time to bring ready-to-eat food home, whether you pick it up or have it delivered. Harmful bacteria can start to grow. To prevent illness, keep hot food hot and cold food cold. If hot food has cooled, reheat it before you eat. For more infomation, see Chapter 21, "Keeping Food Safe to Eat."

The next time you eat out, use your nutrition knowledge to choose a meal that's both healthful and tasty.

Understanding Key Ideas

1. Where might you find information about calories and fat in restaurant foods?
2. What should you consider when choosing between breaded fish and broiled fish?
3. What might you do if you're served more food at a restaurant than you want to eat?
4. What precautions should you take when you bring take-out food home for a meal? Why?

Applying Knowledge and Skills

◆ **Restaurant Skit:** With a partner, write a skit showing two restaurant customers who want to make healthful choices. They might be reading a menu or choosing food from a buffet or salad bar.

◆ **Menu Choices:** Think of a fast-food restaurant that's familiar to you. Using its menu items, plan three meals that each provide servings from at least four food groups. If possible, obtain a nutrition brochure from the restaurant. Calculate the amount of calories, fat, sodium, calcium, iron, and vitamins A and C in your meals. Share your results with the class.

Exploring Further

◆ **Investigation:** Contact the manager of a local restaurant. Find out the portion size of several menu items and why they were chosen. How do the restaurant portions compare to Pyramid servings (on pages 64-68)?

PERSONALIZED NUTRITION

Discover...

★ *how food needs change in a lifetime.*

★ *nutrition needs of athletes.*

★ *the dangers of eating disorders.*

★ *food advice for special health situations.*

Key Terms
eating disorders
food allergy
food intolerance
diabetes

Sometimes special conditions demand changes in food choices. In this chapter, you'll learn about several conditions that require special, or personalized, nutrition.

> **FOOD FOR THOUGHT**
>
> Not everyone has the same nutritional needs. What factors might affect your personal nutritional needs?

NUTRITION THROUGH THE LIFE SPAN

As people move through their life span, their food needs change:

◆ Babies start out with breast milk or formula. It's all the food they need for the first 4 to 6 months. Gradually they can begin eating soft, strained foods, then more solid ones.

◆ Small children need foods from all the food groups. They like to eat small meals and snacks throughout the day. They shouldn't eat small, hard foods, such as nuts and popcorn, which can cause choking. As children get older, they need more food for their growing bodies. Parents and caregivers can help children learn good eating habits.

◆ Teens are growing fast. They need extra servings from the Food Guide Pyramid, especially if they're active.

◆ In adulthood, your food needs will change. Depending on how active you are, you may need less food than you did as a teen.

FOOD FOR ATHLETES

Athletes often believe that special products—such as protein powders, vitamin supplements, or energy bars—will help them be tops in their sports. However, studies show they can get all the nutrients they need just by making healthy food choices.

Athletes do have some special needs. Because they use so much energy, they usually need extra calories. Good sources include grain products, dry beans and peas, and starchy vegetables.

During physical activity, the body loses fluid through perspiration. It's up to you to replace it. Plain water is one of the best and cheapest fluids. Don't wait until you feel thirsty—that's not a reliable sign.

To get the fuel and fluids you need, follow these guidelines:

Before—Eat a high-starch meal about three to four hours before vigorous activity. About two hours before the activity, drink at least 2 to 3 cups of fluids. Just before the activity, drink another 1 to 2 cups.

During—Drink 1/2 cup of fluid every 15 minutes during the activity.

After—Drink about 2 cups of fluid for every pound of weight lost. (To check, weigh yourself before and after the activity.) Within four hours, eat a balanced meal.

Athletes who play seasonal sports don't need as much energy during off-season as they do when they're competing. If you play a seasonal sport, you should either remain as active as when you compete or cut down on high-calorie foods. This will help you maintain your weight until the playing season begins again.

EATING DISORDERS

Eating disorders are illnesses that involve harmful attitudes about the body, self, and food. They also involve actions that can be very dangerous to health. These attitudes and actions depend on the type of eating disorder:

Anorexia nervosa (an-uh-RECK-see-uh nur-VOH-suh). People with this disorder purposely starve themselves. They have an intense fear of gaining weight. They believe they are fat even after becoming extremely thin. Losing weight is the focus of their lives. They often set extreme, strict rules for themselves concerning what, when, and how much they can eat and how long and hard they must exercise.

Bulimia nervosa (boo-LEEM-ee-uh nur-VOH-suh). People with this disorder binge and purge. Bingeing means they eat much more food at one time than normal. Purging means they rid themselves of the extra calories so they don't put on extra weight. They may do this by forcing themselves to vomit, by taking large amounts of laxatives, or by exercising very hard. Some also go on strict diets between binges.

Binge eating disorder. People with this disorder binge regularly, but don't purge. They often go on eating binges when they're emotionally upset.

Eating disorders can occur in people of all ages and backgrounds. The causes are very complex and are still being studied.

All three eating disorders are dangerous to health. Anorexia can lead to serious illness, even death. Binge eating can cause the stomach or esophagus to burst. Purging can cause heart failure. Many other medical problems can result from eating disorders.

Health professionals can treat eating disorders. The first challenge is to recognize the problem. People with eating disorders often go to great lengths to keep their eating habits a secret. Many deny that anything is wrong. Family members and friends can help by:

◆ Being alert to the signs of an eating disorder. These vary, but may include rapid weight loss or changes in eating habits.

◆ Encouraging the person to seek professional help.

◆ Being supportive during the treatment process.

If you think someone you know may have an eating disorder, talk to a trusted adult or health professional.

SPECIAL FOOD NEEDS

The Dietary Guidelines and Food Guide Pyramid provide general nutrition advice that meets most people's needs. Some people, however, have special needs because of a food allergy, food intolerance, or long-term health problem.

FOOD ALLERGIES

A **food allergy** is a bad reaction to a particular food. The reaction occurs in the body's immune system. It can cause different physical symptoms, such as itchy skin, a runny nose, or diarrhea. Some people may find it difficult to breathe.

Allergies aren't common. Some of the foods most often involved are wheat, milk, eggs, shellfish, peanuts, dry beans and peas, and nuts. Usually the problem can be solved by avoiding the particular food and substituting others. An allergist is a health professional who can help people discover the foods they are allergic to. A dietitian can help people plan food choices to avoid the specific food.

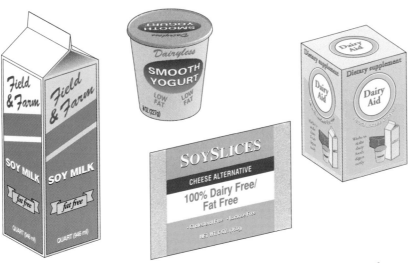

Some people can't tolerate lactose, a natural sugar in dairy products. They can choose lactose-free products or take a supplement that helps them digest the lactose.

FOOD INTOLERANCE

Food intolerance results when a person can't digest certain foods. Food intolerance can result in the same symptoms as a food allergy and is often mistaken for an allergy. Unlike a food allergy, however, food intolerance may not entirely prevent a person from eating a particular food. Often the person can eat the food in small amounts or take supplements that help digest the food.

DIETS TO MANAGE HEALTH PROBLEMS

The right food choices can help lessen or control certain long-term health problems. Here are some examples of special diets that might be prescribed by a health professional:

Low-fat, low-cholesterol diet. Cutting down on fat and cholesterol is especially important for people with heart problems or high blood cholesterol levels.

Low-sodium diet. Eating less salt and sodium can help control high blood pressure in some people. Making sure to get enough potassium, calcium, and magnesium can help, too.

Diabetic diet. Diabetes (die-uh-BEE-tuss) means the body can't control blood sugar properly. Over time, diabetes can damage many parts of the body, including the kidneys and eyes. However, damage can be reduced or prevented by the right eating plan, physical activity, and perhaps medication. A diabetic diet is specially designed for each person's needs.

Following health professionals' advice is important to the success of any treatment plan. If the person is used to a different style of eating, the change may be a challenge at first. Family members can help by giving encouragement. Often it's possible to prepare flavorful meals that not only fit in the special diet, but can be enjoyed by the whole family.

Seasonings such as lemon juice, chives, and dill can add flavor to a low-sodium meal.

FOOD AND MEDICINES

Some types of medicine can interfere with the way the body uses certain foods. Some foods can also keep certain medicines from working properly. To avoid such problems, always read and follow directions for taking medicines. Some must be taken on an empty stomach. Others need to be taken with food. If you have questions, ask your physician or pharmacist.

NUTRITION DURING ILLNESS

When people are ill, they may be unable to eat normally. Medication may cut down on their appetite. However, good nutrition is important because it helps the body fight illness and return to health.

Follow the physician's instructions for what foods and liquids to give the patient. Make meals and snacks as appetizing as possible. Small meals may be easier to handle than large ones. Gradually, as the patient's health improves, so does appetite and the ability to eat normally.

CHAPTER 11 REVIEW

Understanding Key Ideas

1. How do the amounts and types of food you need change throughout your life span?
2. Describe an athlete's schedule for drinking fluids.
3. How are anorexia nervosa and bulimia nervosa similar and different?
4. What is the difference between a food allergy and food intolerance?

Applying Knowledge and Skills

◆ **Pregame Meal:** Plan a meal that would give a teen basketball player energy and nutrients for an after-school game. Explain your choices.

◆ **Identifying Alternatives:** Brainstorm a list of ten different foods that would be off-limits to someone who was allergic to wheat. Then suggest foods that could be eaten instead and would be similar in nutrients.

Exploring Further

◆ **Creative Thinking:** Think of creative ways to make a meal or snack more appealing to a young child. Draw pictures of your ideas.

◆ **Research:** Learn more about one of the eating disorders discussed in the chapter. Include signs of the disorder and how and where to obtain help in your area. Report to the class.

CHAPTER 12

SHOPPING FOR FOOD

If you're like most teens, you shop for food fairly often. It may be just to get snacks for you and your friends, or you may buy food for your entire family.

Discover...

★ *how to plan your food shopping.*

★ *how to use food labels.*

★ *how to shop wisely.*

Key Terms

processing
enriched
fortified
impulse buying
unit price
generic

FOOD FOR THOUGHT

How can you make the most of your time and money when you shop for food?

PLAN YOUR FOOD SHOPPING

Before you shop, you need to make several important decisions. How much can you spend? Where and when will you shop? What will you buy?

CONSIDER YOUR BUDGET

Most families decide on a specific amount to spend on food each month. Before you go shopping, talk with other family members about your food budget.

The cost of food depends on many factors. Some of these are the weather, the time of year, and the costs of packaging and transportation. Many nutritious foods are inexpensive. By planning carefully, you can have appealing and nutritious meals on a limited budget. The shopping strategies you'll learn later in this chapter can also help you get the most for your money.

Hunger can affect your shopping decisions!

WHEN WILL YOU SHOP?

Avoid shopping when you're hungry. Hungry shoppers often buy more food than they need to. Try to shop when the store isn't crowded.

How often you buy food depends on your schedule and the amount of storage space you have at home. In most cases, making many trips to the store during the week takes extra time and energy. It's usually more efficient to plan ahead and make one major shopping trip.

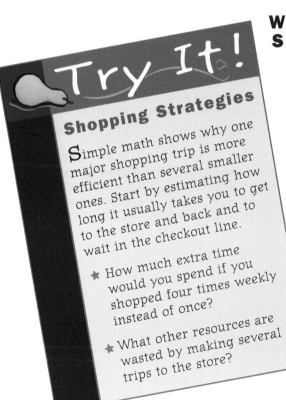

Try It!

Shopping Strategies

Simple math shows why one major shopping trip is more efficient than several smaller ones. Start by estimating how long it usually takes you to get to the store and back and to wait in the checkout line.

★ How much extra time would you spend if you shopped four times weekly instead of once?

★ What other resources are wasted by making several trips to the store?

What type of food store might include a flower shop?

WHERE WILL YOU SHOP?

Depending on where you live, you may be able to choose from different kinds of food stores.

Supermarkets have a great variety of foods attractively displayed. Many offer extra services.

Discount or warehouse stores are similar to supermarkets, but food is often displayed in cardboard boxes. Prices are usually lower.

Co-ops require you to pay a membership fee. The co-op buys food in large quantities and sells it at low prices to its members.

Convenience stores are smaller and usually more expensive than supermarkets.

Compare food stores in your area. Choose a store that's clean, sells good quality food, and offers a good selection. Decide whether you're willing to pay more for convenience and service. If you decide to shop at several stores, be sure it's worth the extra time, effort, and expense.

WHAT WILL YOU BUY?

Suppose you want to buy fruit. Will you choose fresh, canned, or dried? These are examples of different processing methods. **Processing** includes all the steps taken to prepare and package food for sale. Foods may be processed for several reasons, such as:

- To make them safer to eat or drink.

- To make them easier to use.

- To lengthen the time they can be stored.

- To add nutrients or put nutrients back that have been lost. Foods with added nutrients are called **enriched** or **fortified**.

- To turn the food into a particular product. For example, wheat is processed to make flour and breakfast cereal.

Convenience Foods

Convenience foods have been processed to make them more convenient to store or use. The choices range from canned tomato sauce to mashed-potato mix to a complete frozen meal.

When you're busy, convenience foods offer speed and simple preparation. But consider these points as well:

- As food is processed, it loses nutrients. Labels can help you compare the nutritional value of foods.

- Most convenience foods are high in sodium. Many are also high in sugar and fat.

- Convenience foods often cost more. Compare prices.

It's fine to use some convenience foods, as long as you choose wisely. However, if most of the foods you eat are highly processed, it may be difficult to follow the Dietary Guidelines. You need other foods, such as fresh fruits and vegetables, for good health.

This meal was quick to prepare because of convenience foods.

MAKE A LIST

Making a shopping list is one of the most important steps in buying food. When you make the list:

- Plan the meals and snacks you're going to have. (Chapter 24 gives tips for meal planning.)

- As you plan, consider what foods you already have and need to use up. Check newspaper ads to see what foods are on sale.

- Use your plan to make a list of the foods you need to buy.

- Check your supply of staples—basic foods that you always keep on hand, such as milk and flour. Add them to the list if needed.

- If you clip and save coupons, look through them to find any you may be able to use on this trip.

Organize Your List

An orderly list helps speed your shopping. Group items on your list according to the areas of the store, such as:

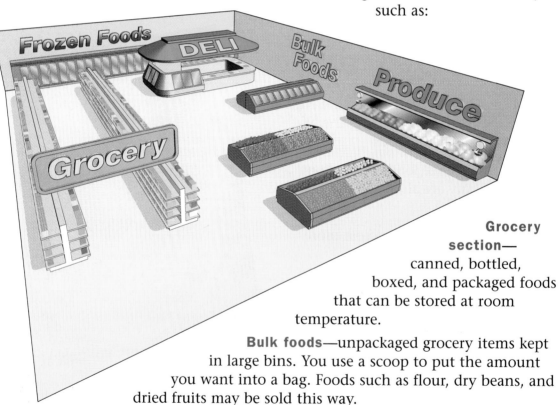

Grocery section—canned, bottled, boxed, and packaged foods that can be stored at room temperature.

Bulk foods—unpackaged grocery items kept in large bins. You use a scoop to put the amount you want into a bag. Foods such as flour, dry beans, and dried fruits may be sold this way.

Produce—fresh vegetables and fruits.

Refrigerated cases—dairy products, juices, and fresh meat, poultry, and fish.

Frozen foods.

Delicatessen (deli)—hot and cold ready-to-eat foods.

UNDERSTANDING FOOD LABELS

Imagine a food store where all the items come in plain brown wrappers without labels of any kind. How would you know what to buy? It's a good thing food packages have label information to help you make wise purchases.

WHAT'S ON A FOOD LABEL?

Food labels give you valuable information for making wise food choices. Here is some of the information you'll find on a typical label.

Description. Helps you make sure you're getting the product you want. For example, do you want "Whole Green Beans" or "Cut Green Beans"? The picture on the label can help you, too.

Quantity. Often given as a net weight—the weight of the food itself, not including the package.

Directions. Tell you how to store or prepare the food.

Nutrition Facts. Helps you choose foods that make up a healthful diet. You'll read more about "Nutrition Facts" later.

Ingredients. Listed by weight, from most to least. Reading the ingredients list can help you avoid foods you don't want or can't eat.

Manufacturer or distributor. The name and address of the company that makes or distributes the product.

UPC symbol. "UPC" stands for Universal Product Code. It's used with computerized checkout systems. A scanner "reads" the bars to identify the item. The price is then rung up automatically.

USING "NUTRITION FACTS"

Most processed foods have a "Nutrition Facts" panel that looks like this one. Here's how to use "Nutrition Facts" to make healthful food choices.

Serving information. Start by checking this area. All the nutrition information given is for *one* serving of the size shown. Is the amount you'll eat the same as the serving size given here? If not, you'll need to do some math as you read the label. For instance, if you eat 1 cup of green beans, that's really two servings. You'll get twice as many calories as shown and twice as much of all the nutrients listed.

Calorie information. Shows the number of calories in one serving of the food. Also tells you how many of those calories come from fat.

Nutrient amounts. Shows how much of each of these nutrients you'll get from one serving of the food. The amounts are measured in grams (g) or milligrams (mg).

Vitamins and minerals. Shows the Percent Daily Value for four of the vitamins and minerals you need each day.

Percent Daily Values. The numbers in this column can help you decide how the food fits into a healthful eating plan. You might not know whether 2 grams of dietary fiber is a lot or a little. This column tells you that it's 8 percent of what the average person needs each day.

- For fat, saturated fat, cholesterol, and sodium, a *low* Percent Daily Value is your goal. Reading labels can help you avoid getting too much of these nutrients.

- For total carbohydrate, dietary fiber, vitamins, and minerals, a *high* Percent Daily Value is your goal. You want your day's food choices to add up to 100% of the Daily Value for these nutrients.

Percent Daily Values explanation. This information is the same on all nutrition labels. It tells what nutrient amounts were used to calculate the Percent Daily Values given above.

Nutrition Facts

Serving Size 1/2 cup (121g)
Servings Per Container 3 1/2

Amount Per Serving

Calories 20   Calories from Fat 0

	% Daily Value*
Total Fat 0g	0%
Saturated Fat 0g	0%
Cholesterol 0mg	0%
Sodium 10mg	0%
Total Carbohydrate 4g	1%
Dietary Fiber 2g	8%
Sugars 2g	
Protein 1g	

Vitamin A 6%	Vitamin C 4%
Calcium 2%	Iron 4%

*Percent Daily Values are based on a 2000 calorie diet. Your daily values may be higher or lower depending on your calorie needs.

As you read the Nutrition Facts panel, remember—it's your overall eating plan that counts. You can't expect just one food to offer "perfect" nutrition. Some foods may be short on vitamins or have more fat than others. Go ahead and enjoy those foods if you like. Just balance them with other choices throughout the day or over several days.

LABEL LANGUAGE

Certain label terms are defined by the government. They can be used on the label only if the product meets the requirements.

Key Words	What They Mean
Fat Free	Less than 0.5 gram of fat per serving
Low Fat	3 grams of fat (or less) per serving
Lean	Less than 10 grams of fat, 4 grams of saturated fat, and 95 milligrams of cholesterol per serving
Light (Lite)	1/3 less calories or no more than half the fat of the higher-calorie, higher-fat version • OR • No more than half the sodium of the higher-sodium version

OPEN DATING

Some food packages have a date stamped on them to help you know whether the food is fresh. For example, the package may say "sell by May 31" or "best if used by June 8." This is called open dating. Look for it on foods such as dairy products, bakery items, and grocery items.

Open dating can't guarantee the quality of the product. Quality is affected by the way the food has been handled and stored. For example, if fresh milk is stored at too warm a temperature, it may lose quality before the date stamped on the package.

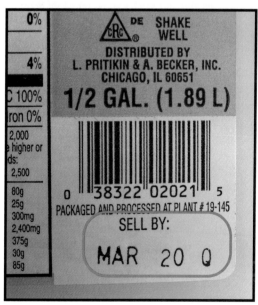

You could still buy this item on March 20. It will stay usable for at least several more days if properly stored.

YOUR SHOPPING TRIP

When you get to the store, follow your shopping list. Avoid **impulse buying**—buying an item you don't need just because it seems appealing at the moment. However, keep your plan flexible. Look for unadvertised specials that could save you money.

USING UNIT PRICES

In many stores, you'll see unit prices posted near items. The **unit price** is the cost per ounce, pound, item, or other unit of measure. For instance, a can of pineapple weighing 8 ounces might cost 56 cents. The unit price would be 7 cents per ounce.

Sometimes the unit price can be found on a shelf tag.

Unit prices make it easier to compare the cost of items, especially those that come in different size packages. If the store doesn't give the unit price, you can figure it out yourself. Divide the price of the item by the number of ounces (or other units). Do the same for other brands or sizes. Then compare the unit price for each.

COMPARISON SHOPPING

You can find the best values using comparison shopping. Compare the unit prices and nutrition of:

Different forms of food. Fresh green beans may be a better buy than frozen this week. At another time of the year the reverse may be true.

Different brands. Name brands are nationally advertised. The price you pay for the food includes the cost of advertising. You can often save money by buying products with the store's own brand name. **Generic** products, which have a plain label, are even less expensive.

Different sizes. Larger sizes often have a lower unit price than smaller sizes, but not always. Besides the unit price, also consider whether you'll actually use the larger amount before it spoils. If not, you waste food and money.

Decision-making skills can help you decide which product to buy.

CHOOSING QUALITY FOODS

Always buy food that's in good condition. Poor quality food wastes money. You'll find information about buying specific types of food in Units 6, 7, and 8. In the meantime, here are some general guidelines.

◆ Avoid containers that are damaged in any way. Give damaged containers to a clerk.

◆ Be sure refrigerated items feel cold when you buy them.

◆ Be sure frozen food packages are frozen hard. Ice crystals may mean that the food has thawed and refrozen.

◆ Buy refrigerated and frozen foods last. Otherwise they'll start to get warm as you shop.

Smart shoppers pass up packages like these!

Shopping for Food 99

MORE SHOPPING TIPS

◆ Be considerate. Don't block traffic by leaving your cart in the middle of the aisle.

◆ Handle food carefully so you don't damage it. If you choose an item and then change your mind, put it back where it belongs.

◆ Don't open packages. If packages of meat or produce contain more than you want, ask a store clerk for help.

◆ Put raw meat and poultry packages in a plastic bag. That will help keep the juices, which may contain harmful germs, from dripping on other foods in your cart.

By not opening packages or damaging items, you help keep prices down.

AFTER SHOPPING

After shopping, bring the food home immediately and store it. If you do errands on your way home, food may begin to lose its quality. For instance, frozen food may start to thaw. In Chapter 21 you'll learn how to store food properly to keep it safe and fresh.

Store all your food purchases as soon as you get home. What might happen if you left some to put away later?

Understanding Key Ideas

1. What are the advantages of making an organized list before you shop for food?
2. What parts of the "Nutrition Facts" panel would be most helpful if you wanted to watch the amount of fat in your diet? Why?
3. How can unit pricing and comparison shopping help you make wise food choices?

Applying Knowledge and Skills

◆ **Shopping List:** Find three recipes in this book or a cookbook. Make one shopping list for all three recipes. Organize your list by area of the store.

◆ **Using Nutrition Facts:** Obtain Nutrition Facts panels for two similar snack foods (such as chips or granola bars). Compare them for serving size, calorie information, nutrient amounts, and Percent Daily Values. Which product would best meet your needs? Why?

Exploring Further

◆ **Product Comparison:** Purchase a national brand, store brand, and generic version of a food item. Calculate the unit price for each. Compare how the items look and taste. Discuss why someone might choose each product.

USING KITCHEN APPLIANCES

Discover...

★ large and small appliances you can use in food preparation.

★ how to use and care for these appliances.

Key Terms

conventional oven
convection oven
microwave oven

Appliances are resources that can help you prepare food faster and more easily. Large appliances, such as refrigerators and ranges, are usually kept in one place. Small appliances, such as toasters, can be used wherever there's an electrical outlet.

FOOD FOR THOUGHT

What kitchen appliances do you use most often? Why?

REFRIGERATOR-FREEZERS

Refrigerator-freezers store food at cold temperatures. There are two basic types:

Two-door model. One door is for the refrigerator, the other for the freezer. The freezer may be at the top, side, or bottom. It's cold enough to freeze fresh foods as well as store those already frozen.

One-door model. This type has only one outer door. Inside there's a small freezer section with a lightweight inner door. The freezer section can store already frozen foods up to two weeks. It's not cold enough to freeze fresh foods well.

USE AND CARE OF THE REFRIGERATOR-FREEZER

Here are some tips to help you get the most efficient use from a refrigerator-freezer.

◆ Wipe up spills right away. Be sure the containers you put in are clean. Spills and dirt breed germs.

◆ Every few weeks, clean the inside of the refrigerator-freezer thoroughly with baking soda and warm water. The outside can be cleaned with mild detergent and water.

◆ Keep the door open for as short a time as possible. You'll save energy and help the appliance maintain the proper temperature.

◆ Don't overload the refrigerator, or food may spoil. The refrigerator compartment works most efficiently when it's about three-quarters full. (The freezer compartment works most efficiently when it's full.)

◆ Don't cover wire shelves to keep them clean. If you do, cold air won't be able to circulate properly.

◆ Read the owner's manual to find out if you must periodically remove food from the freezer and allow the frost to melt. When frost builds up, the freezer has to work harder and use more energy.

An overloaded refrigerator has to work harder. It may not be able to keep food cold enough.

RANGES

A range provides heat for cooking food. A basic range is a single unit with these cooking areas:

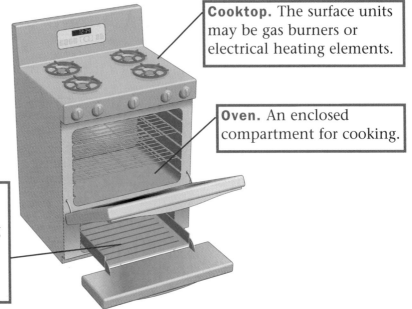

Cooktop. The surface units may be gas burners or electrical heating elements.

Oven. An enclosed compartment for cooking.

Broiler. May be in the oven or in a separate compartment. A heating unit at the top provides direct heat to cook or brown food.

Some ranges are powered by gas, others by electricity. Some have smooth, easy-to-clean cooktops or cooktops with special features, such as a grill. Instead of a single self-contained range, some kitchens have separate cooktop and oven units that are built into kitchen cabinets.

OVEN OPTIONS

There are three basic types of ovens. Each uses different technology to heat food.

A **conventional oven** heats the air in the oven compartment. The hot air circulates naturally around the food. You set the oven control to a specific temperature.

A **convection oven** is similar to a conventional oven except that a fan circulates the air at high speed. It cooks many foods faster than a conventional oven, but not as fast as a microwave oven.

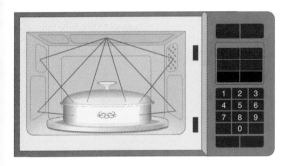

A **microwave oven** cooks with tiny waves of energy that produce heat inside the food. It cooks most foods much faster than other types of ovens and uses less energy. Although a microwave oven is sometimes part of a range, it's more often a separate appliance. You'll learn more about microwave ovens in Chapter 19.

USE AND CARE OF THE RANGE

Before using any appliance, read the owner's manual. It gives information about safe use and care. Here are some tips for using ranges:

◆ Match the pan size to the size of the heating element or burner flame. Otherwise, heat is wasted.

◆ Use pans with flat bottoms. They won't tip over easily.

◆ Turn the surface unit off before you remove a pan.

◆ Adjust oven racks to the desired positions before turning on the heat.

◆ When you open the oven door, stand to one side. This way hot air and steam escaping from the oven won't burn you.

Is this teen using the range safely? Why or why not?

◆ Wipe up any spills after the range has cooled.

SMALL APPLIANCES

Small appliances are available to help with almost any kitchen job. Many small appliances can help you save energy when cooking a small amount. For example, it takes less energy to bake a potato in a small toaster oven than in a large conventional oven.

Here are some of the more common small appliances. Think about how you could substitute them for large appliances.

Slow cooker. Cooks food slowly at low temperatures. A main dish can be prepared in the morning and be ready to eat in the evening.

Electric skillet. Does many different cooking jobs. The heat can be set at a specific temperature.

Toaster. Toasts bread. Comes in two- and four-slice sizes.

Toaster oven. Can be used as a toaster or as an oven. Some models include a broiler.

Mixer. Beats and mixes food. Available as a lightweight portable mixer or a heavier model on a stand.

Blender. Blends, liquefies, or cuts up food quickly.

Food processor. Slices, chops, and shreds a wide variety of foods. Can also be used for mixing ingredients and kneading dough.

USE AND CARE OF SMALL APPLIANCES

Electricity can give you a shock or start a fire if misused. Carefully read and follow the directions in the owner's manual and the guidelines in Chapter 20. Here are some additional tips:

◆ Turn the appliance off before plugging it in or unplugging it.

◆ Always unplug a mixer before putting the beaters in or removing them. Otherwise, the mixer might be turned on accidentally while your fingers are holding the beaters.

◆ Clean appliances after each use. Unplug them first.

◆ Don't put an appliance into water unless it's labeled "immersible." You can damage the appliance and create a safety hazard.

◆ If you get a shock from an appliance, unplug it immediately. Have it repaired.

Look for the UL label. It shows that electrical appliances have been tested for safety.

Underwriters Laboratories, Inc.

CHAPTER 13 REVIEW

Understanding Key Ideas

1. Give three guidelines for using a freezer compartment.
2. Compare and contrast the three types of ovens.
3. How would you choose a pan to use on a cooktop heating unit? Why?
4. When handling a mixer between uses, should it be plugged in? Why or why not?

Applying Knowledge and Skills

◆ **Demonstration:** Show how you would safely and efficiently use one of the appliances discussed in this chapter.

◆ **Recipe Analysis:** Find a recipe for a bread, main dish, vegetable dish, or dessert. List all the large and small appliances used to prepare the recipe. As a class, make a master list for each type of food. What can you conclude about the most useful appliances for each category?

Exploring Further

◆ **Critical Thinking:** Is it always more efficient to use a small appliance rather than perform a task by hand? Why or why not?

◆ **Research:** Identify three special features found in some ranges. For each feature, find out any additional use and care tips the manufacturer gives. Report to the class.

KNOW YOUR EQUIPMENT

When you prepare food, you need certain kinds of equipment to help you work easily, successfully, and safely. In this chapter, you'll learn about equipment for measuring, cutting, mixing, cooking, and baking.

Discover...

★ *some of the equipment you can use for food preparation.*

★ *what the equipment looks like.*

★ *what the equipment is used for.*

Key Terms

colander
casserole

FOOD FOR THOUGHT

Think about some of the kitchen tools you've used. What tasks did you use them for? How would you categorize them?

TOOLS OF THE TRADE

Kitchen equipment is just as important to a cook as carpentry tools are to a builder. To make the best use of your kitchen tools:

◆ Store items close to where you use them. You'll save steps.

◆ Use tools for the jobs they're designed to handle. Otherwise you might damage the tools or injure yourself.

◆ Learn the correct, safe way to use equipment.

◆ Clean and care for equipment properly so it will last a long time.

◆ Put items back in their proper place so they can be found easily.

CUTTING TOOLS

These tools help you cut food into smaller pieces. Each is designed for a particular cutting task, so choose the right tool for the job. When knives are kept properly sharpened, they cut more easily and cause fewer accidents than dull ones.

Utility knife. All-purpose knife. Cuts and slices many foods, such as fruits and vegetables.

Slicing knife. Slices meat and poultry.

Paring knife. Cuts and pares (removes the skin from) fruits and vegetables.

Bread knife. Has serrated (sawtooth) edge. Cuts bread and cakes easily.

Chef's knife. For quick slicing, dicing, and chopping of foods.

Grater. Grates food into tiny pieces.

Cutting board. Protects countertop or table while cutting.

Kitchen shears. Cut foods such as dried fruit and parsley.

Peeler. Removes the skin from fruits and vegetables.

COOKING AND BAKING TOOLS

These tools help you handle food when you cook and bake. Some tools are made of, or coated with, plastic. That's so they won't scratch the surface of pans that have a nonstick finish.

Wire cooling racks. Hold hot food, such as cakes, breads, and cookies, while cooling.

Spatula. Levels off dry or solid ingredients when measuring. Loosens baked goods from pans.

Basting spoon. Used for basting (pouring liquid over food), as well as stirring or serving. Has a long, heatproof handle.

Rolling pin and cover. Rolls out dough for pie crust, biscuits, cookies. Cover keeps dough from sticking to the rolling pin.

Utility fork. Lifts or turns food.

Tongs. Lift and turn hot food without piercing it.

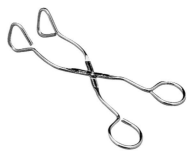

Slotted spoon. Drains liquid from food.

Meat thermometer. Measures internal temperature of food. *Oven-proof thermometer* remains in meat during roasting. *Instant-read thermometer* is used to test food after cooking to be sure it's reached the proper internal temperature.

Turner. Lifts and turns food such as pancakes and hamburgers.

Ladle. Used to dip liquid, such as soup, from pan to bowl or cup.

Colander. Drains liquid from foods such as cooked spaghetti.

COOKWARE

Cookware refers to the wide variety of pans used for cooking and baking. Cookware is made of various materials. Metal, enamel-coated metal, and glass-ceramic cookware can usually be used on top of the range or in the oven. Pottery and some glass cookware is meant for oven use only. Even some plastic cookware is now ovenproof. Microwave ovens have special cookware needs, which you'll learn about in Chapter 19.

Steamer basket. Used for steaming food, especially vegetables. Inserted into a pot or pan to hold food above boiling water.

Saucepans and pots. Saucepans have one long handle. Pots have two small handles. Both styles come in assorted sizes and usually have matching covers.

Skillets. Also called frypans. Made of metal or glass. Size is usually indicated by the diameter. Some have nonstick finish. Some have matching covers.

Roasting pans. Shallow pans with handles on both ends. They usually have a roasting rack on the bottom to hold the meat or poultry out of the juices.

Casseroles. For baking main dish mixtures and other foods. Made of many different materials—glass, pottery, stoneware, glass ceramic. Usually measured by quart or liter sizes.

Baking pans. Usually made of metal or ovenproof glass. They come in a wide variety of shapes and sizes, depending on the product to be baked.

Cake Pans

Loaf Pan

Cookie Sheet

Pie Plate

Muffin Tin

MEASURING TOOLS

Cups and spoons used for eating vary in size. They aren't meant for measuring. For a recipe to turn out right, you need accurate measurements based on standard measuring cups and spoons.

Liquid measuring cup. Made of plastic or glass in different sizes. Has extra space at the top so liquids can be carried without spilling. Has a pouring spout.

Measuring spoons. Used to measure small amounts of liquid or dry ingredients.

Dry measuring cups. Used to measure dry and solid ingredients.

MIXING EQUIPMENT

This equipment is used for mixing ingredients by hand. You can also mix ingredients with electric appliances, such as a mixer or blender.

Wire whisk. Beats, blends. Especially good for beating egg white mixtures.

Sifter. Adds air to flour and other dry ingredients while mixing them. Removes lumps and large pieces.

Mixing bowls. Made of pottery, glass, or metal. Come in different sizes.

Rubber scraper. Removes food from spoons, sides of bowls, pans, jars, and cans.

Rotary beater. Used for light beating, such as beating eggs or pancake batter.

Pastry blender. Cuts shortening into flour when making pastry and biscuits.

Mixing spoon. Beats, mixes, stirs.

OTHER EQUIPMENT

The items discussed in this chapter aren't the only ones needed in a kitchen. For example, you need an apron to protect your clothes from food spots and stains. Potholders and oven mitts protect your hands when working with hot pans. Cleanup equipment also belongs in every kitchen. What other equipment might you need?

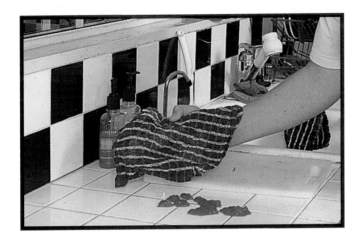

CHAPTER 14 REVIEW

Understanding Key Ideas

1. What would happen if you used a dry measuring cup to measure milk? Why would this occur?
2. Describe how to tell the difference between a chef's knife and a paring knife; a mixing spoon and a basting spoon.
3. Which cutting tools would you use to prepare fresh fruits for a salad? Why?
4. Explain how to tell whether a piece of cookware is meant for oven or cooktop use.

Applying Knowledge and Skills

◆ **Setting Priorities:** The tools you own are usually limited by budget or space. Which kitchen tools do you feel are most important to have? Explain why you chose those items. Tell how they might be used for more than one type of job.

◆ **Foods Lab:** Find a recipe that uses equipment you're familiar with. Gather all the equipment you'd need to prepare the recipe. Explain to the class why you chose the items you did. Discuss other choices that might be made.

Exploring Further

◆ **Other Equipment:** Learn about a kitchen tool not described in this chapter. Bring the item or a picture of it to class and explain its use.

READING RECIPES

Discover...
* *the information given in a recipe.*
* *what basic food preparation terms mean.*

Key Terms
recipe
ingredients
yield

Have you ever had a taco with too much hot pepper or a dry, tough hamburger? What went wrong?

The secret of successful food preparation is knowing how to use recipes correctly. A *recipe* is your guide to help you prepare a certain food. It explains how to put the right amounts of food and seasonings together in just the right way.

FOOD FOR THOUGHT

What might happen if you didn't follow a recipe exactly the first time? When might you want to make changes in a recipe?

CHOOSING A RECIPE

Before you begin to prepare food, look at the recipe carefully. If it's not clear and complete, choose a different one. The example on the next page shows the information a recipe needs to be complete.

FOLLOWING RECIPES

Some recipes are flexible—they can be varied according to your taste. After you prepare a stew, for example, you might decide to use a little more onion and less celery next time. You could also experiment with herbs and spices and give the stew a different flavor. That can be part of the fun of cooking.

What a Recipe Tells You

Recipes can be written in different styles. However, all recipes should include the same basic information.

Ingredients. *Ingredients* are the foods in a recipe. Look for specific details, such as "finely chopped onion" or "light brown sugar." A well-written recipe lists ingredients in the order they are used.

Amounts. The recipe should tell you exactly how much you need of each ingredient. You will learn about units of measurement and their abbreviations in Chapter 16.

Directions. Are there clear, step-by-step instructions for preparing the recipe?

Pan or container. Be sure to use the type and size called for so the recipe will turn out right.

Temperature. You may need to know how to set the controls for the oven or other appliances.

Time. You may need to know how long to cook or chill the food, for example.

Yield. The *yield* is the amount the recipe makes or the number of servings.

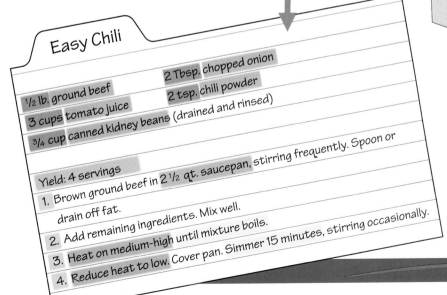

Easy Chili

½ lb. ground beef
3 cups tomato juice
¾ cup canned kidney beans (drained and rinsed)
2 Tbsp. chopped onion
2 tsp. chili powder

Yield: 4 servings

1. Brown ground beef in 2 ½ qt. saucepan, stirring frequently. Spoon or drain off fat.
2. Add remaining ingredients. Mix well.
3. Heat on medium-high until mixture boils.
4. Reduce heat to low. Cover pan. Simmer 15 minutes, stirring occasionally.

However, some recipes can't be changed as easily. That's true of most baked goods, such as breads, cakes, and cookies. For best results, follow these recipes exactly.

What if you don't have an ingredient called for in the recipe? Many cookbooks have substitution charts. The chart may suggest ingredients that can be used in place of the one you're missing. Keep in mind that the results will probably be a little different.

BASIC TERMS AND TECHNIQUES

Here are some of the most common terms and techniques used in food preparation. Become familiar with them. They can help you use recipes more easily and successfully.

TECHNIQUES FOR CUTTING FOODS

When cutting foods, always use sharp tools and a clean cutting board. If you cut directly on a kitchen counter or table, you can damage the surface. After cutting raw meat, poultry, or fish, remember to wash the knife and cutting board with hot, soapy water before using them again. Here are some cutting terms to know:

Pare. Use a peeler or paring knife to cut a very thin layer of peel from fruits or vegetables.

Grate. Rub food on a grater to make very fine particles. Many graters have small holes for grating and larger holes for shredding.

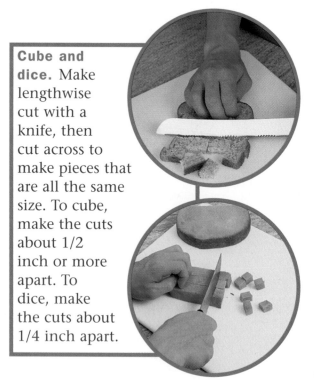

Cube and dice. Make lengthwise cut with a knife, then cut across to make pieces that are all the same size. To cube, make the cuts about 1/2 inch or more apart. To dice, make the cuts about 1/4 inch apart.

Chop and mince. Use a knife, food chopper, kitchen shears, or food processor. To chop, cut food into small irregular pieces. The recipe may tell you what size. To mince, keep chopping until the food pieces are as small as possible.

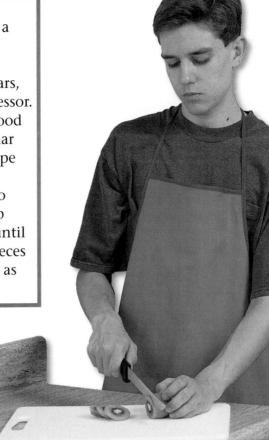

Slice. Cut into thin, flat pieces.

Shred. Cut food into long, thin pieces by rubbing it on the coarse surface of a grater. You can also use a food processor, a knife (to shred lettuce or cabbage), or two forks (to shred cooked meat).

Puree. (pure-RAY *or* pure-EE) Put food through a blender, food processor, food mill, or strainer so that it becomes a smooth, thick mass.

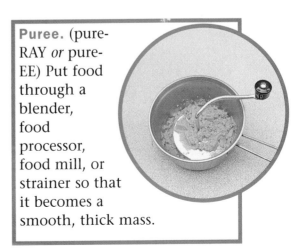

TECHNIQUES FOR COMBINING FOODS

A variety of bowls, spoons, and other tools are used to combine ingredients. The different terms help you know what tool to use and how quickly and completely to combine the ingredients.

Stir. Use a wooden or metal spoon and a circular or figure-8 motion. Stirring may be done to combine ingredients or to distribute heat evenly.

Mix or combine. Both these terms usually mean to stir different ingredients together.

Blend. Mix ingredients together thoroughly until they're completely uniform. You can use a spoon, wire whisk, or electric blender.

Beat. Use a spoon or wire whisk with an over-and-over motion; a rotary beater; or an electric mixer. When beating different ingredients together, continue until the mixture is smooth. Whole eggs or egg whites are often beaten until they take on the desired color and texture.

Cut in. This is a way to mix shortening and flour. Use a pastry blender or two knives and a cutting motion.

Fold in. This is a very gentle way to combine foods. It's often used with ingredients that have air beaten into them, such as whipped cream or beaten egg whites. You don't want the air bubbles to break and release air. Use a wooden spoon or rubber scraper. Cut straight down through the mixture, across the bottom, then up and over. Don't lift the spoon or scraper out of the mixture. Give the bowl a quarter turn. Repeat until the mixture is well blended.

Whip. Some ingredients, such as cream, can be whipped to add air to increase volume. Beat very rapidly with a beater, mixer, or wire whisk.

Cream. This usually refers to combining shortening and sugar. Beat them together using a spoon, rotary beater, or electric mixer until soft, smooth, and creamy.

Toss. Tumble a mixture, such as a salad, very lightly with a spoon and a fork.

Try It!

Fold or Stir?

Does the mixing method really make a difference? To find out, place 1 cup pudding in each of two bowls. Use an electric mixer to whip 1 cup cream. Place half the whipped cream in each pudding bowl. Use a spoon to stir one mixture. Carefully fold the other. Measure each mixture.

* Which mixture has more volume?

* How do you explain the difference?

COOKING TERMS

There are many different ways to cook food. You'll learn more about cooking techniques in Chapters 18 and 19. For now, here are some cooking terms you might see in recipe directions.

Preheat. Turn on an appliance, such as an oven or electric skillet, ahead of time so that it will be at the right temperature when you put in the food.

Brown. Cook food briefly until the surface turns brown. You can brown food in a skillet with a little hot fat, in the oven, or in a broiler. Use the method called for in the recipe.

Boil. When a liquid is heated to boiling, bubbles constantly rise to the surface and break.

Simmer. A simmering liquid isn't quite hot enough to boil. Bubbles form slowly and break before they reach the surface.

OTHER RECIPE TERMS

Here are additional terms you may see in recipes.

Chill. Refrigerate food until it's cold.

Grease. Some recipes call for a greased pan. Spread a thin layer of unsalted shortening in the pan or use a cooking spray.

Baste. To brush or pour liquid over food as it cooks. Basting keeps the food from drying out. Melted fat, sauces, or meat drippings may be used.

Drain. Remove excess liquid by pouring it off or by placing food in a strainer or colander.

Garnish. Decorate a food or dish with a small, colorful food such as parsley or a lemon slice.

CHAPTER 15 REVIEW

Understanding Key Ideas

1. Why are recipes useful?
2. How can you tell whether a recipe gives complete information?
3. Explain the difference between each pair of terms: cube and chop; shred and grate; cut in and fold in; boil and simmer.

Applying Knowledge and Skills

◆ **Recipe Analysis:** Copy a recipe from a cookbook. Circle and label each of the recipe parts described on page 117. Note any parts that are missing. List the food preparation terms found in the recipe and explain the meaning of as many as you can. Do you feel the recipe is clearly written? Why or why not?

◆ **Foods Lab:** Use raw potatoes to practice the following techniques: pare, slice, chop, mince, cube, dice, grate. Be sure to use the correct tools for each job.

Exploring Further

◆ **Creative Thinking:** Choose a recipe for a casserole. Identify at least three ways you might alter the recipe to give it a different flavor.

◆ **Social Studies Connection:** Find a recipe or cookbook from the 19th century. Discuss the differences between recipes from that era and modern ones. What might account for these differences?

RECIPE MATH

Food preparation and math go hand in hand. Basic math skills can help you understand the units of measure given in recipes. They can also help you to make changes in a recipe.

Discover...

★ *two basic systems of measurement.*

★ *units of measurement commonly used in recipes.*

★ *how to increase and decrease recipes.*

Key Terms

customary system
metric system
equivalent

FOOD FOR THOUGHT

When might you want to change the amount a recipe makes? Why would you need good math skills to do this?

THE MATH OF MEASURING

Some people—perhaps you—speak more than one language. Measurement also has different "languages." The **customary system** is the system of measurement most commonly used in the United States. The **metric system** is the standard system in most of the world. It's also used by scientists and health professionals in this country.

Some recipes give customary measurements. Others use the metric system. If you have both customary and metric measuring equipment, you won't need to convert measurements from one system to the other.

Different units of measure can be compared using equivalents. For example, 12 inches is the **equivalent** of, or the same as, one foot.

VOLUME

Many recipe ingredients are measured by volume. Volume refers to the amount of space an ingredient takes up. Basic units for measuring volume include:

Customary: • teaspoon (tsp.) • tablespoon (Tbsp.) • fluid ounce (fl. oz.) • cup (c.) • pint (pt.) • quart (qt.) • gallon (gal.)

Metric: • milliliter (mL) • liter (L)

Equipment for measuring volume includes liquid measuring cups, dry measuring cups, and measuring spoons. Liquid measuring cups come in various sizes. Often they're marked in both customary and metric units. Dry measuring cups and measuring spoons come in the following standard sizes:

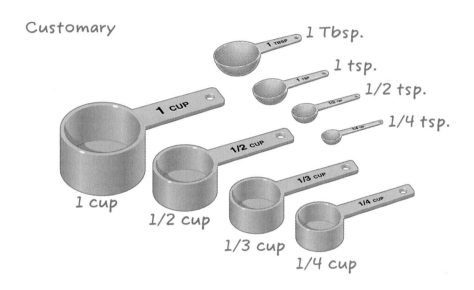

Customary

1 Tbsp.
1 tsp.
1/2 tsp.
1/4 tsp.
1 cup
1/2 cup
1/3 cup
1/4 cup

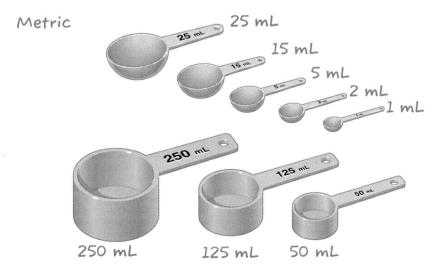

Metric

25 mL
15 mL
5 mL
2 mL
1 mL
250 mL
125 mL
50 mL

VOLUME EQUIVALENTS

Customary Unit	Customary Equivalent	Approximate Metric Equivalent
Dash	Less than 1/8 tsp.	Less than 0.5 mL
1/4 tsp.		1 mL
1/2 tsp.		2 or 3 mL
1 tsp.		5 mL
1 Tbsp.	3 tsp.	15 mL
1 fluid oz.	2 Tbsp.	30 mL
1 cup	8 fluid oz. or 16 Tbsp.	250 mL
1 pt.	2 cups or 16 fluid oz.	500 mL
1 qt.	2 pt. or 4 cups or 32 fluid oz.	1 L or 1000 mL
1 gal.	4 qt.	4 L

WEIGHT

Weight refers to how heavy or light an ingredient is. Scales are used to measure weight. Many food packages are labeled according to how much they weigh.

Here are basic units for measuring weight and their abbreviations or symbols:

Customary system: • ounce (oz.) • pound (lb.)

Metric system: • gram (g) • kilogram (kg)

Notice that the term "ounce" is used in two different ways—to measure weight (ounce) and volume (fluid ounce). Keep in mind that the two kinds of ounces aren't the same. When a recipe calls for ounces, be sure you understand whether you're to measure by weight or by volume.

WEIGHT EQUIVALENTS

Customary Measure	Customary Equivalent	Approximate Metric Equivalent
1 oz.		30 g
1 lb.	16 oz.	500 g
2 lb.	32 oz.	1 kg or 1000 g

OTHER MEASUREMENTS

Temperature. In the customary system, temperature is measured in degrees Fahrenheit (°F). In the metric system, temperature is measured in degrees Celsius (°C). Many thermometers show both types of degrees.

Length. Recipes sometimes include length measurements. You may need to know the length and width of a pan or the size of a vegetable. The customary system measures length in inches (in.), while the metric system uses millimeters (mm) or centimeters (cm).

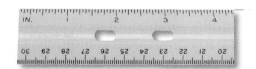

INCREASING OR DECREASING RECIPES

The yield of a recipe tells how many servings it will make. What if you want more or fewer servings? You may be able to change the yield by increasing or decreasing the recipe.

HOW MANY SERVINGS DO YOU WANT?

The first step is to decide on the desired yield—the number of servings you want. Suppose you need enough pasta salad for seven people. The recipe yields four servings. Should you increase the recipe to make seven servings? You could, but the math for eight servings would be easier. You decide that eight servings is your desired yield.

Why might you need to adjust a recipe for a different number of servings?

CALCULATING THE NEW AMOUNTS

Next, use the desired yield and the original yield in this formula:

desired yield ÷ original yield = magic number

Then multiply the amount of each ingredient by the "magic number." To make eight servings of pasta salad instead of four, you would multiply the amount of each ingredient by two.

The same formula works when you're decreasing a recipe. Suppose a recipe makes 12 servings of tuna casserole. How would you adjust it to make four servings? You would multiply each amount in the recipe by 1/3 (because 4 ÷ 12 = 1/3).

Before you start to prepare the recipe, figure out all the new amounts and write them down. Otherwise, you would have to stop and calculate each time you had to measure something. You might forget to change one of the amounts.

Converting Amounts

When adjusting a recipe, you may sometimes need to convert a measurement to an equivalent amount. Suppose the recipe for tuna casserole calls for 1/2 cup of milk. If you multiply 1/2 by 1/3, you get 1/6 cup. However, 1/6 cup is hard to measure. Your liquid measuring cup doesn't have a marking for that amount.

Instead, begin by converting 1/2 cup into tablespoons. Look at the volume equivalent chart on page 126. One cup is 16 tablespoons, so 1/2 cup equals 8 tablespoons.

Now when you multiply by 1/3, you get:

$$8 \times 1/3 = 8/3 = 2\frac{2}{3} \text{ Tbsp.}$$

But how do you measure 2/3 tablespoon? Break the tablespoon down into smaller measures. Remember, one tablespoon equals 3 teaspoons. Therefore, 2/3 of a tablespoon is 2 teaspoons. To measure the milk for the tuna casserole, you measure 2 tablespoons plus 2 teaspoons!

1/6 Cup =

What If It Doesn't Come Out Even?

Sometimes an amount can't be decreased easily. You might end up with an amount like "1/2 egg." What should you do then?

With mixtures such as casseroles, stews, salads, or soups, exact amounts usually aren't critical. You could probably use a whole egg instead of half in a casserole with good results.

However, baked products such as cookies, cake, or bread depend on exact amounts of ingredients. If you have to round off amounts or can change only some of them, the recipe may not work.

If a recipe can't be increased or decreased easily, think of another way to solve the problem. Instead of trying to prepare just half of a recipe, you might prepare the entire amount and freeze half to use later.

Is this the way to halve a recipe that calls for one egg?

USE THE RIGHT SIZE EQUIPMENT

Suppose you double a recipe for brownies. Will you need a larger mixing bowl? If you use a larger baking pan, the brownies will take longer to bake. You may want to divide the mixture into two pans of the same size and shape.

When you decrease a recipe, cook the food in a smaller pan. Otherwise, it may cook too fast or dry out.

After you've adjusted the yield of a recipe, decide whether you need to change the equipment for preparing it.

CHAPTER 16 REVIEW

Understanding Key Ideas

1. If a recipe uses metric measurements, what are your two options for preparing it?
2. What are weight and volume? How is each measured?
3. Tell what each of the following stands for, what it measures (weight, volume, etc.), and whether it is metric or customary: mL, oz., tsp., °C, fl. oz., g, pt.
4. Suppose you are changing a recipe's yield from eight servings to ten. Explain how to determine ingredient amounts.

Applying Knowledge and Skills

◆ **Converting to Equivalents:** Convert each amount to the units shown in parentheses: 4 Tbsp. (cups); 1/2 cup (mL); 1½ pt. (fl. oz.); 1/4 lb. (oz.); 8 oz. (g).

◆ **Changing Yield:** Choose a recipe that makes 4 servings. Rewrite it to make 6 servings. Include all changes needed to help ensure the recipe's success. Show your calculations.

Exploring Further

◆ **Computer Lab:** Explore ways to use a computer to help change the yield of a recipe. Two possibilities are a spreadsheet for converting amounts and recipe software that changes yield automatically. Demonstrate one or more methods to the class. Explain the advantages and limitations of each.

BASIC MEASURING METHODS

Discover...

★ *how to measure dry ingredients.*

★ *how to measure liquid ingredients.*

★ *how to measure solid fats.*

Key Term
sift

Too much or too little of an ingredient can make a big difference! This chapter shows you how to work with measuring cups and spoons to measure ingredients accurately.

FOOD FOR THOUGHT

What might happen if you put too much salt and not enough flour in pancakes?

MEASURING DRY INGREDIENTS

Dry ingredients include flour, sugar, rice, spices, and so on. Measuring spoons are used for small amounts. For larger amounts, use dry measuring cups. Usually, dry ingredients should be level with the top of the measuring cup or spoon. Sometimes, however, a recipe calls for a "heaping" measurement—one that's above the top of the cup or spoon.

Level

Heaping

How to **Measure Dry Ingredients**

1. Hold the cup or spoon over waxed paper or the ingredient's container.

   Why? If any spills over, it will be caught by the paper or the container instead of going into your recipe.

STEP 2

2. Fill the cup or spoon slightly over the top.

   Tip Don't shake or tap the cup to make more room. Don't pack the ingredient into the measuring utensil—*unless* you're measuring brown sugar or the recipe says to.

STEP 3

3. Use a straight edge, such as a spatula, to level off the top of the cup or spoon.

TIPS FOR DRY INGREDIENTS

Brown sugar. Pack the sugar firmly into the cup using the back of a spoon or a rubber scraper. Overfill the cup a little, then level it off. The brown sugar should come out holding the shape of the cup.

Granulated sugar. If sugar is lumpy, put it through a strainer before measuring. Press out the lumps with a spoon.

Sifted flour. Some recipes call for sifted flour. To **sift** means to put a dry ingredient through a sifter to separate the particles. Place waxed paper under the measuring cup. Spoon the flour into the sifter, then sift into the cup. After measuring the amount you need, return any remaining flour to its original container.

Unsifted flour. If the recipe doesn't tell you to sift flour, just stir it with a spoon before measuring. Whole grain flours, such as whole wheat or rye, are never sifted.

MEASURING LIQUID INGREDIENTS

For liquids, such as milk, water, oil, or honey, use a liquid measuring cup. It has a pouring spout and extra space at the top to help prevent spills. For small amounts, use a measuring spoon. Fill it just to the brim.

Syrup and honey are thick and sticky. Before measuring them, you can oil the measuring cup so they'll flow out more easily. You may need to use a rubber scraper to get all the syrup or honey out of the cup.

Hold the cup or spoon away from the mixing bowl. If you pour out too much, the extra won't fall into the bowl.

How to Measure Liquids

1. Place the cup on a flat, level surface, such as a table or counter.

2. Slowly pour the liquid into the cup.

STEP 2

3. Stoop down to check the measurement at eye level.

   Why? If you look down at the cup or lift the cup off the flat surface, you won't get an accurate measurement.

STEP 3

MEASURING SOLID FATS

Solid fats, such as butter, margarine, or shortening, can be measured in several different ways. Two of the easiest are the stick method and the dry measuring cup method.

Stick method. Butter and margarine are sold by the stick. One stick weighs 1/4 pound and is equal to 1/2 cup. The wrappers are usually marked off in tablespoons so you can cut off the amount you need.

Dry measuring cup method. Spoon shortening into a dry measuring cup. Pack it down firmly. Be sure to work out all air bubbles so the measurement is accurate. Pack the cup slightly more than full, then level it off. To get the shortening out of the cup, use a rubber scraper.

CHAPTER 17 REVIEW

Understanding Key Ideas

1. What is the difference between level and heaping measurements?
2. How is measuring flour different from measuring brown sugar?
3. What is the correct way to measure 1/2 cup milk? 1 tsp. vanilla?
4. Describe two methods you could use to measure solid fats.

Applying Knowledge and Skills

◆ **Recipe Analysis:** Choose a recipe and list all the measuring equipment you would need. Explain how you would use each item.

◆ **Demonstration:** Imagine you host a television cooking show. Demonstrate accurate measuring methods.

Exploring Further

◆ **Researching Equivalents:** Locate a list that gives equivalents such as these: How many cups in a pound of brown sugar? How many graham crackers make a cup of crumbs? As a class, make a master list of such equivalents to use in the foods lab.

◆ **Measuring Tool Teamwork:** In small groups, brainstorm ideas for a new type of measuring tool. Decide on one of the ideas and develop a presentation for the class. Explain how the tool would be used and how it would work.

BASIC COOKING METHODS

Discover...

★ *three general types of cooking methods.*

★ *the characteristics of different cooking methods.*

★ *how to save nutrients when you cook.*

Key Terms

dry heat methods
moist heat methods
sautéing

I t was Josh's turn to make dinner. In the refrigerator he found a package of meat and some fresh green beans. Neither one came with cooking directions, and Josh didn't have time to look around for a recipe. "Oh well," he thought. "I know how to bake potatoes or a frozen pizza, so maybe I can cook these the same way." Josh put the meat on a pizza pan, dumped the beans in a dish, and put them both in the oven.

Josh didn't know that different foods need to be cooked in different ways. If he had, his family could have enjoyed a home-cooked meal instead of another night of fast-food burgers.

FOOD FOR THOUGHT

How would you have prepared the foods if you were in Josh's place? What might you have done differently?

TYPES OF COOKING METHODS

When you look through cookbooks, you can find hundreds of different ways to prepare food. However, most recipes use one or more of three basic cooking methods: dry heat, moist heat, and frying.

DRY HEAT METHODS

Dry heat methods are those in which you cook the food uncovered without adding any liquid or fat. Broiling, roasting, and baking are examples of dry heat methods.

Cooking in dry heat improves the flavor, texture, and appearance of many foods. The food usually turns brown and develops a crisp or tender crust.

Baking and Roasting

"Baking" and "roasting" are two terms that mean the same thing—to cook food in dry heat in an oven. Foods that can be baked or roasted include fish, tender meats and poultry, and some fruits and vegetables. Breads, cakes, pies, cookies, and similar foods are also baked.

Baking and roasting can be done in a conventional oven or a convection oven. You can also use a toaster oven or a similar small appliance. A microwave oven, however, doesn't cook with hot, dry air. For this reason, microwaving is not considered a dry heat method.

When you want to bake or roast food, leave the food uncovered. If you add liquid or cover the food, you'll cook it in moist heat, not dry heat.

Broiling

In broiling, food is cooked by direct heat from above. Foods that can be broiled include tender cuts of meat, young poultry, fish, and some fruits and vegetables. The next page shows how foods are broiled.

Broiling is simple and versatile. Just remember these basic points.

The broiler pan. A broiler pan has two parts:

- **A grid**, or tray with holes. The food is placed on the grid.

- **A bottom pan** that is about 1 inch deep. The grid fits over it. As the food broils, fat drains through the holes in the grid and into the bottom pan.

Under the heat.
The broiler pan is placed under the heating unit of an appliance. It might be a range, countertop broiler, or toaster oven. You control how fast the food cooks by how far you place it from the heat. Thicker foods should be placed farther from the heat than thin foods.

Tips for Successful Broiling

- Don't preheat the broiler pan. It should be cold when the food is placed on it to avoid sticking.

- Don't line the grid with foil—the fat will not be able to drain away. The food will fry and the fat could catch fire.

- Check the recipe for the proper distance between the broiler pan and the heat.

- Follow the directions in the owner's manual for the broiler or oven. When broiling in an electric oven, the door is usually left slightly open. If you are using a gas range, the broiler door should be closed.

- Broil for the length of time given in the recipe. Turn food as directed.

Panbroiling

Panbroiling is a cooktop method of broiling food. It can be used for thin, tender cuts of meat, such as pork chops, bacon, or hamburgers.

To panbroil, place the food in an ungreased hot skillet. Cook, uncovered, until browned on one side. Turn and continue cooking until done. Pour off any fat that accumulates during cooking. Don't pour the fat down the drain—it will clog the plumbing. Instead, pour it into an empty can. After the fat cools and hardens, throw the can away.

The only fat used in panbroiling is that found naturally in the meat.

MOIST HEAT METHODS

Moist heat methods use a hot liquid, steam, or a combination of both. You're using moist heat cooking whenever:

- ◆ The food being cooked is a liquid, such as a sauce or cocoa. *Or . . .*

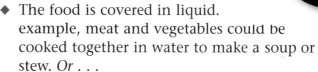

  - ◆ The food is covered in liquid. example, meat and vegetables could be cooked together in water to make a soup or stew. *Or . . .*

  - ◆ The pan or container is covered so that steam and moisture stay inside.

Foods cooked in moist heat don't brown. They also do develop a crisp or tender crust.

Moist heat has many uses. It can tenderize foods, such cuts of meat. It can also help keep food from drying out as it cooks. It's used to cook foods that must absorb liquid, such as noodles or dry beans. Foods may be cooked together in a sauce or broth to blend their flavors.

Many different appliances can be used for moist heat cooking:

Conventional oven. Moist heat can be created by cooking food in a covered dish, sealing in foil, or using a special plastic cooking bag.

Microwave oven. Microwaving is a moist heat method. You'll learn more about microwave cooking techniques in the next chapter.

Small appliances. For example, you can use a slow cooker or a covered electric skillet.

Cooktop. When cooking on top of the range, the most common moist heat methods are boiling, simmering, and steaming.

Why is using a slow cooker a moist heat method?

How can you tell this liquid is boiling?

Boiling

The boiling point of liquid is the temperature at which it turns to steam. The boiling point of water is 212°F. When liquid boils, bubbles rise up continuously and break the surface of the liquid.

There are only a few times when food should be cooked at a boil. For example, noodles must be cooked in a large amount of boiling water. Usually, however, it's better to simmer foods than to boil them. Why? Foods lose more nutrients, flavor, and texture when boiled. Boiling also toughens protein foods.

Simmering

Simmering lets foods cook gently until they're done. The temperature of the liquid is just slightly below boiling. Bubbles rise slowly but don't break the surface.

Some foods, such as corn on the cob, are simmered in enough water to cover them. Others are simmered in just a little water in a covered pan.

Food may be simmered whole or cut into pieces. To make sure the food or liquid is at the right temperature for simmering, first bring it to a boil. Then lower the heat immediately so the bubbles don't break the surface.

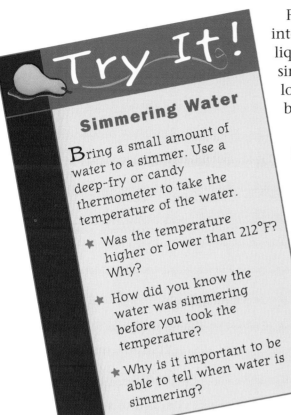

Steaming

Many foods, such as vegetables, can be cooked in steam. The most common method is to place a steamer basket inside a pan with a small amount of boiling water. The basket holds the food above the water, but has holes to let steam flow through and cook the food. After putting the food in the basket, cover the pan at once to keep the steam inside.

Steam cooks foods quickly because of its high heat.

FRYING

Frying means cooking in fat. This cooking method makes food brown, crisp, and flavorful. However, frying isn't as healthful as other methods because the food soaks up fat. Choose other cooking methods, such as broiling or panbroiling, most often.

When you do fry, use as little fat or oil as possible. Avoid using hard fats such as butter or lard for frying. Liquid vegetable oil is lower in saturated fat. Another good choice is vegetable-oil cooking spray, which gives just a light coating of oil.

What are the advantages and disadvantages of frying food?

French fries are deep-fat fried potatoes.

Deep-Fat Frying

One way to fry foods is deep-fat frying, also called french frying. The food is completely covered in a large amount of fat. The fat is heated to a specific temperature, which is checked using a deep-fry thermometer. Of the two frying methods, deep-fat frying adds more fat to food.

Panfrying

Some foods can be fried in a skillet in a small amount of fat. This is called panfrying. You can use this method for tender or quick-cooking foods, such as eggs.

Panfrying is often used to precook foods such as onions, mushrooms, and green peppers before they're used in a recipe. Then it's usually called **sautéing** (saw-TAY-ing). The foods are chopped or sliced so they'll cook quickly. Cook, stirring occasionally, just until the vegetables soften.

What types of recipes might require that ingredients be sautéed first?

COMBINATION METHODS

Braising and stir-frying are two methods that combine frying with moist heat.

Braising means to brown food in a small amount of fat, then finish with long, slow cooking in moist heat. Pot roast, chicken pieces, or vegetables such as carrots, potatoes, and parsnips may be braised.

Stir-frying is a method of frying food quickly in a small amount of oil at a high temperature. The food is stirred constantly to keep it from sticking to the pan. During the last few minutes of cooking, the pan may be covered so the food can steam. Stir-frying, which began in Asia, is most often used to cook mixtures of vegetables and other foods. You'll learn how to stir-fry in Chapter 39.

SAVING NUTRIENTS WHEN YOU COOK

Preparing food can cause it to lose nutrients. How? Some nutrients can be destroyed by heat or by the oxygen in the air. Water-soluble nutrients—the B vitamins and vitamin C—are most easily destroyed. Other times the nutrients are thrown away. For example, if you discard the skin of a potato, you're throwing away the vitamins and minerals found there.

When you prepare food, one of your most important goals will be to save nutrients. Here are some general guidelines. You'll learn more when you study other chapters.

Pare or trim as little as possible. Many of the nutrients in fruits and vegetables are found in the outer portions, such as skins.

Keep food whole or in large pieces when possible. If food is cut into small pieces, more surface area is exposed to air, water, or heat. That often means more nutrients are lost.

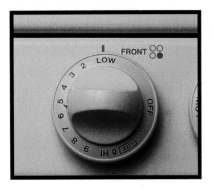

Cook food at the right temperature. Most protein foods, including meat, poultry, fish, eggs, milk, and cheese, are very sensitive to heat. They must be cooked at low temperatures. Otherwise they lose nutrients and may also become too tough or dry to eat.

Save cooking liquids. Water-soluble vitamins may move from food into the water in which it's cooked. If the cooking water is thrown away, the nutrients are lost. Instead, serve the liquid with the food or save it for another use, such as making soup.

Cook food the right amount of time. Overcooking can destroy vitamins or make the food inedible. To be safe, begin to test the food about 5 to 10 minutes before the cooking time is up.

CHAPTER **18** REVIEW

Understanding Key Ideas

1. Name three basic types of cooking methods. Which, if any, cause foods to brown?
2. What is the difference between broiling and panbroiling?
3. Why might you cover the pan when cooking meat in a conventional oven? Why might you leave the pan uncovered?
4. How does panfrying differ from deep-fat frying?
5. How do cooking time and temperature affect nutrition?

Applying Knowledge and Skills

◆ **Cooking Guidelines:** Select four cooking techniques. Create a mini-poster for each, including pictures and basic tips.

◆ **Classifying Methods:** Think of six ways to prepare potatoes. Classify them according to their basic cooking method. (Check a cookbook, if needed.) Discuss the advantages and drawbacks of each.

Exploring Further

◆ **Experiment:** Compare the results of simmering and boiling canned green beans. What conclusions can you draw?

◆ **Nutrient Analysis:** Use nutrition tables or software to compare the amount of calories, fat, vitamins, and minerals when the same food is prepared in different ways. Explain any differences in nutrient content based on what you've learned in this chapter.

CHAPTER 19

MICROWAVE TECHNIQUES

Discover...

★ *how the microwave oven works.*

★ *how to choose cookware for microwaving.*

★ *basic techniques for microwaving.*

★ *safety guidelines for microwaving.*

Key Terms
microwaves
cooking power
standing time

Microwave cooking seems easy—just push a few buttons. As with any other kind of cooking, though, you'll get the best results if you take time to learn a few basic guidelines.

FOOD FOR THOUGHT

In what ways does microwave cooking differ from conventional cooking? How can knowing this help you be a successful microwave cook?

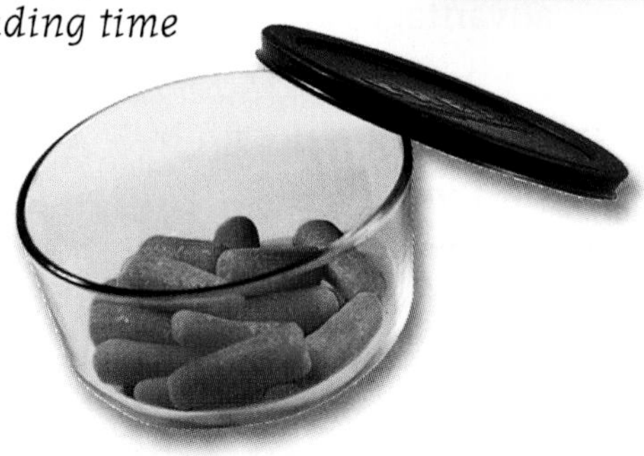

THE MICROWAVE OVEN

Microwave ovens can be great time-savers. They can be used for:

Heating convenience foods. Many canned, packaged, and frozen foods include microwave directions. Some are made just for the microwave oven.

Defrosting frozen foods. Many microwave ovens have a defrost setting. You can thaw frozen meat, poultry, or fish in minutes.

Reheating food. Cooked take-out foods and leftovers can be reheated in a microwave oven in just seconds. They keep much of their original flavor and texture. Test the food with an instant-read thermometer at the end of the cooking time. Be sure it's reached an internal temperature of 165°F.

Cooking fresh foods. Many foods can be cooked two to four times faster than with a conventional range. However, not all foods can be microwaved with good results. As you study other chapters in this book, you'll learn more about which foods can be microwaved successfully.

HOW MICROWAVES WORK

Rub your hands together quickly for about 10 seconds. What do you feel? The heat in your hands is caused by friction. Microwave ovens also use friction to produce heat.

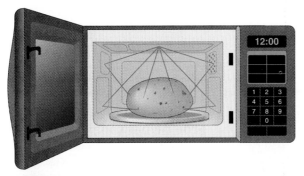

A microwave oven produces tiny waves of energy called **microwaves.** These bounce off the oven walls and into the food.

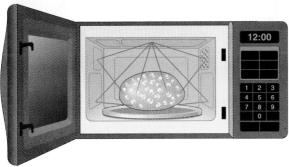

As the microwaves penetrate the food, they cause molecules (tiny particles) within the food to vibrate very fast.

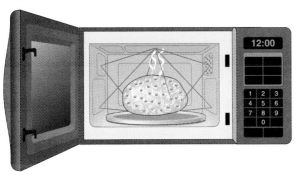

The vibration causes friction between the molecules. The friction produces heat and cooks the food.

COOKING POWER

The amount of electricity the oven uses to create microwaves is known as the **cooking power.** Cooking power is measured in watts of electricity. Most microwave ovens have a cooking power of about 500 to 700 watts. The higher the wattage, the faster the oven cooks.

Power settings control the amount of cooking power. Most microwave ovens have several power settings. Others may have only one or two.

MATERIALS FOR MICROWAVING

Some, but not all, of the cookware you use with a conventional range can be used for microwaving. In addition, many types of paper and plastics can be used. Microwaves pass right through these materials to cook the food inside. However, always check paper and plastics to make sure they're labeled "microwave-safe." If not, they could start a fire.

In general, it's safe to use:

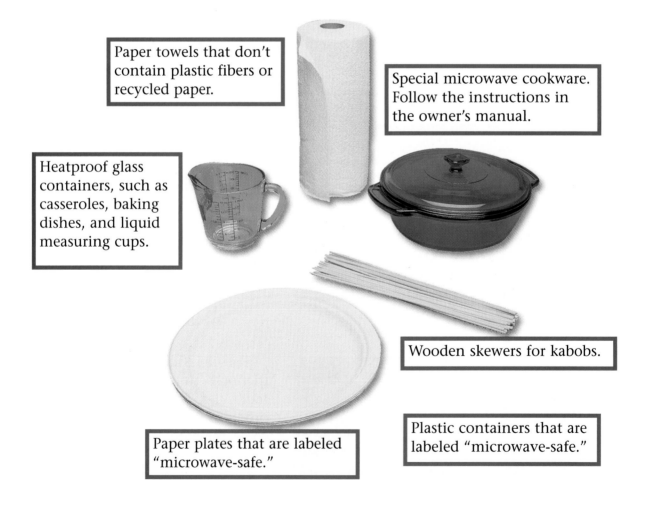

Paper towels that don't contain plastic fibers or recycled paper.

Special microwave cookware. Follow the instructions in the owner's manual.

Heatproof glass containers, such as casseroles, baking dishes, and liquid measuring cups.

Wooden skewers for kabobs.

Paper plates that are labeled "microwave-safe."

Plastic containers that are labeled "microwave-safe."

Some materials can cause problems in the microwave oven. Don't use these materials:

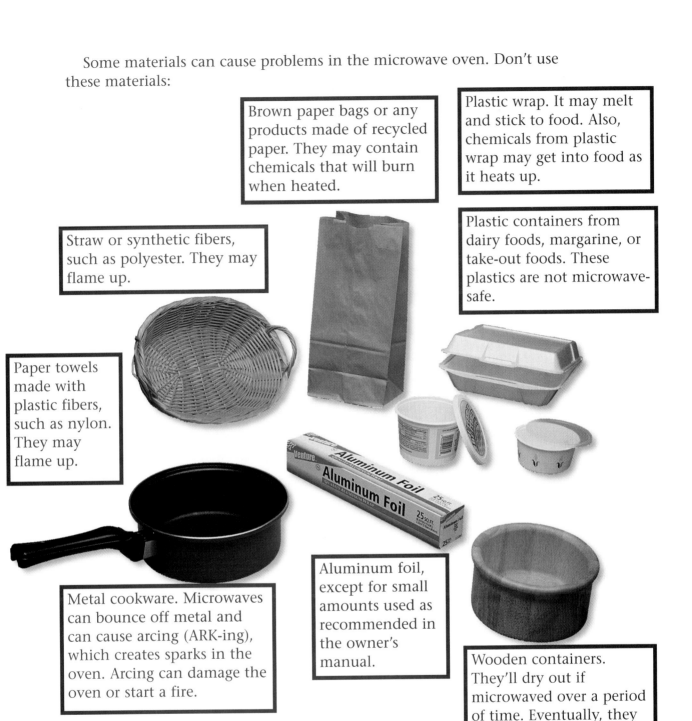

Brown paper bags or any products made of recycled paper. They may contain chemicals that will burn when heated.

Plastic wrap. It may melt and stick to food. Also, chemicals from plastic wrap may get into food as it heats up.

Plastic containers from dairy foods, margarine, or take-out foods. These plastics are not microwave-safe.

Straw or synthetic fibers, such as polyester. They may flame up.

Paper towels made with plastic fibers, such as nylon. They may flame up.

Metal cookware. Microwaves can bounce off metal and can cause arcing (ARK-ing), which creates sparks in the oven. Arcing can damage the oven or start a fire.

Aluminum foil, except for small amounts used as recommended in the owner's manual.

Wooden containers. They'll dry out if microwaved over a period of time. Eventually, they may be damaged.

BASIC STEPS IN MICROWAVING

Most microwave recipes include a number of basic steps. Following these steps correctly will help you make sure the food cooks evenly without overcooking.

CHOOSING A CONTAINER

The instructions should tell you what size container to use. Be sure it's made of microwave-safe material.

Microwave recipes often tell you to use a round, oval, or ring-shaped pan. Why? These shapes allow microwave energy to strike the food from all angles. If you use square or rectangular pans, the energy concentrates in the corners. Food in those areas overcooks.

Remember, microwaves tend to hang around in the corners of pans. To avoid overcooked areas, use round pans.

ARRANGING THE FOOD

For even cooking, it's important to arrange food as specified in the recipe. Individual items, such as cupcakes or whole potatoes, are often arranged in a ring or like the spokes on a wheel.

Make foods as uniform as possible. For example, cut carrots into pieces that are all about the same size and shape. Mixtures such as casseroles should be an even depth.

Some foods, such as a chicken leg, aren't uniform throughout. The parts that are thicker, more moist, or more dense will take longer to cook. Place these parts toward the outside of the container.

Broccoli stems should be placed toward the outside of the dish because they're tougher.

COVERING THE FOOD

The recipe or cooking instructions may tell you to cover the food. A cover helps control the amount of moisture in the food. It also helps keep food from spattering in the oven.

The container you're using may come with a microwave-safe cover. If not, use one of the following:

An upside-down plate. Use a plate or the container's cover when you want to retain as much moisture as possible in the dish. Make sure the plate is microwave-safe.

Waxed paper. Use when you want most of the moisture to evaporate. Cover the dish loosely with the waxed paper.

Paper towel. Towels absorb moisture. They're generally used for heating rolls and sandwiches so the bread doesn't get soggy.

COOKING THE FOOD

Set the oven for the correct power level and cooking time. Timing is especially important when microwaving. Overcooked foods become hard, tough, and chewy. Often, they can't be eaten.

Most recipes give an approximate time for microwaving food. To avoid overcooking, turn off the oven a few minutes before the time is up. Check the food. Then add short cooking periods, if necessary. Once food is overcooked, there's nothing you can do to save it.

The cooking time depends on the number of servings you're making. If you heat two frozen dinners at the same time, for example, they'll take longer to cook than one dinner alone. Check the instructions carefully.

ROTATING, STIRRING, TURNING, AND REARRANGING

Many microwave ovens heat unevenly. They contain "hot spots" in which the microwaves are more concentrated. Food in the hot spots of a microwave oven will cook faster than food in the other parts, and will be overcooked by the time the rest of the food is done.

To make sure food cooks evenly, the instructions may tell you to rotate the food, stir it, turn it over, or rearrange it. Usually this is done after half the cooking time. Here's how:

Stir. Liquids should be stirred thoroughly. For a more solid food, stir from the outside of the dish to the center. Let the food that was in the center of the dish move to the outside.

Rotate. Turn the plate or dish. The instructions may say "rotate one-quarter turn" or "rotate one-half turn."

1/4 turn   1/2 turn

Turn over. Flip the food so the bottom becomes the top. The instructions may say "invert."

Rearrange. Move outside pieces toward the center and inside pieces toward the outside.

Try It!

Microwave Hot Spots

Test a microwave oven for hot spots. If the oven has a part that rotates, take it out. Cover the bottom of the oven with a sheet of waxed paper. Evenly space several large marshmallows on the waxed paper. Microwave on 100% power for one minute. Check the marshmallows. Keep microwaving until all marshmallows are puffed up or melted.

★ What differences did you notice in the marshmallows?

★ Does the oven have hot spots? Where are they?

STANDING TIME

When the oven shuts off after cooking, the molecules in the food continue to vibrate. The food keeps on cooking until it cools slightly. The period when the food continues to cook after microwaving is called **standing time.** Standing time also allows heat to penetrate all areas of the food.

If the instructions say "let stand," leave the food covered for the time specified. If the food needs more cooking after the standing time, return it to the oven.

When cooking and standing time are completed, test meat and poultry with an instant-read thermometer to be sure the food has reached the proper internal temperature. Test the food in several different places in case it hasn't cooked evenly.

Standing time lets the food finish cooking.

SAFE MICROWAVE USE

You don't see an open flame or a reddened heating element with a microwave oven, but you can still get burned or start a fire if you aren't careful. Follow these guidelines for safe microwave use:

PREVENTING BURNS

◆ Always use potholders when handling food during or after microwaving. As the food cooks, the heat from the food passes into the cooking container and can make it extremely hot.

◆ If a food contains a concentration of fat or sugar, like cheese or a jelly filling, don't eat it as soon as it comes out of the oven. The fat or sugar will be extremely hot and could burn your mouth. Let the food cool first.

- Cook in small batches. Large amounts of foods are difficult to handle. Smaller amounts will cook faster and can be handled more easily.

- Be careful when removing covers. Escaping steam can severely burn your fingers, face, and eyes. Lift the cover so the steam flows away from your body. Keep your fingers out of the way. When opening a microwavable bag of popcorn, hold the bag away from your face and follow directions carefully.

KEEP FOODS FROM BURSTING

- Never microwave whole eggs. They may burst, and you could be severely burned.

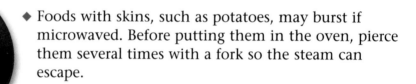

- Don't use containers with tight-fitting covers. Loosen the cover first. Otherwise the container could burst from the pressure of built-up steam.

- Foods with skins, such as potatoes, may burst if microwaved. Before putting them in the oven, pierce them several times with a fork so the steam can escape.

OVEN CARE

- Don't turn on the microwave oven if the door doesn't close properly.

- Don't lean on the oven door or close it with something such as a potholder between it and the oven cavity. You could damage the door.

- Don't attach magnets to the oven. They can damage the electronics.

- Wipe up any spills or spatters after each use. Not only does this help keep food from becoming dried onto the surface, it can help prevent a grease fire.

Don't do this to your microwave! Magnets can damage it. Put them on your refrigerator instead.

Understanding Key Ideas

1. How do foods cook in a microwave oven?
2. What type of container would you use to make a cake in a microwave oven? Why?
3. Name five ways to help foods microwave more evenly.
4. Give three safety tips for cooking and handling a microwaved casserole.

Applying Knowledge and Skills

◆ **Making Decisions:** List advantages and limitations of microwave and conventional cooking. What factors would you consider in deciding when to use each method?

◆ **Microwave Materials:** Identify which materials in the foods lab or your home kitchen would be safe and effective for microwave cooking. Explain why.

◆ **Demonstration:** Place several spoons on a plate. Pretend they are pieces of food. Demonstrate the difference between rotating, turning, and rearranging the items.

Exploring Further

◆ **Consumer Research:** Using appliance store catalogs and advertisements, research the options available in microwave ovens. Which features would be most useful for your family? In the foods lab?

SAFETY IN THE KITCHEN

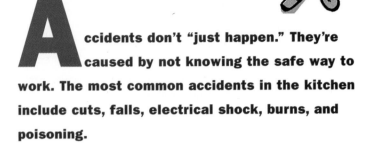

Accidents don't "just happen." They're caused by not knowing the safe way to work. The most common accidents in the kitchen include cuts, falls, electrical shock, burns, and poisoning.

Discover...

* *how to identify safety hazards in the kitchen.*

* *how to prevent kitchen accidents.*

Key Terms

flammable
poison control center

FOOD FOR THOUGHT

What steps can you take to reduce the chance of accidents in the kitchen?

PREVENTING CUTS

Take care to avoid cuts from knives and other sharp objects.

◆ When you use a knife, place the food on a cutting board and cut away from your body. If the knife slips, you won't cut yourself.

◆ Don't cut toward other people. Don't point a knife or other sharp instruments toward others, even in fun. You could injure them.

◆ If a knife starts to fall, don't try to catch it. Get out of the way.

- Use a knife only for cutting food. Don't use it to open a can or tighten a screw. The knife could break and you could injure yourself.

- Wash knives separately from dishes. If you let them soak in soapy water, you can't see them and might cut yourself.

- To open cans, use a can opener that makes a smooth cut, not a jagged edge. Cut off the can top completely and throw it in the trash.

- Sweep up broken glass with a broom or brush. Never pick it up with your bare fingers. To pick up tiny pieces, use a wet paper towel.

When cutting, be sure to keep your fingers out of the way.

USING ELECTRICITY WISELY

If misused, electricity can give you a severe shock or burn. It can even kill you. Remember, water and electricity don't mix.

- Never use an electrical appliance if your hands are wet or if you're standing on a wet floor.

- Keep electrical cords away from the sink and range.

Water and electricity don't mix!

- Keep appliances in good condition. Never use an appliance with a damaged cord. It could cause a shock or start a fire.

- Hold the plug, not the cord, when you disconnect an appliance. If you tug on the cord, you may damage it.

- Don't run electrical cords under a rug. They could get damaged.

- If you can't get food out of an appliance, such as a toaster, first disconnect it. Then try turning the appliance upside down. If the food doesn't shake loose, take the appliance to a repair person. Never insert a fork or other object into the appliance. You could get a shock. Even if the appliance is disconnected, you could damage it.

- Don't plug too many appliances into one outlet. You could get a shock or start a fire.

PREVENTING BURNS AND FIRES

Hot food, steam, grease from cooking, hot appliances—these are just some of the kitchen hazards that can cause burns or fires.

- Wear close-fitting clothes. Roll up long sleeves when you cook. Tie long hair back.

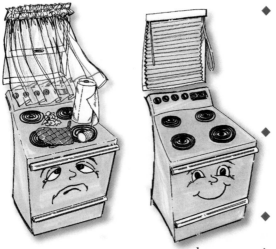

- Keep **flammable** materials (those that burn easily) away from the range. This includes kitchen curtains, towels, paper, potholders, and plastic items. Some plastics burn very fast and give off thick, black smoke and poisonous gases.

- Use potholders or oven mitts to handle hot pans. Be sure they're dry—a damp potholder on a hot pan can cause a steam burn.

- Turn the handles of pans toward the center of the range. If handles are turned outward, someone may bump against them and knock a hot pan off the range.

- When you lift the cover from a hot pan, keep the front edge down as you lift the back of the cover up. This tilts the cover so the steam flows away from you and can't burn you.

- Wait until the range cools before you try to clean it.

- When you open a hot oven, stand to one side as you open the door.

- Before putting a pan in a hot oven, use a potholder to pull out the oven rack. Otherwise, you could burn yourself as you reach inside the oven. Pull out the rack again when you take the pan out.

- Keep aerosol cans away from heat sources. The cans may explode if heated, and their spray may be flammable.

- Learn how to use a fire extinguisher. Every kitchen, at school and at home, should have one.

Avoid reaching into a hot oven, but be careful not to pull the rack out too far.

GREASE FIRES

Fats and oils are very flammable. Keep equipment clean so grease doesn't build up. Watch cooking foods carefully. You must react quickly and correctly to stop a grease fire.

- **Don't** pour water on a grease fire. It will cause the grease to spatter and burn you.

- **Don't** try to carry the burning pan to the sink. You could spill burning grease on yourself or cause the fire to spread.

- **Do** turn off the heat immediately.

- **Do** pour salt or baking soda over the flames. This will cut off the oxygen and smother the fire. You can also put a cover on the pan or use a fire extinguisher.

- **Do** leave immediately if the fire seems out of control. Alert others in the building to get out. Call the fire department.

PREVENTING FALLS

Cover the pan to smother grease fire flames.

Most kitchen falls can be prevented with a few simple precautions.

- If you spill something on the floor, wipe it up right away.

- Use a ladder or stepstool to reach high shelves. A chair can tip over easily.

- If you have a rug in the kitchen, be sure it has a nonskid back.

- If the floor is wet, don't walk on it. Wait until it's dry.

PREVENTING POISONING

Poisons can enter the body through . . .

◆ Drinking   ◆ Eating   ◆ Breathing   ◆ The skin

Many household chemicals are poisonous. These include some products used for cleaning, pest control, personal care, medicine, gardening, and arts and crafts. Be alert for dangerous chemicals. Often you can accomplish the same task with safer products.

◆ Before you buy household chemicals, read the label directions carefully. If you're uncomfortable with the directions or product warnings, choose a safer product.

◆ Don't buy more than you need. Some chemicals change as they age and may become dangerous to use. Disposing of leftover hazardous household chemicals can be a problem.

◆ Follow label directions exactly. You may be told to wear rubber gloves or a mask to prevent skin contact. With pesticides—poisons that kill insects and other pests—you may need to cover or remove food, dishes, and cookware.

◆ If directions call for a well-ventilated area, open windows and use a fan. Otherwise, harmful fumes may build up.

◆ Never mix household cleaners together. Mixtures may release poisonous gases that could cause illness or death.

◆ Never point spray containers toward another person or inhale the spray yourself. Check which way the nozzle is facing before you spray.

Mixing household chemicals can cause deadly gases to form.

- Keep all household chemicals in their original containers. The labels tell how to use and store them and what to do in case of an accident.

- Never store chemicals in the same cabinet with food. The chemicals could spill into the food or someone could pick up the wrong container.

- If there are children in the household, buy products in childproof containers. Keep them in a locked cabinet.

- If someone is poisoned, call the nearest **poison control center** right away. It has a staff specially trained to deal with poison emergencies. You'll be asked what the poison is and about how much was taken or used. Have the container with you when you call.

Store chemicals away from food and out of children's reach. Before using any household chemical, read the label carefully.

CHAPTER 20 REVIEW

Understanding Key Ideas

1. Describe how to practice safety when slicing an onion.
2. What steps can help prevent damage to electrical appliances? Why is this important?
3. What two dangers are associated with wet kitchen floors?
4. Suppose you're about to use an oven cleaner. Identify two safety rules you should follow as you work.

Applying Knowledge and Skills

- **Demonstration:** Pretend you're cooking at the range, but do not turn the range on. Show how you would prepare to work, place hot pans on the cooktop and in the oven, and uncover hot pans. Then imagine a grease fire has started. Show exactly what you would do and explain why.

- **Chemical Survey:** Survey the household chemicals in the foods lab or your home kitchen. What types of products did you find? Explain whether they are stored correctly. Read the labels carefully. What warnings and special instructions are given? In class, discuss whether the benefits of the products outweigh the hazards.

Exploring Further

- **Research:** Contact local or state agencies to find out how to dispose of dangerous chemicals safely and legally. Report your findings to the class and your family.

Safety in the Kitchen 159

KEEPING FOOD SAFE TO EAT

Discover...

★ *how harmful bacteria make food unsafe.*

★ *how to keep food safe when you work in the kitchen.*

★ *how to store food properly.*

Key Terms
foodborne illness
bacteria
food safety
cross-contamination
danger zone
perishable

Have you ever heard someone say, "It must have been something I ate"? If food isn't stored and handled properly, it can cause illness. By following some simple, but important, guidelines, you and your family and friends can enjoy food that's safe to eat.

FOOD FOR THOUGHT

What responsibility do you have when you store, prepare, and serve food? How can you meet this responsibility?

FOODBORNE ILLNESS

Illness caused by food that's not safe to eat is called **foodborne illness**. Some foodborne illnesses are mild. They may seem like a case of the flu and last just a day or two. Others can cause more serious illness, even death.

Anyone can get a foodborne illness. However, some people may be more at risk than others. These include infants and children, the elderly, pregnant women, and people with certain health problems.

FACTS ABOUT BACTERIA

Most foodborne illness is caused by harmful bacteria. **Bacteria** (bak-TEER-ee-uh) are tiny living things that can be seen only with a microscope.

Which bacteria cause foodborne illness? Not all bacteria are harmful. In fact, helpful kinds are used to make cheese, yogurt, and medicine. Some of the bacteria that cause foodborne illness are:

- *E. coli* (ee-KOH-lie)
- *Salmonella* (sal-muh-NELL-uh)
- *Campylobacter* (kam-pih-low-BAK-tur)
- *C. botulinum* (bah-chuh-LIE-num)
- *Listeria* (liss-TEER-ee-uh)
- *Staphylococcus* (staff-ih-low-KAH-kus), or "staph"

How do harmful bacteria get into food? Bacteria are everywhere. They're carried on people, animals, objects, raw food, and in the air. They can get into foods before you buy them or when you store, prepare, or serve them.

What happens then? Usually, a few bacteria aren't enough to make someone sick. But bacteria can multiply rapidly to dangerous levels. All they need is food, moisture, and warm temperatures. In just a few hours, one bacterium can become tens of thousands. However, you still can't see, smell, or taste them.

Bacteria multiply by dividing. One splits into two, then two become four, and so on.

THE FOOD SAFETY TEAM

Fortunately, harmful bacteria can be stopped before they cause foodborne illness. **Food safety**—taking steps to prevent foodborne illness—is a team effort. The food industry and the government work to keep food as safe as possible before you buy it. After that, it's up to you to handle food properly. You can do this by practicing cleanliness and keeping food at the right temperatures.

PRACTICING CLEANLINESS

Cleanliness helps keep bacteria from getting into food before they have a chance to multiply. Follow these simple guidelines to keep yourself and the kitchen clean.

WASH YOUR HANDS

Washing your hands is one of the most important ways to prevent the spread of bacteria. Always wash your hands:

◆ Before you begin to prepare food.

◆ Before setting the table.

◆ After using the toilet.

◆ After touching a pet or your hair.

◆ After you cough, sneeze, or blow your nose.

◆ After handling raw meat, poultry, fish, or eggs.

◆ As often as needed to keep your hands clean during food preparation.

How to Wash Your Hands

1. Wet your hands with warm water. Apply soap and work up a lather. Scrub for at least 20 seconds.

STEP 1

DON'T SPREAD YOUR GERMS

Even after washing your hands, your body carries bacteria. Keep these bacteria away from food and dishes.

◆ If you have an open cut or sore on your hand, cover it with a clean waterproof bandage. Then use clean rubber or plastic gloves. Wash gloved hands just as often as bare hands.

◆ If you have open cuts or sores on other parts of your body, don't touch them while you handle food.

◆ Be sure your clothes are clean. Wear a clean apron to protect your clothes from spots and stains.

◆ If your hair is long, tie it back to keep it out of food.

◆ Don't cough or sneeze into food. Turn away and cover your nose and mouth with a clean handkerchief or disposable tissue. Scrub your hands immediately.

◆ When you taste food, use the tasting spoon only once. Wash it before using it again. (Don't taste meat, poultry, fish, or eggs when raw or during cooking. These foods aren't safe until thoroughly cooked.)

◆ When you set a table, don't touch surfaces that come in contact with food or beverages. Examples are the rim or inside of a glass, the tines of a fork, or the center of a plate.

2. Rinse well under running water.

3. Dry with a clean towel.

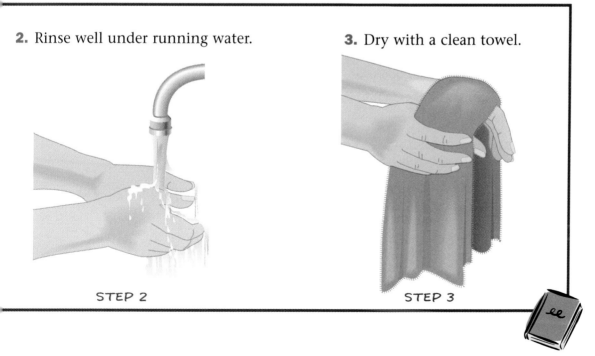

STEP 2

STEP 3

KEEP THE KITCHEN CLEAN

Make sure your kitchen is a clean place to work. Dirt, spills, and crumbs can breed germs. They can also attract insects and mice. These pests leave harmful bacteria wherever they go.

◆ Clean kitchen surfaces, appliances, and storage areas regularly.

◆ Wash the countertop before you begin preparing food and after you're finished.

◆ Wipe up spills and spots immediately.

Wipe up spills right away. If you let them sit, they can breed germs. They'll become harder to wipe up, too.

◆ Use clean tools, cookware, and dishes.

◆ Wash cutting boards after every use. Scrub them with soap and a stiff nylon brush under hot running water, or use a dishwasher.

◆ Replace cutting boards that are worn and scratched. They're difficult to clean thoroughly.

◆ Use a clean towel to wipe dishes, or let dishes air dry. Don't use the same towel for wiping dishes and your hands.

◆ Use a clean dishcloth every day. Wash dishcloths and towels in the hot cycle of the washing machine.

◆ Keep dirty dishes, pots, and pans away from the area where you prepare food.

◆ Wash the can opener often. Food often sticks to it. Wipe off the tops of cans before opening them to keep dirt and dust out of the food.

◆ Keep pets away from food, kitchen appliances, and work surfaces. Pet hairs carry harmful bacteria and can get into food easily.

◆ Keep kitchen garbage in a can with a tight cover. Empty the garbage can daily—more often if needed.

DON'T CROSS-CONTAMINATE

Raw meat, poultry, fish, and eggs can contain harmful bacteria. Cooking kills the bacteria in the food itself. But while you prepare these foods, the harmful bacteria get on your hands, utensils, and work surfaces. They can spread to other foods. Letting harmful bacteria spread from raw foods to other foods is called **cross-contamination**.

After working with raw meat, poultry, fish, or eggs:

◆ Wash equipment used for the raw food before it's used again. It's also best to use separate cutting boards for raw meats and other foods.

◆ Use a paper towel to wipe up any scraps, spills, or meat juices from the counter. Then wash the counter and your hands with hot, soapy water before handling other foods.

◆ Never put cooked food back on the same plate that held the raw food. Instead, use a clean plate.

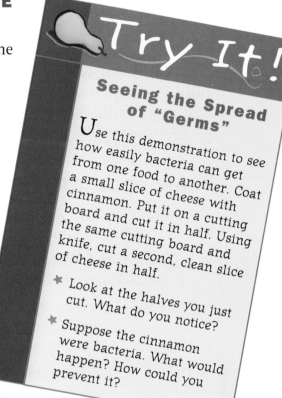

Try It!

Seeing the Spread of "Germs"

Use this demonstration to see how easily bacteria can get from one food to another. Coat a small slice of cheese with cinnamon. Put it on a cutting board and cut it in half. Using the same cutting board and knife, cut a second, clean slice of cheese in half.

★ Look at the halves you just cut. What do you notice?

★ Suppose the cinnamon were bacteria. What would happen? How could you prevent it?

Bacteria can really get around if you're not careful!

CONTROLLING TEMPERATURES

Cleanliness can't keep all harmful bacteria out of food. Your next line of defense is temperature control.

Bacteria multiply fastest in a temperature range called the **danger zone**—40°F to 140°F. Find the danger zone in the illustration on the next page. Notice that normal room temperature is in this range. For food safety, don't let food stay in the danger zone.

THAW FOOD SAFELY

Never thaw frozen food by letting it sit at room temperature. Instead, use one of these methods for thawing:

◆ Place the food in the refrigerator. It will thaw slowly, so allow plenty of time. A frozen turkey, for example, may take several days to thaw.

◆ Place the package of food in a water-tight plastic bag. Then put the bag in a container of cold water. Keep the bag completely under the water. Change the water every 30 minutes.

◆ Defrost the food in a microwave oven. Follow the manufacturer's directions. Food that's been thawed in the microwave must be cooked right away.

What would happen if you let food thaw on the countertop?

Temperature Guide to Food Safety

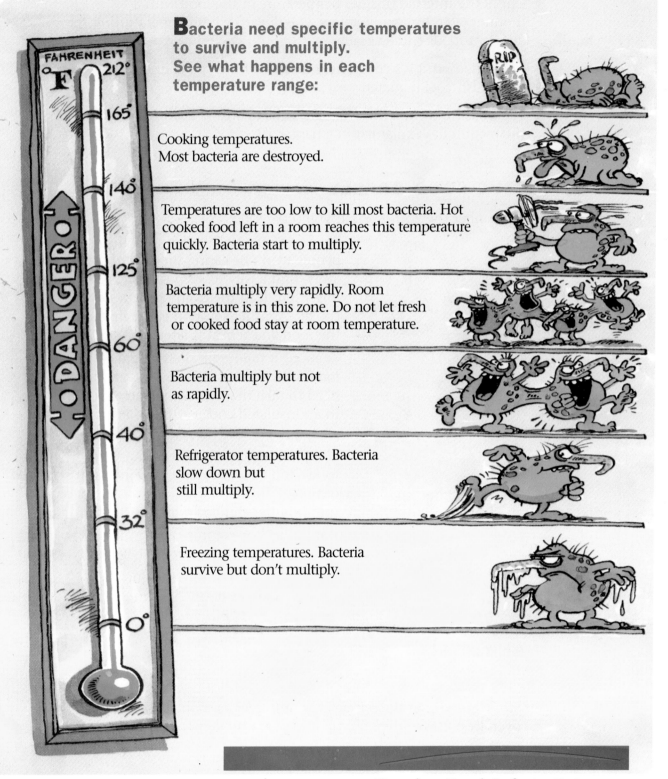

Bacteria need specific temperatures to survive and multiply. See what happens in each temperature range:

FAHRENHEIT °F

212°
165°

Cooking temperatures.
Most bacteria are destroyed.

140°

Temperatures are too low to kill most bacteria. Hot cooked food left in a room reaches this temperature quickly. Bacteria start to multiply.

125°

Bacteria multiply very rapidly. Room temperature is in this zone. Do not let fresh or cooked food stay at room temperature.

60°

Bacteria multiply but not as rapidly.

40°

Refrigerator temperatures. Bacteria slow down but still multiply.

32°

Freezing temperatures. Bacteria survive but don't multiply.

0°

DANGER

COOK FOOD THOROUGHLY

When you cook foods, make sure they reach the high temperatures that destroy bacteria. How?

◆ Check the internal (inside) temperature of the food with a thermometer. In later chapters, you'll learn what temperature different foods should reach.

◆ Cook food until it's completely done. Don't try to cook it partway and finish cooking later.

◆ When using the microwave, take steps to ensure even heating. Use the techniques explained in Chapter 19.

SERVE FOOD SAFELY

Remember these rules when you serve food:

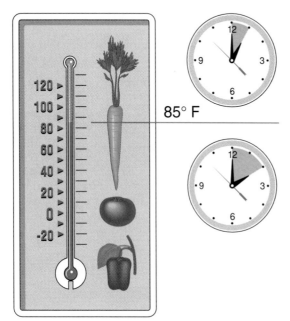

85° F

Serve hot food while it's hot. If some people won't be eating the food right away, find a way to keep it over 140°F. You might put it in the oven or use a slow cooker. Another solution is to refrigerate the food and reheat it later.

Keep cold food cold. Refrigerate cold food until you're ready to serve it. If you need to take the food somewhere, put it in an insulated cooler with ice or freezer packs.

Limit serving time. When you serve food—indoors or outdoors—don't let it sit out on a table or counter too long. Check the thermometer and watch the clock.

• If the air temperature is 85°F or higher, keep food out no more than 1 hour.

• If the air temperature is below 85°F, keep food out no more than 2 hours.

HANDLE LEFTOVERS PROPERLY

Leftovers need special handling so they'll be safe to eat later.

◆ Store leftovers in the refrigerator or freezer as soon as the meal is over. Don't leave them at room temperature to cool first.

- Divide large amounts into small containers for quick cooling.

- Use refrigerated leftovers in three to four days.

- Bring leftover soups, sauces, and gravies to a rolling boil before eating. Reheat other leftovers to an internal temperature of 165°F.

STORING FOOD

Storing food properly helps prevent foodborne illness. It also preserves the food's flavor and nutrients. It keeps food from becoming too moist or dry and keeps dirt, dust, and insects away.

REFRIGERATOR STORAGE

The refrigerator provides short-term storage for foods that spoil easily. These **perishable** foods include meat, poultry, fish, milk, eggs, butter, and leftovers. Many other foods, including fresh fruits and vegetables, are also refrigerated to keep them fresh longer.

Check the temperature inside the refrigerator regularly. It should be between 32°F and 40°F. Inside shelves stay colder than shelves on the door. For this reason, perishable foods should go on inside shelves.

Cover refrigerated foods so they don't dry out. Place packages of raw meat, poultry, and fish on a plate, in a plastic bag, or on the bottom shelf. Then their juices won't drip on other foods.

Perishable foods will keep in the refrigerator from a day to a few weeks, depending on the food. For longer storage, many foods can be frozen.

Keep a thermometer in the refrigerator. Is this refrigerator cold enough? How do you know?

FREEZER STORAGE

Proper freezing allows many foods to keep their safety and quality for weeks or months. Check the temperature of the freezer. It should be 0°F or below.

Not all foods freeze well. Avoid freezing cooked egg whites, foods made with mayonnaise or salad dressing, gelatin, and raw vegetables you don't plan to cook.

Foods must be properly wrapped for the freezer. Otherwise, they can dry out and lose flavor and texture. Foods you buy already

Before storing food in the freezer, label it with the date. Then you'll know how long the food has been stored.

Keeping Food Safe to Eat 169

frozen should be left in their original packages. To protect other foods, use freezer paper, heavy-duty aluminum foil, freezer-quality plastic bags, or plastic freezer containers. Make the wrapping or container airtight. Avoid lightweight plastic tubs from foods such as cottage cheese, margarine, and yogurt. They don't provide enough protection in the freezer.

DRY STORAGE

Foods that don't need refrigeration or freezing, such as unopened cans and many packaged foods, are stored in a dry storage area. This area can be a cabinet or shelves. It should be cool, dry, and clean.

Don't store food in cabinets above the refrigerator or range or near a radiator or furnace outlet. The temperatures will be too warm.

Don't store food under the sink. Openings around pipes can't be sealed, so insects and other pests may crawl through. Water leaking from pipes can cause damage or spoilage.

Once packages are opened, close them tightly before storing to keep out insects. You may also put the food in tightly covered containers.

STORING GROCERIES

When you return from grocery shopping, store food right away. Check labels carefully for proper food storage instructions. If you bought frozen food, put it away first so it doesn't thaw. Then store foods that belong in the refrigerator. Finally, store foods that belong in the dry storage area. If you bought bulk foods, put them into containers with tight-fitting covers to keep out dirt, pests, and moisture.

When you put away your groceries, put new packages behind older ones of the same kind. This makes it easy to follow the rule "first in, first out." By using up the older packages first, you'll save food and money.

Why is it a good idea to put new packages of food behind older ones?

IF FOOD SPOILS

When food is stored improperly or too long, it may spoil. Spoilage is caused by certain kinds of bacteria and by other organisms, such as mold. They can make food unsafe or unpleasant to eat.

Food that has spoiled may have an unusual color, odor, texture, or flavor. If food shows any of these signs, discard it. Also discard any dented or bulging cans.

However, spoiled foods may not show any signs. Don't take a chance. If leftovers are old, or you suspect they haven't been stored properly, discard them. Follow this rule: "When in doubt, throw it out!"

CHAPTER 21 REVIEW

Understanding Key Ideas

1. In general, how are foodborne illnesses caused?
2. How often should you wash your hands when preparing food?
3. Give three food safety guidelines for using cutting boards and explain the reasons behind them.
4. What temperature range is called the "danger zone" and why?
5. Describe safe short-term and long-term storage of perishable foods.

Applying Knowledge and Skills

- **Communication:** Write a song, rap, poem, or public service announcement about one aspect of food safety.

- **Food Safety Checklist:** Prepare a food safety checklist for use in your home or school kitchen. Organize it according to what should be done before, during, and after preparing food. Use the checklist the next time you work in the kitchen and report the results.

Exploring Further

- **Critical Thinking:** Lack of knowledge is one reason people don't always follow safe food practices. What are some others? What can you do to help?

- **Research:** Find information on one of these topics and report to the class: (A) What to do if you suspect an illness is caused by unsafe food. (B) What to do if the refrigerator-freezer stops working or loses power.

CHAPTER 22

GETTING ORGANIZED

Discover...

* how to plan for preparing food.

* how to work efficiently in the kitchen.

* the basic steps in cleaning up.

* how to work as a team in the foods lab.

Key Terms
work plan
pre-preparation
dovetailing

Have you ever watched a cooking show on television? Think about how smoothly the chef works. Successful food preparation calls for good management skills. Take a tip from television chefs—learn to be organized when you work in the kitchen.

FOOD FOR THOUGHT

In what ways do television chefs organize their work? How might you do the same?

PLANNING YOUR WORK

When you think ahead and get ready before you start to work, food preparation is more successful and enjoyable. The first step is deciding what to prepare.

CHOOSING A RECIPE

Before you decide on a recipe, read through it carefully. Make sure it's clear and complete (see page 117). Also consider your resources:

Skills. If you choose a recipe that calls for skills you've mastered, you can prepare it with confidence.

Time and energy. How long will the recipe take to prepare? If time and energy are short, choose a simple recipe. Think about using convenience foods or preparing some things ahead of time.

Food. Check to see if you have all the ingredients on hand. If not, add them to your shopping list.

Money. Will the recipe fit into your food budget? Perhaps you can find a recipe using foods that are on sale.

Equipment. Do you have the equipment you'll need? Be sure you have the size pan called for in the recipe.

MAKING A WORK PLAN

Another way to plan ahead is to make a **work plan**—a list of what you have to do to prepare the food. Each task is listed in the correct order so you don't miss a step.

Most tasks are given as steps in the recipe. However, you may also have to do some tasks that aren't in the recipe directions. Suppose the ingredients list says "2 cups cooked rice." Cooking the rice is an example of **pre-preparation**—getting the food or equipment ready to use in the recipe. Other examples are cleaning and chopping vegetables, greasing baking pans, and browning meat. Read the recipe carefully to find pre-preparation tasks. Then list them in your work plan.

Work Plan— Sloppy Joes for potluck

Friday night
Put meat in refrigerator to thaw

Saturday afternoon
Wash hands
Gather food and equipment
Chop onions
Brown meat and onions
Measure and add other ingredients
Simmer

MAKING A SCHEDULE

Once you have a work plan, you can use it to make a schedule. Here's how:

1. Next to each task in the work plan, write down how long you think it will take. Cooking times are usually given in the recipe or package directions. For other tasks, make an estimate. Keep in mind that it's better to allow too much time than too little.

2. Write down what time to start each task. Work backward from the time you want the food to be ready. For example, if you want the food ready at 6:00 and the last item in your work plan takes 5 minutes, you'll need to start that task at 5:55. Then figure out what time to start the next-to-last task, and so on.

A schedule can be very helpful when you're just learning to prepare food. As you gain more experience, you may not need to make one every time. But even experienced cooks often make a work plan and schedule when they prepare a new dish or a special meal.

A schedule is especially useful when you're preparing a whole meal rather than just one recipe. Chapter 24 will help you learn to schedule a meal so that all the food is ready at the same time.

WORKING EFFICIENTLY

Now it's time to prepare the recipe. Before you begin, make sure you and your work area are clean. Review the cleanliness guidelines in Chapter 21.

As you work, think about whether there's a faster or better way to do the job. However, be sure to follow the rules of safety and cleanliness. Don't take shortcuts that may endanger you or the people who eat the food.

Here are some guidelines for working efficiently:

Gather equipment and ingredients first. By having everything you need at hand, you'll be able to work without interruption. Arrange the items on the counter or table where you'll work.

Learn to use equipment properly. Choose the right tool for the job and use it in the correct way. Otherwise, you'll waste time and might damage the equipment.

Set a timer. If food must cook for a certain amount of time, don't rely on your memory.

Use your work plan and schedule. Check off each task as you complete it.

Dovetail tasks. You may be able to work ahead on some steps while others are still going on. This is called **dovetailing.** For example, while waiting for water to boil, you can measure ingredients or chop vegetables.

Clean up as you work. Have a clean, wet dishcloth handy to wipe up spills. Keep hot, sudsy water in the sink or dishpan. When you have a few moments between tasks, wash any equipment you've finished using.

FINISHING THE JOB

After the food has been prepared and enjoyed, there's one more job left to do. The kitchen and eating area should be left clean and ready to use again.

When you serve the food, scrape it out of the pan thoroughly. Then rinse the pan. If food is stuck in the bottom, soak the pan in hot water.

After the meal, store leftovers properly. (To review how, see pages 168-169.) Then scrape all food off dishes into the garbage container or disposal.

If the kitchen has an automatic dishwasher, follow the directions in the owner's manual. Some items can't be put in the dishwasher because it may damage them.

Working together makes cleanup go faster.

To wash dishes by hand, follow these guidelines:

◆ Use hot, sudsy water and a clean dishcloth.

◆ For hard-to-clean spots on pots and pans, use a scouring pad. Abrasive scouring pads shouldn't be used on some cookware. There are nonabrasive pads for these materials.

◆ Wash glassware first, then other dishes used for eating. Save greasy or heavily soiled items for last.

◆ Rinse thoroughly in hot water.

- If possible, keep the dishes in the rack until they dry by themselves. Otherwise, dry them with a clean dish towel.

- Put all dishes and equipment away as soon as they're dry. Otherwise, they may gather dust and bacteria.

After the dishes have been washed, wipe up any crumbs or spills from the table and counters. Sweep the floor. If the kitchen is clean, the job is done!

TEAMWORK IN THE FOODS LAB

When you prepare food in the school foods lab, you work in a group with other class members. You use a work plan and schedule, just as you've already learned. The difference is that the work is divided among the group members. For example, as one person preheats the oven and greases the baking pans, another may measure ingredients, while a third sets the table. The different tasks must be timed so that the work flows smoothly.

Teamwork is the key to success in the foods lab. Everyone in the group must cooperate if you're to reach your goal. That means all team members must do their share of the work to the best of their ability.

Here are some suggestions to help your lab group work well together:

- Prepare your work plan together. Be sure you all understand and agree on it.

- As you plan, look for ways to work efficiently. Remember that your time in the lab is limited.

- Be sure the work is divided equally. Making one person do most of the work is not only unfair, it slows the whole group down.

- Try to stick to the plan as you work. However, be prepared to make changes if an unexpected problem comes up.

- Take responsibility for your share of the work. Remember, the whole team is depending on you.

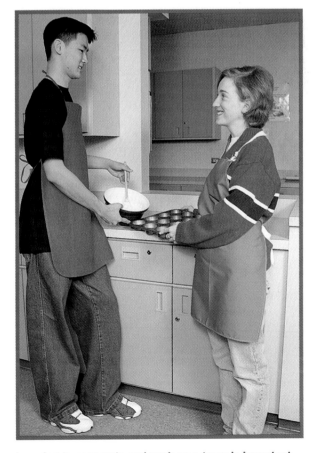

Learning to cooperate and work as a team is important to the success of any foods lab.

◆ When you finish your part of the job, ask your partners how you can help them.

EVALUATING THE LAB

As part of the foods lab, you'll evaluate the food you prepared. Rate it according to its appearance, texture, and flavor.

It's just as important to evaluate how well you worked together. Evaluating the lab will help you be even more successful in the future. Get together with the other members of the team. Ask yourselves:

◆ Did the work go smoothly?

◆ Was the project completed on time?

◆ Did we leave the kitchen clean?

◆ Did any unexpected problems arise? How well did we handle them?

◆ How might we change the plan next time? Why?

Why is it important to evaluate both the finished product and how well you worked as a team?

Understanding Key Ideas

1. What's the difference between a work plan and a schedule? Why might you need both?
2. Describe two ways to make the most efficient use of cooking equipment.
3. Identify the tasks involved in cleaning up after a meal and the order in which you'd do them.
4. Describe three signs that a foods lab group is using good teamwork.

Applying Knowledge and Skills

◆ **Evaluating Recipes:** Find a recipe you haven't tried. Based on your resources, would this recipe be a good choice for you to prepare? Why or why not?

◆ **Foods Lab:** In small groups, select a simple recipe to prepare in the foods lab. Develop a work plan and schedule for preparing this recipe as a team. If possible, use your plan and evaluate how well it worked.

Exploring Further

◆ **Watching the Pros:** Watch a television cooking show. Record all examples of efficiency and teamwork that you notice. Share your observations with the class.

◆ **Family Teamwork:** Select a recipe to prepare at home. Make a work plan and schedule for preparing the recipe alone. Make another work plan and schedule for preparing the recipe with one or two family members using teamwork. Test both plans by making the recipe. Evaluate the results. Which method was more efficient? Which was more enjoyable? Explain your answers.

Getting Organized 179

CONSERVING AND RECYCLING

Discover...

★ *how to conserve fuel and water in the kitchen.*

★ *what you can do to cut down on trash.*

★ *how to reduce food waste.*

Key Term
disposables

Our planet has a limited supply of natural resources. You can do your part to conserve them by developing a few simple habits. The example you set can encourage others to do their part as well.

FOOD FOR THOUGHT

What natural resources do you use when preparing meals? How can you use them more responsibly?

CONSERVE FUEL

By using less fuel, you help ensure a supply for the future. You also help prevent pollution. Here are some ways to conserve fuel in the kitchen.

◆ When using appliances, carefully follow the directions in the owner's manual. Keep appliances clean and in good condition. Appliances that are dirty or not working properly use more fuel than normal.

- Use small appliances, such as a toaster oven or electric skillet, when you can. They're often more efficient than either the cooktop or a large oven.

- When using the oven, cook an entire meal at the same time so you get the most use of the fuel. For instance, you could bake meat loaf, potatoes, and a green bean casserole together.

- Keep the oven door closed. If you open the oven door frequently to see how the food is cooking, heat escapes, fuel is wasted, and the food takes longer to cook.

CONSERVE WATER

Communities depend on having a source of clean, fresh water. In some areas there isn't enough water to go around. Droughts—unusually long periods with no rain or snow—can create a water shortage. Pollution can ruin the water supply.

Even though your community may not have a shortage now, learn to conserve water. That way, you'll help ensure a supply of good drinking water for the future.

- Have dripping faucets repaired. One drop a second can waste 700 gallons of water a year.

- Don't run a dishwasher with only a few dishes in it. Wait until you have a full load. You'll save energy, too.

- Don't let water run while you're doing something else.

- Use detergents and other cleaning compounds only as directed. If you use more than needed, you can pollute the water supply.

- Use detergents and other cleaners that don't contain phosphates. Phosphates are chemicals that pollute water.

Fresh, clean water is a valuable resource.

- Dyed paper pollutes water. Buy plain white paper towels, napkins, and toilet paper.

- Use household chemicals completely before you throw out the container. Leftover chemicals in landfills can leak into the water supply.

- Don't pour household chemicals down the drain. Contact your sanitation or health department and ask how to dispose of them.

CUT DOWN ON TRASH

Every American produces about 4 pounds of trash every day! Why is this a problem? Throwing items away costs resources. For example, most plastics are made from petroleum (oil), a resource that's limited. The more plastic products that are made and thrown away, the faster the petroleum is used up.

The way people get rid of trash also affects the environment. Trash is normally buried in landfills or dumps. Many communities are running out of space for landfills and are looking for solutions.

What can you do to help? Practice the environmental 3Rs:

Reduce • Reuse • Recycle

Disposable items add up faster than you may realize. What are some alternatives?

REDUCE

First, look for ways to reduce the amount of paper, plastics, and other products you use. The less you use, the less you have to get rid of.

Consumer packaging makes up about 50 percent of the trash people create. When you shop, look for items without a lot of packaging.

Disposables are products that are used once or perhaps a few times and then thrown away. Many people are in the habit of using them, but habits can be changed. Try making the switch yourself. Use cloth napkins instead of paper ones. Wash a glass instead of using a paper cup. Can you think of other ways to use fewer disposables?

REUSE

Many items that you'd normally throw away can be reused in the home. Reusing old items instead of buying new ones saves money as well as natural resources. Here are a few suggestions:

◆ Use large paper bags for trash. Smaller bags can be used to line wastepaper baskets, carry a lunch, or ripen fruit.

◆ Reuse foil containers from frozen foods for baking.

◆ Use plastic plates from frozen foods as saucers under potted plants.

Reusing empty jars reduces the need to buy special containers to store leftovers.

◆ Save glass jars and covers. After washing, use them to store food in a cabinet or refrigerator.

◆ Community centers, schools, and senior citizens centers always need materials for arts and crafts projects. Donate reusable items such as margarine tubs, juice cans, and cardboard rolls from paper towels.

RECYCLE

When items are recycled, they're put through a special process. The materials from these products are used to manufacture other items. It usually takes less fuel to make a product from recycled materials than from new ones.

If an item can be recycled or is made from recycled materials, it carries the recycling emblem shown on page 184. Try to buy items with this emblem as much as possible. Fewer products will end up in the trash.

If your community has a recycling program, you can collect items to be recycled instead of throwing them away. First, find out what materials the local program accepts. They might include newspapers, other paper, cardboard,

Try It!

Reusing Items Creatively

How many other ways to reuse items can you think of? Time yourself for 5 minutes. See how many ideas you can come up with.

★ Review the ideas on your list. By carrying them out, what resources would you help conserve?

★ Does reusing items always conserve resources? Explain.

★ How might you encourage others to reuse items?

aluminum and other metals, glass, and some plastics. Then find out what to do with the items you save. In some communities, you put them out at the curb to be picked up on certain days. In others, you take them to a collection station.

When you save items to be recycled:

◆ Rinse containers thoroughly so there's no food left to attract mice, insects, and other pests.

◆ Prepare the items as directed. For example, you may have to remove labels from cans or sort glass by color.

◆ Save space by flattening cans, crushing plastic containers, and breaking cardboard boxes down.

Does your community have a recycling program? If not, perhaps you could help start one.

CONSERVE FOOD

Food is scarce in many parts of the world. Yet a surprisingly large amount of edible food in the United States is thrown away as garbage. You can help prevent this needless waste.

- Don't buy more food than you can use up before it spoils. Buy food that's in good condition and store it properly. Use it before it loses quality.

- Use correct cooking procedures. Food that's poorly cooked may end up in the garbage can.

- When you help yourself to food, take only as much as you're sure you'll eat.

- When serving food to others, keep portions small. Let people ask for seconds if they want them.

- Store leftovers properly so that they stay safe and in good condition. Plan how you'll use them.

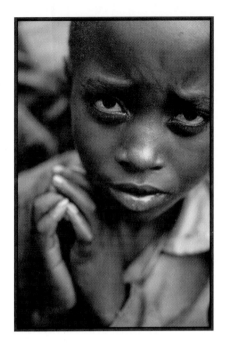

Sadly, food is not plentiful for everyone. The less food you waste, the more there will be to go around.

CHAPTER 23 REVIEW

Understanding Key Ideas

1. Give three tips for saving energy when you use kitchen appliances.
2. Explain how using household cleaners wisely helps ensure a clean water supply.
3. What is the difference between recycling and reusing an item? Explain why both are important.
4. How can your knowledge and skills in choosing and preparing food help prevent food waste?

Applying Knowledge and Skills

- **Communication:** Design a message that will encourage other teens to conserve resources. The format might be a poster, magazine ad, radio or television commercial, or web site design. Include specific reasons for conserving and ways to conserve.

- **Reducing Disposables:** Make a list of all the disposables used in the foods lab or your kitchen at home. For each disposable, list at least one reusable alternative.

Exploring Further

- **Critical Thinking:** Do you think your personal actions can really make a difference to the environment? Explain.

- **Community Resources:** Find out about the recycling options in your community. How can you help your family and neighbors take better advantage of them?

CHAPTER 24

MEAL MANAGEMENT

Menu

Discover...

★ *what to consider when planning a menu.*

★ *how to make meals appealing.*

★ *how to time meal preparation.*

Key Terms

meal management
menu

Have you ever prepared an entire meal for your family or friends? If you haven't yet, you will one day. Making a meal is a little more of a challenge than making just one recipe. You'll need to plan what to serve and how to have the food ready on time. The key is *meal management*—using your management skills to help you prepare good meals.

FOOD FOR THOUGHT

What types of management skills can help make a meal a success?

PLANNING A MENU

Menu planning is the first step in meal management. A **menu** is a list of the foods you plan to serve at a meal. Many families find it's helpful to plan menus for several days or weeks at one time. Long-range planning helps you:

◆ Build variety into your food choices.

◆ Be sure of getting all the food group servings you need each day.

◆ Plan your shopping and get better food bargains.

◆ Save time and reduce stress by being prepared.

The best meals are made up of nutritious foods that not only look and taste good, but go well together. Where do you begin? It's often easiest to start by choosing a main dish. Then you can select other foods that will complement, or work well with, the main dish. As you make your choices, keep these points in mind:

Meal pattern. People often prefer different foods for breakfast than for lunch. Will this be a light meal or the main meal of the day?

Nutrition. Include foods from the five groups in the Food Guide Pyramid. Choose foods that are nutritious without extra amounts of fat, sugar, and sodium.

Individual needs. Who will be eating the meal? What do they like and dislike? Does anyone have special nutritional needs?

Your own resources. Consider time, energy, food, money, skills, and equipment, as you learned in Chapter 22.

MENUS WITH APPEAL

Another important consideration is meal appeal. The food you serve should look and taste good so that everyone will enjoy eating it. Think about:

Flavor. Have a variety of flavors in the meal. Balance strong, spicy flavors with milder ones.

A well-planned meal is appetizing as well as nutritious. What gives this meal its appeal?

Color. Try to include at least one brightly colored food in each meal, or a pleasing variety of colors. You can add color with a garnish such as parsley, a wedge of lemon, radish slices, carrot curls, or a sprinkling of paprika.

Texture. Texture means whether the food is crunchy or tender, hard or soft. A meal should have a mixture of textures.

Temperature. On a very hot day, a chilled salad would be more appealing than steaming soup. However, a variety of temperatures can make a meal interesting.

Size and shape. What's wrong with a meal of meatballs, peas, rolls, and melon balls? Use a variety of sizes and shapes in meals. Many foods can be cut into slices, strips, or cubes to add interest.

TIMING A MEAL

Once you've planned what to serve, you need to plan how you'll prepare it. Suppose you're going to make the menu shown at the right.

Broiled Fish
Broccoli
Brown Rice
Fresh Spinach & Tomato Salad
Whole Wheat Rolls
Baked Apple
Skim Milk

Begin by thinking about your options for each food. Will you use fresh or frozen broccoli? Will you cook it on the range or in the microwave oven? The choices you make will affect your shopping list and your plan for preparing the meal.

In Chapter 22, you learned how to make a work plan and schedule for just one recipe. Planning to prepare a whole meal requires a little extra thought. That's because your goal is to have all the foods ready to eat at the same time. It can be easy if you follow these three steps:

1. Identify the tasks you need to complete for each menu item.

2. Arrange those tasks into a combined work plan for the whole meal.

3. Make a schedule based on the combined work plan.

IDENTIFY PREPARATION TASKS

First, consider the menu items one at a time. Look at the recipe or the package directions for each. What are the basic tasks in preparing the food? List them, as shown in the example on the next page. Also write down how much time you'll need to complete each task.

Preparation Tasks

Food	Tasks	Time needed
Broiled Fish	• Thaw fillets in refrigerator	Overnight
	• Rinse thawed fillets; put on broiler grid	10 min.
	• Broil in oven	15 min.
Frozen Broccoli	• Remove from package; put in container	5 min.
	• Microwave	10 min.
	• Let stand	1–2 min.

Remember to include tasks that relate to the meal as a whole. Washing your hands, gathering food and equipment, setting the table, and putting food into serving dishes should all be on your list.

MAKE A COMBINED WORK PLAN

Next, turn your list of tasks into a work plan for the whole meal. Why not just do all the tasks in the order you've listed them? Think about what would happen. After the fish had finished broiling, you'd start on the broccoli. By the time the broccoli was done, the fish would be getting cold. Also, the whole meal would take longer than necessary to prepare. You wouldn't be using your time efficiently.

How can you decide on the most efficient sequence for your work plan? Here are some suggestions:

◆ Look for tasks that can be done ahead of time. You might make the salad early, then refrigerate it until it's time to eat.

◆ Look for ways to dovetail tasks, or fit them together efficiently. Can you prepare another food while the salad vegetables are draining? Can the dessert microwave while you eat the rest of the dinner?

◆ Don't try to dovetail two tasks that require your full attention. Look for another solution. Perhaps one food could be prepared first, then reheated at the last minute.

◆ If someone will be helping you prepare the meal, divide the work so you each have specific jobs to do.

The more food preparation experience you have, the easier it becomes to dovetail tasks.

MAKE A SCHEDULE

Once you have a combined work plan, it's easy to turn it into a schedule. Just work backward from the time you want to serve the meal. Figure out what time you'll need to start the last task in your plan, then the next-to-last task, and so on.

Here's how your finished schedule might turn out:

Schedule	
Night before	Put fish in refrigerator to thaw.
4:25	Wash hands, get ready to cook.
4:30	Set table.
4:45	Gather food and equipment
4:55	Rinse apples and salad vegetables; let vegetables drain.
5:00	Prepare apples for microwaving; set table.
5:10	Assemble salad; refrigerate.
5:20	Prepare fish for broiling.
5:30	Start water heating in saucepan; measure rice.
5:35	Prepare broccoli for microwaving.
5:40	Add rice to pan; cover and let stand. Put pan of fish in broiler; set timer. Put broccoli in microwave.
5:50	Set rolls on table. Remove salad from refrigerator. Pour milk.
5:55	Check fish for doneness. Put food in serving dishes. Put apples in microwave.
6:00	The meal is ready!

EVALUATING THE MEAL

Planning a menu, writing out a work plan, and making a schedule take time and thought. But the few extra minutes you spend can make the meal preparation go much more smoothly.

After the meal, evaluate how successful it was. Did your plan work as you expected? Did everyone enjoy the food? If so, save your menu and schedule to use again. If not, think about what you might change next time. Then try again. With practice, you'll soon be skilled at making appealing, nutritious, well-managed meals.

Preparing meals is a skill you can be proud of. It will help you now and in the future.

Understanding Key Ideas

1. How would you evaluate whether a menu is suited to the people who will prepare and eat the meal?
2. Describe how to use variety to make a meal appealing.
3. How would you determine what tasks to include in the work plan for a meal?
4. What are two strategies for making the best use of time as you prepare a meal?

Applying Knowledge and Skills

◆ **Analyzing Meal Appeal:** Find pictures or menus for three complete meals in magazines or cookbooks. Analyze what makes the meals appealing or how the appeal could be improved.

◆ **Menu Planning:** Plan a menu for a simple meal your family would enjoy. Explain why you chose those foods, referring to the points discussed in the chapter.

◆ **Making a Schedule:** Make a work plan and schedule for the meal you planned in the above activity. If possible, prepare and serve the meal at home and evaluate the results.

Exploring Further

◆ **Social Studies:** Using ethnic cookbooks or other sources, find a menu for a traditional meal from another culture. In what ways does it reflect the chapter's guidelines for meal appeal? In what ways does it differ? What might explain the differences?

Meal Management 191

SERVING A MEAL

Discover...

★ basic methods for serving a meal.

★ how to set a table.

★ guidelines for table manners.

Key Terms
stemware
tumblers
flatware
place setting

Mealtime should be relaxing and enjoyable. This is true whether the meal is casual or formal, eaten at home or away. The table setting and the way food is served can help make any meal more pleasant. Good conversation and simple courtesy also add to the enjoyment.

FOOD FOR THOUGHT

Besides the food itself, what makes a meal more enjoyable for you? Why?

SHARING MEALS

Many families feel that mealtime is more than just a time to eat. Preparing and eating meals together builds family bonds. You can talk about your day, share ideas, and just enjoy one another's company. Even the busiest families can plan to eat some meals together.

The mealtime customs of some families might differ from yours. Learn to respect and appreciate these differences. For example, the foods in this Middle Eastern meal are meant to be eaten with the fingers.

All around the world, mealtime is a time for sharing. However, specific customs for serving and eating meals vary from one culture to another. The guidelines given in this chapter are followed by many people in the United States and elsewhere. Remember, though, that other customs are followed in some homes near and far. Whatever the customs, what matters most is being thoughtful of others.

TYPES OF MEAL SERVICE

Every family has its own customs about who sits where and how most meals are served. A well-planned routine can help mealtime be an orderly, relaxed, and comfortable time. Most people serve meals in one or more of these basic styles:

Family style means the food is placed in serving dishes on the table. People help themselves, passing serving dishes to each other.

Plate service means the food is already on each person's plate when it's brought to the table.

When you serve food buffet style, remember food safety. Keep cold foods cold and hot foods hot.

Buffet service is often used for larger gatherings. Serving dishes of food are arranged on a table or counter, with the tableware stacked at one end. People line up and serve themselves. Then they carry their food to an eating area.

Families may use a combination of meal service styles. For instance, if most of the foods are served buffet style, rolls and relishes may be passed around the table and dessert brought out on plates.

TABLEWARE

The items you need to serve and eat food are called tableware. The tableware you need for a meal depends on the food you serve and the way you serve it. Tableware includes:

Plates. Large plates are used for the main course. Salads, bread, and desserts are often served on separate, smaller plates. That way they're not next to hot foods that could make them wilt, melt, or get soggy.

Other dishes. Bowls are needed for foods such as cereal, soup, and some salads and desserts. Hot beverages are served in a mug or in a cup with a saucer. If you serve the meal family style, you'll also need serving dishes, such as large bowls and platters.

Glasses. These come in two basic shapes. **Stemware** has a stem between the base and the bowl. It's fragile because the stem breaks easily. Hold stemware by the bowl, not by the stem. **Tumblers** are glasses without stems. They come in many shapes and sizes.

Flatware. Items such as forks and spoons are called **flatware.** The basic items include a dinner knife to cut meat and spread butter, a dinner fork, and a teaspoon for beverages and some desserts. You might add another, smaller fork for salad or dessert. A larger-bowled soup spoon is used for soups.

Table linens. These include napkins, place mats, and tablecloths.

SETTING THE TABLE

Each piece of tableware has a specific place where it should be put on the table. The arrangement of tableware for each individual is called a **place setting,** or cover. It's designed for the convenience of the person eating.

Setting a table is easiest if you do it in this order:

1. Decide what tableware will be needed for each person to eat the meal.

2. Put a tablecloth or place mats on the table. Add a table decoration, if desired.

3. Put the plate in the center of each place setting. Or, if the food is being served on plates from the kitchen, allow enough space for the plate.

4. Arrange the flatware next.

5. Finally, add other items around the outside of the setting.

The next two pages show how to arrange items in the place setting correctly.

The Place Setting

Each place setting should be arranged as shown here. As you look at these pages, think about how the placement of each item adds convenience for the person who is eating.

❖ The salad plate goes above the forks.

❖ Put the napkins to the left of the forks. The folded edge should be farthest away from the forks. The napkin can then be picked up by the corner edge and unfolded easily.

❖ Place the dinner plate in the center of each place setting. The edge of the plate should be about 1 inch from the edge of the table.

❖ Place the forks to the left of the dinner plate.

❖ What if you need a salad fork and a dinner fork? A basic rule is to arrange flatware so that the piece you use first is farthest from the plate. If the salad is to be eaten before the main course, you would place the salad fork on the outside.

Table Decorations

A table decoration in the center of the table, no matter how simple, can make a meal more pleasant. Ordinary items in your home can be the beginning of a table centerpiece. Here are some ideas:

❖ An arrangement of fruit in a bowl or basket or on a cutting board. You might serve the fruit as a dessert.

❖ Flowers in an attractive container, such as a teapot, a pitcher, or an old, unusual coffee pot.

❖ A grouping of several different candles on a place mat.

❖ Put the water glass just above the tip of the knife. If there is another beverage glass, place it to the right and slightly in front of the water glass.

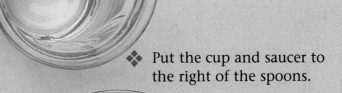

❖ Put the cup and saucer to the right of the spoons.

❖ Place the knife to the right of the plate with the blade facing the plate.

❖ Put the spoon to the right of the knife. If there is more than one, place the spoon that will be used first (such as a soup spoon) farthest from the plate.

❖ Be sure the handle of each flatware piece lines up with the lower edge of the plate.

MAKING MEALS PLEASANT

When you gather around the table with family or friends, set a pleasant tone for the meal. Try soft music or a quiet background instead of the television. Good conversation can make the meal more enjoyable—and easier to digest, too. Help keep the conversation cheerful and positive. Save any disputes or problems for after the meal.

BASIC TABLE MANNERS

Table manners are really a matter of courtesy. They make everyone more comfortable so the meal is more enjoyable. Remember to use good table manners every day, not just on special occasions. Soon they'll become a habit.

Eating with someone whose manners are poor can ruin your appetite. How are your manners?

Here are some guidelines for good table manners:

◆ Sit up straight instead of slouching.

◆ Place your napkin in your lap. Use it to wipe your hands and mouth when needed.

◆ If you're in a small group, be sure everyone has been served before you begin to eat. In a large group, you may start to eat as soon as three or four people have been served.

◆ Take small bites and chew quietly with your mouth closed. Don't talk or drink your beverage with food in your mouth.

◆ Reach for food only if you don't have to lean too far across the table or reach in front of anyone. Otherwise, ask your neighbor to pass it to you. Be sure to say "please" and "thank you."

◆ Use serving utensils, not your flatware, to serve yourself.

◆ Avoid putting your elbows on the table as you eat. However, you may rest your elbows on the table between courses if you like.

- Some foods, such as corn and peas, may be difficult to get onto a fork. Push them on the fork with a piece of bread or a knife.

- If you cough or sneeze, turn your head away from the table. If you have a coughing or sneezing spell or must blow your nose, excuse yourself and leave the table.

- When you're not eating, rest your fork and knife on the plate. When you're through eating, put them in the center of the plate.

CLEARING THE TABLE

After everyone is finished eating, it's time to clear the table. Stand to the side of each person as you pick up dishes from the place setting. Then carry the dishes to the cleanup area. Don't scrape or stack dishes at the table. Follow the guidelines for cleanup explained in Chapter 22.

CHAPTER 25 REVIEW

Understanding Key Ideas

1. What is the value in eating meals as a family?
2. Explain how a casserole would be served in each of the three basic styles of meal service.
3. Suppose you're serving individual green salads along with the main course. What tableware items are needed for the salad? Where should they be placed?
4. Describe good manners specifically related to serving food family style.

Applying Knowledge and Skills

- **Tableware Choice:** Find or plan a menu for a complete meal. What serving style would you use? What tableware would you need? Explain your answers.

- **Place Setting:** Correctly arrange a place setting using a dinner plate, water glass, teaspoon, dinner fork, dinner knife, dessert fork, and napkin. Explain the placement of each item.

- **Table Manners:** In small groups, demonstrate good table manners while eating a meal. After your demonstration, discuss which tips from this chapter you used.

Exploring Further

- **Social Studies:** Find out about a culture in which serving methods, tableware, or table manners differ from those described in the chapter. Describe or demonstrate the customs to the class. If possible, learn how they originated.

PACKING A LUNCH

Food on the go can be fun. Many people enjoy taking food along on special outings, such as a picnic or football game. Perhaps you bring your lunch to school every day.

FOOD FOR THOUGHT

What should you consider when you make a packed lunch or any other portable meal?

PLANNING A PACKED LUNCH

A well-planned packed lunch gives you energy and nutrients for a busy day away from home. Include plenty of nutritious food group servings, especially fruits, vegetables, and whole grains. You might add a high-protein food, such as lean meat, cooked dry beans, or peanut butter. A dairy food, such as low-fat milk, yogurt, or cottage cheese, can round out the meal.

To keep packed lunches interesting from day to day, be creative. Vary sandwich breads and fillings to make different combinations. How about packing leftover pizza or chicken pieces and eating them cold? You can pack salads or even hot, hearty dishes such as chili or spaghetti. First, however, be sure you know how to keep hot foods hot and cold foods cold when you pack a lunch.

Sandwich Ideas

Breads: Whole wheat • Multi-grain • Rye • Bagel • Tortillas • English muffin • Pita (pocket) bread • Roll • Biscuit

Main fillings: Leftover cooked poultry, fish, or meat • Mashed cooked dry beans • Low-fat cheese • Peanut butter

Additions: Lettuce or other salad greens • Sliced or chopped tomatoes, cucumbers, onions • Shredded carrots • Green pepper rings • Well-drained sauerkraut • Sliced or chopped fruit

FOOD SAFETY FOR PACKED LUNCHES

As you learned in Chapter 21, food must be kept either cold or very hot. Otherwise harmful bacteria multiply and could cause serious illness. Your lunch container may have to sit at room temperature for several hours. To keep the food inside safe, you need to take the proper steps when you pack it.

USING A VACUUM BOTTLE

A **vacuum bottle** is an insulated bottle that keeps foods at their original temperature. Narrow-mouth vacuum bottles are used for beverages. Wide-mouth vacuum bottles are used for foods such as soups, casseroles, and chili. Bottles with a glass or stainless steel lining do a better job of keeping foods hot than those with plastic interiors.

If you can't buy a nutritious beverage at lunch time, take one along in a prechilled vacuum bottle.

Prechill or preheat the vacuum bottle to help keep food and beverages at the right temperature. For cold foods and beverages, you can fill the bottle the night before and refrigerate. For hot foods and beverages, pour hot water into the bottle in the morning. Let it stand a few minutes while you heat the food to be packed. Pour out the hot water and fill with the heated food or beverage.

MORE WAYS TO KEEP FOOD COLD

This gel pack can be frozen, then packed in your lunch container to help keep foods cold.

◆ Keep cold foods in the refrigerator or freezer until you're ready to pack your lunch in the morning.

◆ Pack a tightly-sealed container of frozen water or juice with your lunch. (Caution: Small cans of juice may break during freezing.) You can also use freezable gel packs.

◆ Freeze individually wrapped sandwiches ahead of time. Then pack one, still frozen, in your lunch. It will keep other foods cold. By lunch time, it will be thawed. (Sandwiches made with eggs, jelly, mayonnaise, or raw vegetables don't freeze well.)

◆ Pack your lunch in an insulated bag or box.

◆ Store your lunch in as cool a place as possible. Keep it out of sunny areas and away from heat sources, such as a radiator.

Try It!

Keeping Beverages Cold

Fill a vacuum bottle with ice and cold water. Put the same amount of ice and cold water into an ordinary glass jar. Stir well, then check the temperature of the water in each container. Close both containers and let them sit at room temperature several hours or overnight. Then check the temperature of the water again.

✳ How much has the temperature changed in each container?

✳ How do you explain the results?

TIPS FOR PACKING YOUR LUNCH

◆ Airtight wrapping or containers help keep your packed food fresh and in good shape. You can use plastic bags, plastic wrap, waxed paper, or reusable plastic containers.

◆ If you use a lunchbox or lunch tote, wash it in warm, soapy water, rinse, and dry after every use. Do the same with plastic containers. Let them air dry to get rid of previous food odors.

◆ Remember to wash fresh fruits and vegetables before packing them.

◆ To save time in the morning, prepare some lunch items the evening before. Refrigerate them until you're ready to pack your lunch bag.

- Pack fresh vegetables for your sandwich, such as lettuce and tomato slices, in separate bags or containers. Add them to the sandwich just before you eat it. Otherwise, they may wilt or make the bread soggy.

- Pack salad and salad dressing in separate containers. Add the dressing just before you eat.

- Remember to pack a napkin and a fork or spoon, if needed.

You can wash and slice celery sticks the night before, then refrigerate them. In the morning they'll be ready to pop into your lunch bag.

CHAPTER 26 REVIEW

Understanding Key Ideas

1. What types of foods are the basis of a nutritious packed lunch?
2. Explain why your packed lunches can include more variety if you have a vacuum bottle.
3. Besides saving time in the morning, why might you make and freeze sandwiches to use in packed lunches?
4. Describe how to pack a salad in your lunch.

Applying Knowledge and Skills

- **Menu Planning:** Assume you'll be taking a packed lunch to school every day for a week. Plan five menus that are varied, nutritious, appealing, and quick to prepare. For each menu, explain what equipment you'd need to keep all the foods safe to eat and in good condition.

- **Packing Food Safely:** Explain all the steps you would follow, and why, to pack a lunch that includes hot vegetable soup; a chicken, lettuce, and tomato sandwich; cottage cheese; and a whole peach.

Exploring Further

- **Creative Thinking:** Write recipes for five original sandwiches that each include a protein food, at least two vegetables or fruits, and a spread or other flavor booster. Don't repeat any ingredients.

- **Math:** Compare the cost of packing a homemade lunch to buying a similar lunch at a restaurant or supermarket deli. Make a chart of your findings.

MILK

Discover...

★ *how milk fits into a healthful eating plan.*

★ *how to select and store milk.*

★ *how to cook with milk.*

Key Terms
pasteurized
homogenized
curdle
reconstitute

FOOD FOR THOUGHT

How many ways can you think of to use milk in meals and snacks? Make a list.

NUTRITION NOTES

Remember that you need two to three servings from the Milk, Yogurt, and Cheese group each day. Milk is a good source of nutrients such as:

◆ Protein for growth and repair of the body.

◆ Calcium, phosphorus, and vitamin D for strong bones and teeth.

◆ Vitamin A and B vitamins for growth and health.

The fat content of milk varies, depending on the type of milk.

Whole milk has 8 grams of fat per serving. Children under age two need whole milk for proper growth.

Reduced-fat milk has 5 grams of fat per serving.

Low-fat milk has 2.5 grams of fat per serving.

Fat-free milk, also called skim milk, has almost no fat.

 # CONSUMER POWER

You can choose from many different kinds of milk in fresh, canned, or dry form. The type of milk you choose depends on how you plan to use the product. If several types would suit your purpose, compare the price and advantages of each before you decide.

BUYING FRESH MILK

Fresh milk is found in the refrigerated case at the store. It comes in glass bottles, paper cartons, or plastic jugs. You can choose from fat-free, low-fat, reduced-fat, or whole milk. There are also flavored milks, such as chocolate milk. Buttermilk has a thick texture and tangy flavor.

When buying fresh milk you may see the following on the label:

◆ Grade A means the milk meets quality standards set by the U.S. Public Health Service.

◆ **Pasteurized** (PASS-tyoor-ized) milk has been heat-treated to kill harmful bacteria.

◆ **Homogenized** (huh-MAH-jen-ized) means the fat is broken into tiny drops and mixed permanently with the milk. Otherwise, the fat would rise to the top as cream.

The label also tells you what nutrients have been added. Most milk is fortified with vitamin D. Vitamin A is always added to fat-free and low-fat milk. It replaces the vitamin A that was removed along with the fat. Sometimes extra protein is added.

When you buy fresh milk:

Check the date on the package. It tells you the last day the milk should be sold.

Mar 23

Read the label to be sure you're getting the type of milk you want.

SKIM MILK
LOW CHOLESTEROL

Pasteurized
Vitamin A & D

QUART (946 ml)

SKIM MILK
LOW CHOLESTEROL

Pasteurized
Vitamin A & D

QUART (946 ml)

Buy milk that is pasteurized and fortified with vitamin D.

Be sure the container doesn't leak.

STORING FRESH MILK

Refrigerate fresh milk in its original container. Why? If you pour milk into another storage container, it might pick up harmful bacteria. Then it will spoil more quickly.

To keep milk fresher longer, keep it cold. As soon as you've poured the amount of milk you need, close the container tightly. Return it to the refrigerator at once.

OTHER FORMS OF MILK

Fresh milk is convenient because it's ready to use. Other forms of milk are more convenient to store than fresh milk.

UHT Milk

◆ Processed at ultra-high temperature to kill all bacteria. Packaged in sterile (bacteria-free) cartons.

◆ Unopened packages can be stored at room temperature up to 3 months. Refrigerate after opening.

◆ Similar in taste and nutrition to fresh milk.

◆ Usually costs more than fresh milk.

Canned Milk

◆ Low in cost.

◆ Evaporated milk—Whole or fat-free milk with half the water removed. Use full strength in place of cream, or mix with water to use as fresh milk.

◆ Sweetened condensed milk—Concentrated milk with at least 40 percent sugar added. Use in candy and dessert recipes.

◆ Store unopened cans in a dry, cool area. After opening, cover and refrigerate.

Nonfat Dry Milk

◆ A powder made by removing most of the fat and water from milk.

◆ Low in cost.

◆ Mix with water to use as fresh fat-free milk, or use dry in cooking.

◆ Store unopened packages in a dry, cool area. After opening, put dry milk in an airtight container. After mixing with water, refrigerate.

FOOD SKILLS

As a beverage, milk goes well with meals and snacks. It can even be a snack in itself. You can make refreshing, nutritious blender drinks with milk. (See Chapter 37 for some ideas.)

Milk also has many uses in cooking. You can make hot milk beverages, such as cocoa. You can thicken and flavor milk to make sauces and puddings. Milk is often an ingredient in soups, casseroles, and baked goods.

Milk contributes flavor and nutrients to many kinds of dishes, such as pudding.

PRINCIPLES OF COOKING WITH MILK

Milk is a protein food, and protein is sensitive to heat. Therefore, milk must be cooked slowly at low temperatures. When milk is cooked properly, the product should have a smooth, creamy texture. It should have a rich, mild, pleasant flavor.

What happens if you cook milk at too high a temperature for too long a time? The solids in milk will brown and then scorch, or burn. This gives the milk a burnt flavor and robs it of nutrients. To prevent scorching, use low heat and watch carefully.

Keeping a Skin from Forming

When milk is heated, a skin sometimes forms on the surface. The skin is made up of milk solids and fat. Because the skin prevents steam from escaping, the milk may boil over. To keep a skin from forming, cover the pan or stir the milk frequently as it cooks.

What if a skin forms? Some people throw the skin away because it's tough and chewy. Others prefer to stir it back into the milk because it contains valuable nutrients.

How can you prevent this from happening?

Keeping Milk from Curdling

Milk sometimes **curdles**, or separates into many small lumps and a watery liquid. Milk will usually curdle if you add it too quickly to a mixture that's hot or acidic, such as tomato soup. That's because heat and acids tend to make particles of milk protein stick together.

Try It!

Acids and Milk

Pour about 1/4 cup of vinegar into a clear glass container. Add a tablespoon of milk. (Don't stir.) Can you see what happens to the milk? You may need to look through the bottom of the container or gently tilt it. Now try pouring the mixture through a coffee filter or a fine strainer.

★ How did the milk change after you added it to the vinegar?

★ Why do you think this happened?

How to Keep Milk from Curdling

1. Measure out the amount of milk and pour it into a bowl.

2. Slowly pour some of the hot or acid mixture into the milk, stirring constantly.

   Why? This warms the milk or makes it more acid so it won't curdle easily.

3. Slowly add the milk to the remaining mixture, stirring constantly.

STEP 2

STEP 3

MAKING WHITE SAUCE

White sauce, or cream sauce, is milk thickened with flour. When flour is cooked with a liquid, the grains of flour swell up and thicken the liquid.

White sauce can be used to make casseroles and other main dishes. It's also used for creamy gravies, creamed vegetables, cream soups, and as a base for other sauces.

Here are some ideas for varying the basic white sauce recipe:

◆ For a thinner sauce, use less butter or margarine and less flour. For a thicker sauce, use more. Just be sure to use equal amounts of each.

◆ For cheese sauce, stir 1 cup grated cheddar cheese into the hot white sauce. Season with paprika and a dash of cayenne pepper.

How to Make White Sauce

STEP 1

1. Melt 2 Tbsp. butter or margarine in a saucepan over low heat.

2. Blend in 2 Tbsp. flour and a dash of pepper.

Tip Use a mixing spoon.

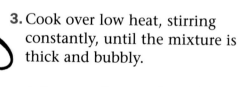
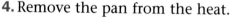

3. Cook over low heat, stirring constantly, until the mixture is thick and bubbly.

4. Remove the pan from the heat.

STEP 2

STEP 3

5. Pour 1 cup fat-free milk into the flour mixture, a little at a time. Then stir constantly to make a smooth mixture.

6. Return the pan to the heat. Cook and stir until the mixture bubbles and thickens. Yield: about 1 cup white sauce.

STEP 5

MICROWAVING MILK

Many recipes made with milk, such as beverages, sauces, soups, and casseroles, can be heated in the microwave oven. Unless it's overcooked, milk is less likely to scorch in the microwave than on the range.

Remember, milk should not be overcooked, and microwaves cook quickly. Follow power level and temperature directions in recipes.

Milk boils over easily when microwaved. Use a container large enough to keep the milk from foaming over into the oven. Watch closely during cooking. Turn the power off as soon as the milk begins to foam.

Be sure to stir milk beverages before heating. Stirring breaks up a thin film on the surface of the liquid. If not stirred, the film holds heat in. It could cause the milk to splatter as it heats. Stir again after microwaving to distribute the heat evenly. Otherwise, if one part is hotter than the rest, you could burn your mouth.

White sauce should be microwaved long enough to cook the flour. Otherwise the mixture will have a raw flour flavor. Stir the sauce several times during heating to keep it from getting lumpy.

Microwave Hints

* A temperature probe is convenient to use when heating milk. Soups and beverages with milk should be heated to 140°F.

* If lumps form in white sauce, use a mixing spoon to press them against the side of the container until they disappear.

A cup of cocoa is a great way to warm up on a cold day! On a warm day, chill the cocoa and serve it over ice.

◆ List the equipment needed for this recipe. How would it differ if you were making eight servings?

◆ Why is the cocoa stirred after the cooking time?

Almond-Spice Cocoa
Yield: 4 servings, about 1 cup each

1/4 cup	unsweetened cocoa powder	4 cups	fat-free milk
1/4 cup	sugar	1/2 tsp.	almond extract
1/4 cup	water	1/2 tsp.	ground cinnamon
		dash	ground nutmeg

1. Combine cocoa powder, sugar, and water in a 2-qt. microwave-safe container. Stir until mixed.
2. Microwave at 100% power, uncovered, for 30 seconds to 1 minute until cocoa and sugar dissolve.
3. Stir in milk, almond extract, cinnamon, and nutmeg.
4. Microwave at 50% power, uncovered, for 4 to 5 minutes or until thoroughly heated but not boiling. Stir after 2 minutes and again at the end of cooking.
5. Pour into mugs and serve hot.

Nutrition Notes
Per serving: 146 calories, 1 g fat
Good source of: potassium, magnesium, iron, vitamin A, vitamin D, riboflavin, vitamin B_{12}, calcium, phosphorus

USING NONFAT DRY MILK

To **reconstitute** means to replace water that's been removed from a food. To reconstitute dry milk, follow the directions on the package. Use as you would fresh fat-free milk.

For more nutrients, especially calcium, add nonfat dry milk to recipes. You can add it to either dry or liquid ingredients. Mix well. Here are some suggestions:

- Ground meat, chicken, or turkey: Mix in 1/2 cup dry milk for every pound of meat.

- Grain products: Mix equal amounts of dry milk and rice, cereal, or other grain products before cooking. Cook as directed on the package.

- Mashed vegetables: Add 1/3 cup dry milk to mashed vegetables, such as potatoes or squash. If necessary, add cooking water.

What types of recipes could you make more nutritious by adding nonfat dry milk?

CHAPTER 27 REVIEW

Understanding Key Ideas

1. Describe the benefits of including milk in your eating plan.
2. Is milk high in fat? Explain.
3. When you buy a carton of milk, how can you tell whether it's fresh and safe to drink?
4. Compare and contrast two types of milk that can be stored without refrigeration.
5. Describe two problems that can occur when you cook with milk. Explain how to prevent them.

Applying Knowledge and Skills

- **Communication:** Create a magazine ad for milk. Include facts about nutrition and tips for including milk in an active lifestyle.

- **Recipe Analysis:** Find three recipes, each for a different type of food, in which milk is heated. Do the recipe directions reflect the chapter guidelines? Explain. What tips would you add?

- **Foods Lab:** Modify a recipe or convenience food by adding nonfat dry milk as suggested in the chapter. Prepare the new version and evaluate the results.

Exploring Further

- **Critical Thinking:** When would UHT milk be especially helpful?

- **Creative Thinking:** Suppose you are starting a restaurant. You want to offer menu items that people can't find anywhere else. Think of at least five original beverage ideas using milk. Write the menu descriptions for your beverages.

YOGURT AND CHEESE

Discover...

* how yogurt and cheese fit into a healthful eating plan.

* how to select and store yogurt and cheese.

* how to use yogurt and cheese..

Key Terms
curd
whey

Yogurt and cheese have been around for centuries. They were invented as a way to preserve milk. Today we have refrigerators to keep milk from spoiling quickly. However, people still enjoy the varied flavors and textures of yogurt and cheese.

> ### FOOD FOR THOUGHT
>
> How many different kinds of yogurt and cheese have you tasted? What others might you like to try?

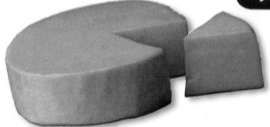

MAKING YOGURT AND CHEESE

Yogurt and cheese are both made from milk. Yogurt is made by adding a special "good" bacteria to milk. This process gives it a smooth, thick texture and a tangy flavor.

There are many ways to make cheese, but all of them include the same basic steps: First, milk is thickened. Then the solid part, or **curd**, is separated from the liquid, or **whey**. The curd is made into cheese.

NUTRITION NOTES

Yogurt and cheese offer another way to get servings from the Milk, Yogurt, and Cheese Group. Like milk, yogurt and cheese are an important source of nutrients, such as:

◆ Protein for growth and repair of the body.

◆ Calcium and phosphorus for strong bones and teeth.

◆ Vitamin A and B vitamins for growth and health.

Yogurt is generally low in fat and sodium. Many cheeses, however, are not. High-fat cheese should be eaten in moderation. Often just a small amount of cheese is added to a dish for flavor and added nutrients.

CONSUMER POWER

You have many choices when it comes to yogurt and cheese. To get the most for your money, shop carefully and store products properly.

TYPES OF YOGURT

Yogurt is available plain or with flavorings added, such as fruit and sugar. You can choose low-fat or fat-free yogurt.

Frozen yogurt is a popular dessert. It's made from yogurt with added flavorings and sweeteners.

Some yogurt—regular or frozen—is labeled "contains live and active yogurt cultures." This means the "friendly" bacteria used to make yogurt are still alive and active. The live, active cultures may offer extra health benefits, such as aiding the body's digestive system. Scientists are working to find out for certain.

Frozen yogurt makes an easy-to-fix, great-tasting dessert. Read the label to check the fat and sugar content.

TYPES OF CHEESE

Hundreds of different cheeses are available. They vary in color, texture, and flavor. However, they can be grouped into three general types:

Unripened cheese. Cottage cheese and cream cheese are examples. They're soft and stay fresh only a few days after purchase.

Ripened cheese. This type can be stored longer than unripened cheese. Some popular ripened cheeses are cheddar, brick, Swiss, and Parmesan.

Process and cold-pack cheese. These products are made from ripened cheeses and blended with other ingredients. They're smooth, melt quickly, and can be stored even longer than ripened cheese. Process American cheese is the most common example.

Cheese is sold in a variety of forms. For example, you can buy blocks or loaves, slices, shredded cheese, grated cheese, and containers of cheese spread.

BUYING YOGURT AND CHEESE

When you buy yogurt and cheese, keep these guidelines in mind.

◆ Read labels carefully. Compare nutrients, fat content, and calories in different types and brands. If you want live, active yogurt cultures, look for a statement on the label.

◆ Compare prices. Some ripened cheeses are very expensive. Process cheeses are usually lower in cost.

◆ Decide whether you're willing to pay more for cheese that's already sliced or shredded.

◆ Look for a freshness date on the package. Buy only as much as you can use within the storage life of the product.

STORING YOGURT AND CHEESE

Most types of yogurt and cheese must be refrigerated. Keep them in the original package, or wrap ripened cheese in foil or plastic wrap. Use yogurt and soft unripened cheese within a few days. Use other cheeses within a few weeks.

🍳 FOOD SKILLS

Yogurt and cottage cheese make delicious snacks, salads, or light desserts. Here are some ideas:

◆ Eat them as is. They taste good chilled.

◆ Mix plain yogurt or cottage cheese with fruit.

◆ Blend low-fat cottage cheese with a little lemon juice. Use as a topping for baked potatoes.

What other ideas can you think of?

You can make a dip from plain yogurt or cottage cheese and seasonings. Serve with fresh vegetables.

YOGURT CHEESE

Cream cheese is sometimes used for dips and sandwiches. However, cream cheese is high in fat. You can make a delicious low-fat substitute from yogurt. Yogurt cheese can be used whenever cream cheese is called for, except in cooking.

How to Make Yogurt Cheese

1. Line a colander with two layers of clean cheesecloth. Place the colander over a pan (such as a cake pan).

2. Place 1 pint *plain* fat-free or low-fat yogurt in the colander. Cover with waxed paper.

3. Refrigerate. Allow yogurt to drain for about 8 to 10 hours.

4. Remove yogurt cheese from cheesecloth. Pack it into a storage container. Cover tightly and refrigerate. Discard the liquid that dripped into the pan.

STEP 2

USING RIPENED AND PROCESS CHEESE

Ripened cheese can be added to sandwiches or salads, served with fruit for dessert, or eaten by itself as a snack. The cheese will taste best if you remove it from the refrigerator about an hour ahead of time.

A combination of cheese and other foods makes a tasty appetizer or salad. How many food groups are represented here?

COOKING WITH CHEESE

Cheese adds special flavor to many cooked dishes. For example, it can be mixed with chili or melted into a sauce. You can use it to top casseroles, pizza, or burgers. For cooking, ripened or process cheese is usually used.

How would you rate the appearance of this melted cheese?

Try It!

Ripened and Process Cheese

Cut a small slice of a ripened cheese, such as natural cheddar. Cut a slice the same size of a process cheese, such as American. Place each on a cracker or corn chip. Put both in a toaster oven at 300°F. Watch closely until both are melted.

★ What differences do you notice in how the two cheeses melt?

★ How might you use ripened and process cheeses differently?

Because cheese is a protein food, it should be cooked at low temperatures. Cheese doesn't have to cook a long time—only long enough to melt.

Properly cooked cheese has a smooth, tender texture. It should be evenly melted with no hard pieces or brown spots.

Recipe File

Here's a different way to have baked potatoes—sliced and topped with a combination of cheeses!

◆ Why aren't the cheeses added before you bake the potatoes?

◆ What other types of cheese could be used in this recipe?

Cheesy Potato Bake

Yield: 4 servings

2	large baking potatoes
1 Tbsp.	melted butter or margarine
1/8 tsp.	garlic salt
1/8 tsp.	pepper
1 Tbsp.	chopped fresh parsley
2/3 cup	shredded Swiss cheese
1 Tbsp.	grated Parmesan cheese

1. Preheat oven to 500°F. Lightly grease a 9 x 1-inch pie pan.
2. Peel potatoes. Slice crosswise into 1/8-inch slices. Arrange potato slices in pie pan by overlapping them from the outside edge toward the center.
3. In a small bowl, combine melted butter or margarine, garlic salt, and pepper. Brush mixture over potatoes.
4. Bake 20 minutes or until potatoes are tender when pierced with a fork. Remove from oven and turn oven off.
5. Sprinkle potatoes with parsley, Swiss cheese, then Parmesan cheese.
6. Place potatoes back in hot oven for 1 minute or until cheese is melted. Serve hot.

Nutrition Notes

Per serving: 172 calories, 8 g fat
Good source of: protein, vitamin C, vitamin B_6, calcium, phosphorus

If you overcook cheese, some of the protein is lost. The cheese becomes tough and rubbery. Here are some ways to keep cheese from overcooking:

◆ Use low heat.

◆ Add cheese near the end of cooking time.

◆ Layer the cheese between other ingredients to protect it from direct heat.

You can use the microwave oven to prepare a hot cheese sandwich without the added fat of grilling.

Microwaving Cheese

The principles of cooking cheese are similar for conventional and microwave cooking. Cheese overcooks easily in the microwave. If it does, it gets tough and stringy. To keep this from happening:

◆ Use the power level specified in the recipe.

◆ If possible, grate the cheese, add it near the end of cooking time, or layer it between other ingredients.

◆ Check often for doneness. Stop cooking when the cheese starts to lose its shape.

Microwave Hints

* Process cheese is less likely to overcook in the microwave than ripened cheese.

* For an "ungrilled" cheese sandwich, put sliced cheese between toasted bread slices. Microwave at 50% power for about 20 seconds to melt the cheese.

CHAPTER 28 REVIEW

Understanding Key Ideas

1. Compare and contrast the nutritional value of yogurt and cheese.
2. What advice would you give someone who's looking for an inexpensive cheese?
3. Compare and contrast the storage guidelines for yogurt, cottage cheese, and Swiss cheese.
4. How could you keep cheese from overcooking when adding it to a sauce?

Applying Knowledge and Skills

◆ **Newspaper Article:** Write an article encouraging teens to snack on yogurt more often. Include facts on nutrition, buying, and storing.

◆ **Foods Lab:** In small groups, create a dip by adding ingredients of your choice to plain yogurt. Serve with fresh vegetables or other foods. Evaluate the results.

◆ **Cheese Ideas:** Suggest specific ways to enhance recipes or convenience foods with a small amount of cheese. How do you think the flavor, texture, and nutrition would be affected? If possible, try out your ideas and evaluate the results.

Exploring Further

◆ **Research:** Choose a specific type of cheese and find out how it's made. Report to the class.

◆ **Experiment:** Plan and carry out an experiment to compare fat-free and regular cheese. What conclusions can you draw?

GRAIN PRODUCTS

Discover...

★ how grain products fit into a healthful eating plan.

★ how to select and store grain products.

★ how to prepare grain products.

Key Terms

whole grain products
enriched grain products
pasta

Grains are the kernels, or seeds, of plants known as cereal grasses. They're the major food source on this planet. Grains are processed to make an endless variety of grain products, including breads, cereals, rice, and pasta.

FOOD FOR THOUGHT

Besides wheat, corn, rice, and oats, what other grains can you name? Think about how you can use them to provide variety in meals.

NUTRITION NOTES

Foods in the Bread, Cereal, Rice, and Pasta Group are an important source of carbohydrates. You may recall that carbohydrates are the best source of energy for your body.

Grain products also supply incomplete protein. They provide some, but not all, of the amino acids you need to make complete protein. The missing amino acids can be obtained from cooked dry beans and peas as well as foods from animal sources.

In addition, grain products can be a good source of:

◆ B vitamins for growth and health.

◆ Iron for healthy red blood cells.

◆ Phosphorus for strong bones and teeth.

Foods in the Bread, Cereal, Rice, and Pasta Group are generally low in fat, sugar, and sodium. However, the way they're processed, prepared, and served can make a difference. For example, many breakfast cereals contain added sugar and sodium. If you spread bread with butter, margarine, or cream cheese, or serve pasta with a rich sauce, you add fat and calories.

PARTS OF THE GRAIN KERNEL

All grain kernels have three basic parts. Each part contains valuable nutrients.

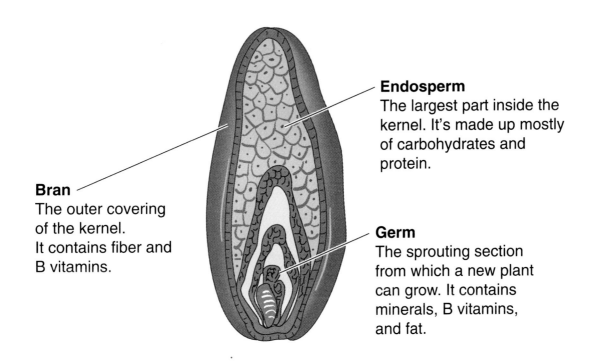

Endosperm
The largest part inside the kernel. It's made up mostly of carbohydrates and protein.

Bran
The outer covering of the kernel. It contains fiber and B vitamins.

Germ
The sprouting section from which a new plant can grow. It contains minerals, B vitamins, and fat.

WHOLE GRAIN OR PART?

Which parts of the grain kernel go into grain products? The answer depends on the particular grain products you buy.

Whole grain products are made using all three parts of the kernel. Some examples of whole grain products are brown rice, oatmeal, and bread made with whole wheat flour. Whole grain products contain most of the grain's original nutrients. They're good sources of fiber.

Some other grain products are made from only the endosperm. For example, all-purpose white flour is the ground endosperm of wheat. When the bran and germ are removed, so are the nutrients and fiber they contain. To make up for some of these losses, iron and B vitamins are added back in to make **enriched grain products.**

You can also find grain products that contain only the bran. (Have you ever had bran cereal for breakfast?) Still others are made from a mixture of different grains and grain parts. For example, a bread may include white flour, whole wheat flour, and oat bran.

When choosing grain products, remember:

◆ Both whole grain and enriched products supply carbohydrates, protein, vitamins, and minerals.

◆ To add fiber to your diet, choose products made with whole grains or bran.

How might you use these breads in meals or snacks?

CONSUMER POWER

Dozens of different grain products fill the store shelves. Knowing about the available choices can help you decide what type of bread, cereal, rice, or pasta to buy.

BREADS

There are many different types of bread. For example:

◆ Loaves, rolls, and buns come in different shapes and sizes.

◆ Bagels are doughnut-shaped rolls with a chewy texture.

◆ Pita is a thick, flat bread that forms a pocket.

◆ Tortillas are a thin, flat bread made from corn flour or wheat flour.

Breads can be bought in fresh loaves, either sliced or unsliced. Some bagels and English muffins are refrigerated to preserve their freshness. In addition, look for frozen breads and refrigerated or frozen dough.

BREAKFAST CEREALS

Supermarket shelves offer dozens of breakfast cereal choices. Ready-to-eat cereals need no preparation. Some have fruits, nuts, sugar, or other flavorings added. Other cereals, such as oatmeal, require cooking and are eaten hot. They may come in regular, quick-cooking, and instant varieties. Some instant cereals have added sweeteners and flavorings.

RICE

Three basic types of rice are available: long-grain, medium-grain, and short-grain. Long-grain rice cooks dry and fluffy. Short-grain and medium-grain rice have moister kernels and tend to stick together.

Rice is sold in boxes and bags. You can choose from rice processed in different ways.

Brown rice is whole grain rice. It has a rich, nutty flavor and a chewy texture.

Enriched rice is also called white rice. It has less fiber than brown rice.

Instant rice is precooked, rinsed, and dried. It takes only a short time to prepare. Both enriched and brown instant rice are available.

You can also buy rice packaged along with a seasoning or sauce mix. Other convenience forms include cooked rice in cans or frozen packages.

PASTA

Pasta is a general term for spaghetti, macaroni, noodles, and similar products. In fact, pasta comes in about 200 different shapes. Some of them are shown below. Most pasta is simply a combination of enriched or whole wheat flour and water. Noodles also contain eggs for added tenderness.

Dried pasta is sold in bags and boxes. You can also buy refrigerated fresh pasta, fresh-frozen pasta, and frozen cooked pasta. Some canned, frozen, or packaged main dishes and meals include pasta.

BUYING GRAIN PRODUCTS

When shopping for any type of grain product, remember these tips:

◆ Read labels carefully. For more fiber, look for whole grains or bran. Choose products that are low in fat, sugar, and sodium.

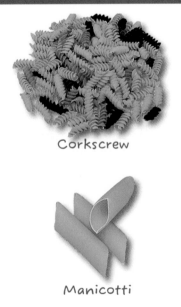

Corkscrew

Manicotti

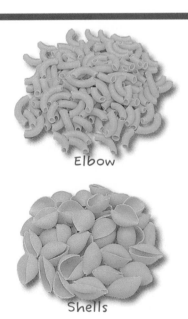

Elbow

Shells

- You might think a dark-colored bread called "Harvest Wheat" is made with whole wheat flour. In fact, it may be enriched bread with color added. Don't guess—look for "whole wheat" on the ingredients list.

- Compare prices. Grain products with many added ingredients usually cost more than simpler kinds.

- Cereals with large amounts of added vitamins and minerals are often expensive. The extra nutrients aren't needed. Good nutrition comes from eating a balanced diet each day, not from one bowl of cereal.

- Check the date on the package.

STORING GRAIN PRODUCTS

- Bread can usually be left in the store wrapper and kept in a cool, dry place. Most breads stay fresh longer at room temperature than in the refrigerator.

- If the kitchen is hot and humid, or if the label tells you to, refrigerate bread to keep mold from growing.

- Freeze bread for longer storage. Keep products purchased frozen in the freezer until used.

- Refrigerate whole grains. They contain oils that can spoil at room temperature.

- Store most other grain products in a cool, dry place. The package or container should be tightly sealed.

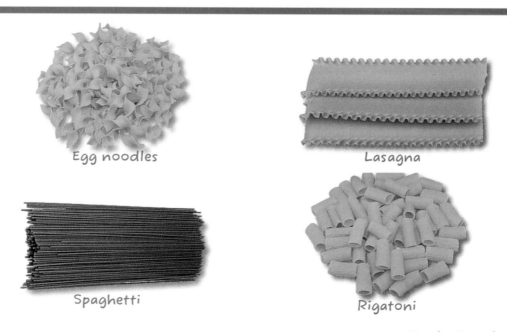

Egg noodles

Lasagna

Spaghetti

Rigatoni

FOOD SKILLS

Grain products play a versatile role in meal planning. Think about what you've eaten in the last day. How many main dishes, salads, side dishes, breakfast foods, and snacks contained grain products?

USING READY-TO-EAT GRAIN PRODUCTS

A nutritious sandwich is easy to make.

Ready-to-eat breads and cereals can be used right from the package. They don't require cooking. Still, they can be prepared in many different ways.

Bread can be warmed in the oven or toasted, if desired. All types of bread can be used to make sandwiches. (See Chapter 26 for creative sandwich ideas.)

For a nutritious breakfast, serve fat-free milk with whole grain, ready-to-eat cereal. If you like, add nuts and fresh, canned, or dried fruits.

Whole grain cereals can also be used in other ways to add fiber to your food choices. For example, you can add crunchy cereal to yogurt. Mix several cereals and add seasonings for a nutritious snack. Try using crushed cereal instead of bread crumbs in a recipe.

COOKING GRAIN PRODUCTS

Grain products such as rice, pasta, and oatmeal are cooked in water. As they cook, they absorb water and swell to double or triple their original size. For example, one cup of raw rice becomes three cups of cooked rice.

Different grain products require different cooking times and methods. Follow the instructions on the package.

When properly cooked, grain products are tender throughout. Undercooked grains are hard or chewy. If overcooked, the grains become soft and sticky.

Don't rinse grain products before or after cooking. Rinsing washes away valuable nutrients.

When cooking rice, stir as little as possible. Stirring scrapes the starch off the grains and makes the rice sticky.

Have you ever tried couscous? This fine-grained pasta is a staple grain product in North Africa.

◆ How does the cooking method for couscous compare to other grain products?

◆ What other types of grain products could you use instead of couscous?

Moroccan Couscous

Yield: 4 servings

³/₄ cup	vegetable broth or low-fat chicken broth
1 cup	couscous (uncooked)
2 Tbsp.	chopped onion

1 tsp.	olive oil
2 cups	frozen mixed vegetables
1 cup	chopped fresh tomatoes
³/₄ tsp.	ground ginger
¹/₂ tsp.	ground turmeric

1. In a medium microwave-safe bowl, microwave broth on 100% power for 3 to 4 minutes or until it boils.

2. Stir in couscous. Cover and let stand 5 minutes.

3. Combine onion and oil in another medium microwave-safe bowl. Microwave at 100% power for 1 minute or until tender.

4. Add vegetables, tomatoes, ginger, and turmeric to onion mixture. Stir until combined. Cover and microwave at 100% power for 4 to 4¹/₂ minutes or until vegetables are tender-crisp.

5. Fluff couscous with a fork. Place it in a serving bowl and spoon vegetable mixture into the center. Serve hot.

Nutrition Notes

Per serving: 181 calories, 2 g fat
Good source of: protein, vitamin A, vitamin C, niacin

Cooking Pasta

Properly cooked pasta is tender but still firm in the center. An Italian phrase for this is *"al dente"* (ahl-DEHN-tay), meaning "to the tooth." However, if the pasta is to be used in a recipe that will be cooked, shorten the boiling time slightly. Remove the pasta before it's completely cooked.

How to Cook Pasta

1. Bring water to a boil in a large pot.

   Tip Use 2 quarts water for every 8 ounces of pasta.

2. Add the pasta slowly so the boiling doesn't stop.

   Why? The rapid boiling helps the pasta cook evenly and helps it keep from sticking together.

   Tip Some people also add a few drops of oil to prevent sticking.

STEP 2

3. Cook until tender. Stir occasionally to keep pasta from sticking.

4. Drain pasta in a strainer or colander without rinsing.

   Why? Rinsing washes away nutrients.

STEP 4

Microwaving Grain Products

Cooking grain products such as pasta and rice in the microwave oven takes almost as long as conventional cooking. Why? The grains need time to absorb water so they can soften. With most grain products, this process can't be speeded up. However, you may find products specially designed for microwave cooking.

Some cooked cereals can be prepared in the microwave oven. Follow directions on the package.

Microwave Hints

* Remember that grain products double or triple in size as they cook. Be sure to use a microwave dish that's large enough to allow easy stirring and prevent sticking.

* Use the microwave to reheat leftover cooked rice or pasta. Check a microwave cookbook for directions.

CHAPTER 29 REVIEW

Understanding Key Ideas

1. How do whole grain and enriched products differ in how they're made? In nutritional value?
2. Describe five types of rice.
3. Which grain products should be refrigerated? How should others be stored?
4. How does preparing rice differ from preparing pasta?

Applying Knowledge and Skills

◆ **Analyzing Recipe Nutrition:** Find recipes for main dishes featuring grain products. With what other foods are the grain products combined to supply complete protein? Why are grain products popular protein extenders?

◆ **Parts of the Grain:** Find several labels from breads or breakfast cereals. Identify the ingredients that come from grains. What part(s) of the grain does each represent? Are differences in ingredients reflected in the nutrient content? Explain.

◆ **Preparing Grains:** Prepare two different forms of a grain product, such as enriched and brown rice. Compare preparation time, flavor, and texture. When might you use each product?

Exploring Further

◆ **Social Studies:** Learn what grains and grain-based dishes are common in another culture. Report to the class.

◆ **Creative Thinking:** Brainstorm ways to add more whole grains to your meals and snacks.

FRUITS

Discover...

★ *how fruits fit into a healthful eating plan.*

★ *how to select and store fruits.*

★ *how to prepare fruits.*

Key Terms
peak season
ripe

Fruits add color and flavor to meals and make delicious snacks. They're nutritious, easy to prepare, and can be low in cost.

FOOD FOR THOUGHT

What are your favorite fruits? What are some others that you might like to try?

NUTRITION NOTES

Remember, you need two to four servings from the Fruit Group each day. Fruits are a good source of carbohydrates for energy and fiber for good digestion and health.

Fruits are low in sodium and fat and have no cholesterol. Most are low in calories. Fruits also provide many of the vitamins and minerals you need for good health, such as:

Vitamin C. Citrus fruits are especially good sources of this vitamin. So are melons, kiwis, and strawberries.

Vitamin A. Some vegetables provide beta carotene, which the body uses to make vitamin A. Good sources include deep yellow fruits, such as mangoes, cantaloupes, apricots, and peaches.

Potassium. Bananas, cantaloupes, oranges, and nectarines are good sources.

CONSUMER POWER

Fruits are sold in several forms: fresh, canned, frozen, and dried. Fruit juice, another form of fruit, is discussed in Chapter 41.

Fresh fruits in good condition have the most nutrients, but other forms of fruit are still nutritious. Frozen fruits often cost more than fresh or canned fruits. However, prices will vary depending on the time of year and the kind of fruit.

BUYING FRESH FRUITS

Fresh fruits are found in the produce section of the store. They may be sold loose or in packages. If a package of fruit is too large for you, ask the clerk to open the package so you can select the amount you want. Don't open the package yourself.

Fresh fruits are very perishable. Buy only the amount you'll use in a few days. Handle fresh fruits very gently—they're easily damaged.

Peach of a deal!

Buying in Season

Most fruits have a **peak season**—a certain time of year when the supply is greatest and the quality is highest. During these months, the fruit is said to be "in season." For example, peaches and cherries are in season during summer. Cranberries are in season during autumn.

Since the supply is greatest when fruits are in season, prices are usually lower then. Knowing when fruits are in season can help you find the best buys.

For best quality and value, take advantage of times when particular fruits are in season.

Ripeness

Fruits that are **ripe** are ready to eat. They've developed their full flavor and sweetness. They're not too hard or too soft.

Fruits begin to ripen while they're still growing. Some fruits stop ripening when they're picked. Examples are apples, berries, and grapes. Buy these fruits fully ripe.

Some other fruits, such as bananas, peaches, and pears, continue to ripen after being picked. Choose these fruits according to when you'll use them. For immediate use, buy ripe ones. Choose slightly underripe fruits to use several days later.

Signs of Quality

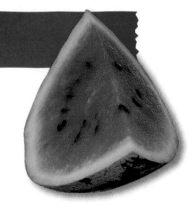

High-quality fresh fruits have the best flavor and nutrition. Low-quality fruits are no bargain. They have already lost nutrients and flavor. How can you judge quality and ripeness? Look for fruits that have these characteristics.

Full size. Fruits that are smaller than normal were picked too soon and will not ripen properly.

The right color. Fruits should have good, full color.

Plump and heavy for their size. This usually means they are juicy.

Firm to the touch. Press the fruit gently so you do not damage it. Very soft fruit may be overripe and lack flavor. Hard fruit may not ripen.

Free of decay, damage, or mold. Avoid fruits with mushy brown spots or powdery areas.

BUYING FROZEN, CANNED, AND DRIED FRUITS

When buying these forms of fruit, remember to read labels carefully and avoid damaged containers.

◆ Frozen fruits are sold in cartons or bags. Some have sugar added.

◆ Canned fruits may be bought whole, halved, sliced, or in pieces. Whole fruits are generally the most expensive. Decide what form is best suited to your needs.

◆ Some fruits are canned in a sugar syrup. Look for fruits packed in water or juice instead.

◆ Dried fruits, such as raisins and dried apricots, are sold in packages or in the bulk foods section. They should be fairly soft and moist, not hard.

STORING FRUITS

Follow these guidelines for storing fruits:

◆ Don't wash fresh fruits until you're ready to use them.

◆ Refrigerate ripe fruits as soon as you bring them home. Put them in a plastic bag or in the crisper section. Use within a day or two.

Fruits ripen faster in a paper bag.

◆ Let slightly underripe fruits stand at room temperature. To speed ripening, put them in a paper bag. When fully ripe, use them at once or refrigerate them.

◆ Store cut fruits in an airtight container or wrap them in foil or plastic. Use as soon as possible.

◆ Store frozen fruits in the freezer until needed. Thaw in the refrigerator.

◆ Store unopened cans of fruit in a cool, dry place.

◆ Refrigerate leftover canned fruit in an airtight container, not in the can.

◆ Store dried fruits in an airtight container in a cool, dry place.

🍳 FOOD SKILLS

Fruits can be served plain or fancy for breakfast, lunch, or dinner. They can be used in salads and main dishes. They make flavorful, nutritious desserts and tasty snacks.

PREPARING FRESH FRUITS TO EAT RAW

Most fresh fruits should be washed before they're eaten or cooked. Washing removes dirt and bacteria that could cause illness. To wash fruits, hold them under running water.

Fresh fruits may be cut into halves, wedges, or slices for serving. Use a sharp knife and a cutting board. Remember that when fruits are pared or cut, they quickly lose some of their vitamin C. Don't let them sit too long before they're eaten.

Some cut fruits, such as sliced apples or bananas, turn brown quickly. To keep them looking fresh, try coating them with lemon, grapefruit, or orange juice. The acid in the juice prevents the chemical reaction that causes browning.

Wash fruit to remove dirt and bacteria that could cause illness.

Try It!

Preserving the Color of Cut Fruits

Slice a Red Delicious or Pippin apple. Dip half of the slices in lemon juice. Lay the slices on a plate. Wait ten minutes.

★ How do the slices dipped in lemon juice differ from the others?

★ In what situations might you want to treat slices of apple or banana with citrus juice?

USING FROZEN, CANNED, AND DRIED FRUITS

Convenience forms of fruit can be used in most of the same ways as fresh fruit. Here are some tips:

◆ Frozen fruits are soft and lose their shape when completely thawed. Many people prefer to serve them before they thaw completely. Ice crystals help the fruits hold their shape.

◆ If canned fruits are packed in natural juices, take advantage of the nutrients in the juice. Serve the juice over the fruits or save it for another use.

◆ Dried fruits are as sweet as candy but more nutritious. Try mixing several kinds together.

These easy-to-prepare baked apples make a simple dessert or snack.

◆ Name two reasons why the apples are cored before they are microwaved.

◆ How can you keep from overcooking fruits in the microwave oven?

Spicy Baked Apples

Yield: 4 servings

4 medium	baking apples (such as Rome Beauty or Granny Smith)
2 Tbsp.	raisins
1 Tbsp.	cinnamon red hot candies
½ cup	apple juice

1. Core apples without cutting through the bottom skin. If necessary, cut a thin slice from the bottom of each apple so it will stand straight. Arrange apples in a shallow, microwave-safe baking dish.

2. Combine raisins and candies in a small bowl. Divide mixture evenly and spoon into apples.

3. Pour juice over apples. Cover baking dish with waxed paper.

4. Microwave apples at 100% power for 9 to 11 minutes, rotating dish every 3 minutes. Let stand, covered, for 5 minutes.

5. Serve warm with juice spooned over the top.

Nutrition Notes

Per serving: 116 calories, 1 g fat
Good source of: vitamin C, fiber

COOKING FRUITS

Cooking affects fruits in several ways. It:

◆ Breaks down the fibers and softens the fruits.

◆ Makes the flavor more mellow and less acid-tasting.

◆ Changes the color.

When properly cooked, fruits should be soft and tender. They should retain as much of their natural color as possible and be pleasantly flavored. Overcooking causes fruits to lose nutrients, color, and flavor. They become mushy and unappetizing.

Fruits can be cooked in a variety of ways. Here are some ideas:

◆ Simmer dried apricots or prunes in water. Serve them with the cooking liquid.

◆ Bake sliced bananas and pears together in an orange juice sauce.

◆ Make a fruit sauce, such as applesauce.

For an easy and nutritious dessert, try baked bananas and pears.

How to Make a Fruit Sauce

1. Pare and slice the fruit. Remove the core and seeds.

2. Put the fruit in a saucepan. Add just enough water or fruit juice to cover the bottom of the pan 1/4 to 1/2 inch deep. Cover.

STEP 2

Tip Don't add sugar yet. If you do, the sugar will help the fruit hold its shape instead of turning into a sauce.

3. Simmer, stirring occasionally, until the fruit breaks down into a sauce.

4. Add sugar to taste. You can also add a spice such as cinnamon or nutmeg.

STEP 3

Tip Remember to use a clean spoon each time you taste.

STEP 5

5. If you prefer a smoother sauce, mash the cooked fruits by putting them through a food mill, a strainer, or a blender.

Microwaving Fruits

Many popular fruit dishes can be prepared using the microwave oven. Fruits cook very quickly in a microwave oven because they're high in sugar and water. Quick cooking helps fruits keep their nutrients and flavor.

Unless the recipe tells you otherwise, cover the fruits when microwaving them. Time cooking carefully. If overcooked, fruits will be hard and dry.

Microwave Hints

* Pierce or slit the skin of whole fruit to allow steam to escape. Otherwise the skin may burst.

* Try this easy dessert: Pour canned fruit pie filling into a microwave-safe baking dish. Cook on full power until heated through. Top with granola or another crunchy cereal.

CHAPTER 30 REVIEW

Understanding Key Ideas

1. What are the nutritional advantages of fruits?
2. If you were buying fresh pears for your family, what quality characteristics would you look for?
3. How should fresh, ripe peaches be stored? Unripe bananas? Dried apricots?
4. Why is it important to avoid overcooking fruits?

Applying Knowledge and Skills

◆ **Demonstration:** Show how to wash, slice, and serve fresh fruits to be eaten raw.

◆ **Menu Planning:** Plan an appealing, nutritious mixed fruit bowl for a brunch. Describe what forms of fruit you'd buy, what you'd look for when buying, and how you'd prepare the fruits. If possible, carry out your plan.

◆ **Foods Lab:** Make a fruit sauce following the directions on page 238. Evaluate it for appearance, flavor, and texture.

Exploring Further

◆ **Experiment:** Prepare two baked apples: one Red or Golden Delicious and one Rome Beauty, Granny Smith, or Winesap. Compare the flavor and texture of the two baked apples. Which type of apple would you recommend for baking? Why?

◆ **Critical Thinking:** Surveys have shown that many people don't eat enough servings from the Fruit Group each day. Why do you suppose this is true? What might happen as a result?

VEGETABLES

Vegetables are colorful, flavorful, and nutritious. Hundreds of different kinds can be prepared in many different ways. Take advantage of these choices by eating a variety of vegetables. Your meals and snacks will be not only more healthful, but more interesting, too.

Discover...

★ *how vegetables fit into a healthful eating plan.*

★ *how to select and store vegetables.*

★ *how to prepare vegetables.*

Key Term

tender-crisp

FOOD FOR THOUGHT

What are the most unusual vegetables you've ever tried? The most colorful? The sweetest tasting? The crunchiest?

NUTRITION NOTES

You need three to five servings from the Vegetable Group each day. Why? Fresh vegetables are low in fat, sodium, and calories. They have no cholesterol. Yet they're an excellent source of the carbohydrates your body needs for energy. In addition, they're an excellent source of fiber. Vegetables are among the best source of vitamins and minerals, such as:

Vitamin A. Your body can make vitamin A from beta carotene. Deep yellow or orange vegetables (such as carrots) and deep green ones (such as spinach) are excellent sources of beta carotene.

Vitamin C. Good sources include raw broccoli, raw cabbage, kale, sweet potatoes, tomatoes, and green peppers.

Calcium. Broccoli, kale, and turnip greens can help supply the calcium you need for strong bones and teeth.

CONSUMER POWER

Did you know that vegetables come from many different parts of plants? Vegetables can be:

- Fruits of a plant—such as tomatoes, eggplants, and peppers.

- Flowers of a plant—such as broccoli and cauliflower.

- Stems—such as asparagus and celery.

- Roots—such as potatoes, carrots, beets, and onions.

- Leaves—such as cabbage, greens, kale, and spinach.

- Seeds—such as beans, corn, and peas.

FORMS OF VEGETABLES

Vegetables can be purchased fresh, frozen, or canned. High-quality fresh vegetables have the most nutrients, but frozen and canned vegetables aren't far behind. Compare the prices of different forms when you shop.

You can also buy convenience products such as instant mashed potatoes, potato and sauce mixes, and vegetables in microwavable packages. What might be some advantages and disadvantages of these products?

BUYING FRESH VEGETABLES

Fresh vegetables are found in the produce section of the store. They're sold loose or in packages, just as fruits are. Sometimes several pieces are held together with a band or tape and sold as a unit.

Many fresh vegetables are available in supermarkets all year round. Because they're shipped from wherever they can be grown, there's a steady supply. Locally grown vegetables can be bought only during their growing season. These are usually fresher and lower in price than those shipped from other areas.

SIGNS OF QUALITY

When you buy fresh vegetables, buy only the amount you can use during their storage life. Look for these signs of quality:

♦ Solid—should feel heavy in relation to its size.

♦ Good color—not too pale or too dark.

♦ Crisp or firm.

♦ In good condition—no decay, soft spots, or damage.

STORING FRESH VEGETABLES

♦ Store potatoes and onions separately in a cool, dry, dark area. They'll keep for several weeks.

♦ Other vegetables should be refrigerated as soon as you bring them home. If they're wet, shake off the excess water. Too much moisture can make vegetables spoil faster. If they're dirty, you may rinse them briefly, then drain or pat dry. Otherwise, don't wash them yet. Store the vegetables in the crisper or in plastic bags or containers. For best quality, use within a few days.

BUYING AND STORING OTHER FORMS OF VEGETABLES

Frozen vegetables are available in a wide range of choices. You can buy one kind of vegetable or packaged mixed vegetables. Some are frozen in a sauce.

Canned vegetables are available whole, sliced, or in pieces. Some are packed in special sauces. Canned vegetables are already cooked. They need only be heated by following label directions.

🧑‍🍳 FOOD SKILLS

There are many ways to include vegetables in daily menus. Vegetables are popular as side dishes and in salads. They appear in many main dishes, such as stews, soups, and casseroles. Besides being an important part of a meal, vegetables make delicious snacks.

PREPARING RAW FRESH VEGETABLES

Many vegetables, such as carrots, cauliflower, broccoli, mushrooms, and peppers, can be eaten raw. Before you prepare fresh vegetables, wash them thoroughly to remove dirt and harmful bacteria. Hold the  vegetables under cold running water. Hard vegetables, such as carrots, should be scrubbed with a vegetable brush. To preserve nutrients, don't soak the vegetables.

Cut off damaged spots and parts that can't be eaten. Remember to trim or pare vegetables as little as possible. The outer portions often contain the most nutrients.

To make the vegetables easier to pick up and eat, you can cut them into wedges, slices, strips, or chunks.

Refrigerate the cut vegetables in a covered container until it's time to eat. Keeping them crispy fresh will preserve their appearance, flavor, and nutrients.

Raw fresh vegetables make appetizing, nutritious snacks and party foods.

COOKING VEGETABLES

Cooking makes vegetables easier to chew and digest. Many vegetables, such as green beans and potatoes, must be cooked before you can eat them. Remember to wash fresh vegetables before cooking.

When vegetables are cooked properly, they...

◆ Lose few nutrients.

◆ Stay a bright, attractive color.

◆ Are **tender-crisp**—tender but still firm.

◆ Have a mild, mellow flavor.

When vegetables are overcooked, many nutrients are lost. The vegetables become mushy and unappetizing. They may lack flavor or have a strong, unpleasant flavor.

Cooking Method Choices

Consider nutrition when choosing a cooking method. Deep-fried vegetables soak up large amounts of fat. You can choose other cooking methods that preserve nutrients while adding little or no fat. Here are some ideas:

When vegetables are steamed properly, they keep most of their nutrients.

◆ Many fresh vegetables can be cooked using a steamer basket. Follow the general directions in Chapter 18. Let the vegetables steam until tender-crisp.

◆ Stir-frying is a quick and fun way to cook vegetables. Although few nutrients are lost, stir-frying does add a small amount of fat. You can combine different kinds of vegetables for color, flavor, and nutrition. You can also add fish, poultry, or meat to turn the stir-fry into a main dish. For more on stir-frying, see chapter 39.

◆ Some vegetables, such as potatoes and squash, can be baked right in their skin. You can also bake vegetables in a dish along with a sauce, topping, or other foods. Have you ever had scalloped potatoes, green bean casserole, or stuffed peppers?

Two other healthful ways to cook vegetables are simmering and microwaving.

Baking is a popular method of cooking vegetables such as sweet potatoes and stuffed green peppers.

This flavorful dish reflects French and German food traditions.

◆ Why aren't the vegetables covered with water to simmer them?

◆ How would you change this recipe if fresh green beans weren't available?

Favorite Green Beans

Yield: 4 servings

³/₄ lb.	fresh green beans	2 tsp.	cornstarch
½ cup	water	½ tsp.	dry mustard
2 slices	bacon	1 Tbsp.	vinegar
1 Tbsp.	packed brown sugar	2 Tbsp.	chopped onion

1. Remove stems from beans. Cut into 2-inch pieces.
2. Bring water to a boil in 2-qt. saucepan. Add the beans. Simmer, covered, over medium heat until tender-crisp, about 15 minutes.
3. Meanwhile, cook bacon in medium skillet until crisp. Drain, crumble, and set aside. Keep skillet out for step 6.
4. Combine brown sugar, cornstarch, mustard, and vinegar in a small bowl. Set aside.
5. When beans have finished cooking, drain the liquid into a measuring cup. Measure 1/3 cup of liquid.
6. Cook onion in skillet until tender, about 1 minute. Stir in reserved liquid. Add cornstarch mixture, stirring constantly. Cook until mixture thickens and looks clear, about 1 minute.
7. Add beans and bacon. Stir until coated with glaze. Serve hot.

Nutrition Notes

Per serving: 69 calories, 2 g fat
Good source of: vitamin C

Simmering Vegetables

Fresh or frozen vegetables can be simmered in a small amount of water. The less water used, the fewer water-soluble nutrients will be lost. For most vegetables, there should be just enough water to cover the bottom of the pan.

How to **Simmer Vegetables**

1. Bring a small amount of water to a boil.

2. Add the vegetables.
   Cover the pan and turn down
   the heat.

3. Simmer the vegetables just
   until they're tender-crisp.

STEP 2

4. Serve the cooking liquid along
   with the vegetables.

Why? The cooking liquid contains some of the nutrients that
were lost from the vegetables. It will also help keep the
vegetables warm.

Use a pan with a tight-fitting cover. This keeps the steam in the pan.
The vegetables that aren't in the water cook in the steam.

Don't add baking soda to vegetables. Although it can brighten the
color of green vegetables, it makes them mushy and destroys vitamins.

Microwaving Vegetables

Microwaving is an excellent cooking method for most vegetables. The
short cooking time preserves flavor and nutrients.

Basic microwave methods for vegetables are simple. Fresh or frozen
vegetables are usually placed in a covered microwave-safe dish with a
small amount of water. Most microwave cookbooks include a chart that
tells how to cook each type of vegetable.

You can also use the microwave oven to prepare vegetable casseroles
and other dishes. Check a microwave cookbook for directions.

★ It's easy to "bake" a potato in the microwave oven. Scrub a whole potato and pierce it with a fork in several places. Place on a paper plate. Microwave at full power 4 to 6 minutes. Let stand a few minutes to finish cooking.

Fresh vegetables can be microwaved with only a few tablespoons of water. Why is this an advantage?

CHAPTER 31 REVIEW

Understanding Key Ideas

1. Explain why choosing a variety of vegetables is important for good nutrition.
2. How do high-quality fresh vegetables look and feel?
3. Should all fresh vegetables be stored in the same way? Explain.
4. Describe how to cook green beans in water on top of the range while keeping as many nutrients in them as possible.

Applying Knowledge and Skills

◆ **Create a Recipe:** Plan a mixed vegetable dish that's a good source of beta carotene, vitamin C, and calcium. Describe the vegetables and other ingredients you'd use and how you'd prepare the dish.

◆ **Storage Guide:** Create a small poster that shows how to store vegetables properly. Display it on your refrigerator at home or in the foods lab.

◆ **Foods Lab:** Choose a vegetable and cook it by two different methods. Compare the cooking time, flavor, and texture. When might you use each method?

Exploring Further

◆ **Local Research:** Find out when various vegetables are in season in your community. Make a "Seasonal Vegetable" chart or poster.

LEGUMES

Discover...

★ how legumes fit into a healthful eating plan.

★ how to select and store legumes.

★ how to prepare legumes.

Key Terms
legumes
tofu

Dry peas and dry beans are examples of *legumes* (leh-GYOUMZ), or seeds that grow in a pod. As peas and beans mature, they dry out and turn into seeds. If planted, the seeds would provide a storehouse of food for the sprouting plant.

FOOD FOR THOUGHT

Dry peas and beans have more nutrients than fresh, green ones. Why do you think this is true?

NUTRITION NOTES

Legumes fit into two of the food groups:

Meat, Poultry, Fish, Dry Beans, Eggs, and Nuts Group. Like other foods in this group, legumes are an excellent source of protein. Your body needs protein for growth and repair. Remember, however, that plant protein is incomplete. To meet your complete protein needs, include grain products, such as bread or rice, in your daily diet.

Vegetable Group. Like other vegetables, legumes are high in complex carbohydrates and fiber. You need complex carbohydrates for energy. Fiber plays an important role in preventing health problems.

Legumes are also a good source of vitamins and minerals, such as:

◆ Iron to strengthen the blood.

◆ Calcium and phosphorus for strong bones and teeth.

◆ B vitamins and vitamin E for growth and health.

Legumes have no cholesterol. Most are low in fat. They're easy to fit into a healthful diet.

CONSUMER POWER

Even if the term "legumes" is new to you, you've probably eaten legumes before. Get to know the different types of legumes and how to buy and store them.

KINDS OF LEGUMES

Dry peas and beans come in a wide range of sizes, shapes, and colors. Some of the more popular ones are:

Split peas. Yellow or green. Mild flavor. Used mainly in soups.

Black-eyed peas. Small, oval, white with black spots. Mild flavor. Many uses.

Lima beans. Small or large size. Mild, buttery flavor. Many uses.

Kidney beans. Large beans. Light or dark red. Hearty flavor. Uses include chili, red beans and rice, and salads.

Navy beans. Small, white beans. Mild flavor. Many uses, including baked beans and soups.

Garbanzo beans. Also known as chickpeas. Round with rough texture. Nut-like flavor. Many uses, especially in Middle Eastern foods.

Pinto beans. Small, oval beans with pink dots. Mild flavor. Used for chili, refried beans, and other Mexican foods.

FORMS OF LEGUMES

Uncooked legumes are sold in plastic bags, in boxes, or in the bulk food section. You can also buy canned beans that are already cooked. Some are plain for use in recipes. Others have flavored sauces, such as pork and beans in tomato sauce.

How can you decide whether to buy uncooked beans or canned ones? Here are some points to consider:

◆ Uncooked beans are easy to prepare, but the cooking may take several hours. Canned beans are ready to use.

◆ Both uncooked and cooked beans are inexpensive—especially when compared to other protein sources, such as meat. However, uncooked ones cost less.

◆ You'll probably find more varieties of uncooked beans than canned ones.

◆ Uncooked beans take less storage space.

◆ Canned beans are often high in sodium. However, you can look for low-sodium versions or rinse the beans to remove some sodium.

You can also buy convenience products made with legumes. Examples include canned split pea soup, bean salad, and refried beans. Another product made from legumes is tofu.

Tofu

Soybeans are members of the legume family. They're used to make **tofu** (TOE-foo), a custard-like product. Tofu is very high in protein and low in calories and sodium. Many types of tofu are a good source of calcium, too—check the Nutrition Facts panel.

Tofu has a mild flavor. It can be used in many different ways, such as in soups, stir-fried dishes, dips, and casseroles. It needs only enough cooking to heat through and absorb the flavors of the other foods in the dish.

Tofu comes in a choice of textures, soft or firm. When shopping, look for packages of tofu in the refrigerated section or store shelves. Refrigerated tofu is perishable and must be used within a week. Special packaging allows some tofu to be stored longer. Read and follow package directions carefully. Leftover tofu can be frozen for longer storage.

Tofu (right) can be used in many delicious dishes. This salad (left) is made with tofu and orzo, a rice-shaped pasta.

BUYING AND STORING LEGUMES

When buying legumes, remember to read labels and compare prices as you learned in Chapter 12. Uncooked legumes should have good color and equal size.

Store uncooked legumes in a tightly covered container in a cool, dry place. Use one package completely before opening a new one. Why? Older peas and beans need a longer cooking time than newer ones. You'll get better results when cooking legumes that come from the same package.

Leftover cooked legumes will keep for several days in the refrigerator. For longer storage, freeze them in serving-size portions.

FOOD SKILLS

Legumes can add flavor, texture, and variety to your daily food choices. They can be used for quick, nutritious meals or snacks.

Legumes can perk up the flavor of a salad while adding nutrients.

USING CANNED BEANS

Canned beans are cooked and ready to use. If you're concerned about sodium, rinse the beans first. Here are some ideas for using them:

◆ Add garbanzo beans to a salad.

◆ Mash beans into a paste to use in spreads or dips.

◆ Use beans in soups, chili, and main dishes such as beans and rice.

◆ Serve beans as a side dish. Popular seasonings include tomato sauce, onions, molasses or brown sugar, and spices.

USING DRY LEGUMES

What can you do with uncooked legumes? Plenty! You can find many ideas in cookbooks. For example, dry peas are good in soups. They take just 30 to 45 minutes to cook.

Dry beans are very versatile. Follow basic directions to cook them. Then you can use them in any of the ways described for canned beans.

Keep in mind that legumes expand when cooked. One cup of dry beans makes about 2¼ to 3 cups when cooked.

Preparing dry beans involves three basic steps: sorting, soaking, and simmering.

Sort the Beans

Before cooking beans, sort them carefully. Remove any foreign materials, such as pebbles. Remove beans that are discolored, wrinkled, cracked, or that have holes.

Rinse beans several times to wash off dirt and dust. Swish them in a bowl of cool water or use a sprayer. Check to be sure the beans smell clean, not musty.

Soak the Beans

If desired, soak the beans overnight before cooking. Soaking will cut the cooking time by 15 to 30 minutes. It can also help prevent the beans from causing gas to form in the digestive system.

To soak, place beans in a large pot. Add about 5 cups of water for every 1 cup of dry beans. Cover and let stand overnight. After soaking, pour off the water. Use fresh water for cooking.

Some beans don't require soaking because they're preprocessed. Check the label on the package.

Simmer the Beans

Beans should be simmered until they're tender. This will take from 1 to 3 hours on the range, depending on the type of beans. Check the package for guidelines. If not cooked long enough, the beans may feel gritty or hard. If overcooked, the beans get mushy and fall apart.

If you don't mind a longer cooking time, you can use a slow cooker. Check a cookbook or the recipe book that came with the appliance.

How to **Simmer Beans**

1. Combine water and beans in a large pot with a cover.

   Tip As a general rule, use 3 cups cold water for each cup dry beans. If you've soaked the beans, you may be able to use less water.

   STEP 1

2. Put the cover on, but leave it slightly ajar so that steam can escape.

   Why? This keeps the beans from boiling over.

STEP 2

3. Simmer gently until done.

   Tip If necessary, add enough hot water to keep the beans covered.

Tips for Cooking Beans

◆ Time management skills can help you make more use of dry beans. Cook a large amount of beans at one time. Divide the beans into smaller portions and freeze for future use.

◆ Undercook beans if they'll be cooked again later as part of a recipe.

◆ Overcook beans slightly if you plan to use them for dips or sandwich spreads. That way they'll be easier to mash.

◆ Salt, sugar, and acid foods, such as tomatoes and vinegar, toughen beans. If you want to use these seasonings, add them near the end of the cooking time.

◆ Don't add baking soda when cooking dry beans. The baking soda cuts down a little on the cooking time. However, it destroys thiamin, one of the B vitamins found in beans.

Southwestern cooking combines the wonderful flavors of Native American, Mexican, and European cultures.

◆ What are some reasons for including both black beans and corn in this recipe?

◆ Why does the recipe tell you to rinse and drain the black beans?

Southwest Salad

Yield: 4 servings

1 can (15 oz.)	black beans, rinsed and drained
1 can (11 oz.)	sweet corn, drained
2 Tbsp.	chopped green onions
2 Tbsp.	chopped cilantro leaves
1/2 tsp.	chili powder
1/4 tsp.	ground cumin
1/4 cup	prepared low-fat vinaigrette salad dressing

1. In a large bowl, stir together all ingredients except salad dressing until well combined.
2. Divide mixture evenly among four salad plates.
3. Drizzle 1 Tbsp. dressing over each salad. Serve immediately.

Nutrition Notes

Per serving: 222 calories, 3 g fat
Good source of: protein, potassium, magnesium, iron, zinc, vitamin E, vitamin C, thiamin, folate, phosphorus, fiber

Microwaving Legumes

Legumes need time to absorb water and soften. Therefore, they take about as long to cook in a microwave oven as they do on the range.

The procedure for cooking dry beans in the microwave oven is similar to the conventional method. Soak the beans overnight, drain them, then simmer them in fresh water until tender. Check a microwave cookbook for complete directions.

* Cooked beans are easy to reheat in the microwave oven. Cook on full power for 15 seconds. Stir. Repeat until heated through.

* Thaw frozen beans in the microwave oven. Check a microwave cookbook or owner's guide for instructions on how to defrost food.

CHAPTER 32 REVIEW

Understanding Key Ideas

1. Into which food groups do legumes fit? Why?
2. Compare the advantages of canned and uncooked legumes.
3. How should cooked and uncooked legumes be stored?
4. Describe the benefits of using tofu.
5. Suppose you plan to make a seasoned bean dip from uncooked beans. What tips will help make your recipe easier and more successful?

Applying Knowledge and Skills

◆ **Promoting Legumes:** Design an advertising campaign to promote legumes. Include messages that focus on nutrition, convenience, and preparation.

◆ **Foods Lab:** With your lab group, think of two simple ways to use canned legumes or tofu. Each should be for a different type of dish, such as main dish, salad, or dessert. Try out your ideas and evaluate the results.

Exploring Further

◆ **Critical Thinking:** Legumes are the main source of protein for many of the world's people. Why do you think this is true? Why aren't legumes more popular in the United States? How might their popularity be increased?

◆ **Math:** How much water would you use to soak 2½ cups of uncooked dry beans? What size pot would you need? About how much water would you need for cooking? How many cups of cooked beans would this yield? Show your calculations.

Legumes 255

POLTRY

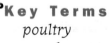

Discover...

★ *how poultry fits into a healthful eating plan.*

★ *how to select and store poultry.*

★ *how to prepare poultry.*

Key Terms
poultry
cured

Many people enjoy poultry in main dishes. *Poultry* refers to birds raised for food, such as chickens and turkeys. Poultry is nutritious, relatively low in cost, versatile, and flavorful.

FOOD FOR THOUGHT

Do you think of turkey as something to roast on holidays? What are some other ways to prepare and enjoy turkey?

NUTRITION NOTES

Poultry is part of the Meat, Poultry, Fish, Dry Beans, Eggs, and Nuts Group. It provides important nutrients, such as:

◆ Protein for growth and repair of the body.

◆ Iron for healthy red blood cells.

◆ B vitamins for a healthy nervous system.

◆ Phosphorus for healthy bones and teeth.

Chicken and turkey contain less total fat and saturated fat than some meats. Most of the fat is located in and just under the skin. If you remove the skin before eating, you'll eat less fat.

The amount of fat in poultry also depends on the cooking method. Frying adds considerable fat. Other cooking methods, such as broiling and roasting, can give poultry a delicious flavor and crispy texture without extra fat.

Many people use chicken or turkey instead of beef or pork in recipes. For instance, you could use ground turkey in chili instead of beef. Substituting poultry for meat can make favorite dishes lower in fat. However, the amount of cholesterol is about the same.

CONSUMER POWER

Chicken and turkey are the most common kinds of poultry. Turkeys are much larger than chickens, and their meat has a stronger flavor.

Both chicken and turkey have white and dark meat. White meat, which comes from the breast, is more tender and milder in flavor than dark meat. White meat also has less fat.

FORMS OF POULTRY

Uncooked chicken and turkey are sold fresh or frozen. You can choose:

◆ A whole bird.

◆ A bird cut in halves, quarters, or individual pieces.

◆ Parts packaged separately, such as breasts, legs, or thighs.

◆ Boneless parts and ground poultry.

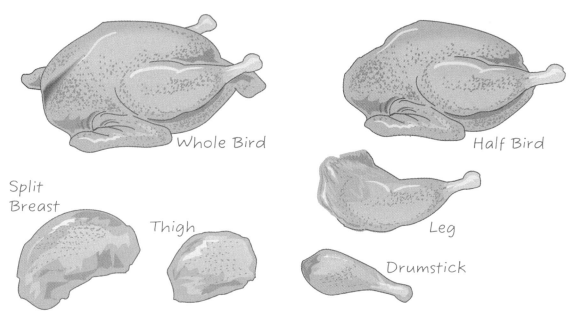

Whole Bird

Half Bird

Split Breast

Thigh

Leg

Drumstick

The form of poultry you buy may depend on how you want to use it.

Chicken and turkey are also available in a wide variety of convenience forms. (You'll read about these on page 260.) Consider cost and nutrition before deciding what form of poultry to buy.

BUYING FRESH AND FROZEN POULTRY

Here are some tips to help you find quality and value in fresh or frozen poultry.

◆ Check the label for the type of bird. The most common type of chicken is usually called "broiler" or "fryer." It's tender and can be broiled, roasted, braised, or fried. A "stewing chicken" or "hen" is less tender and should be simmered in liquid.

◆ Look for a grade shield. Grade A poultry is meatier than Grade B poultry. Not all poultry is graded.

◆ Choose fresh poultry that has a clear, bright color and no bruises. Frozen poultry should be frozen hard.

◆ When buying ground poultry, read the label carefully. Some contains skin, which adds fat.

What does the Grade A symbol tell you?

Reading Price Labels

Most packages of poultry, fish, and meat carry similar price labels. Understanding the label is a basic shopping skill. The label shows:

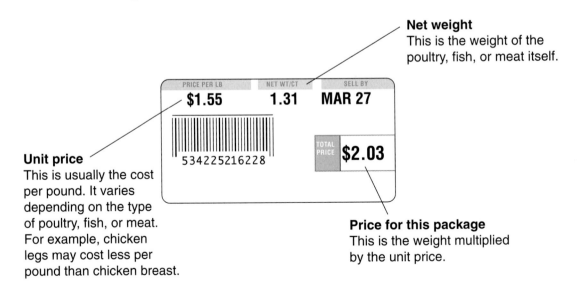

Net weight
This is the weight of the poultry, fish, or meat itself.

Unit price
This is usually the cost per pound. It varies depending on the type of poultry, fish, or meat. For example, chicken legs may cost less per pound than chicken breast.

Price for this package
This is the weight multiplied by the unit price.

Finding the Cost per Serving

To find the best value in poultry, fish, or meat, you need to consider more than just the cost per pound. Why? Imagine two packages of chicken. The first package contains 1 pound of boneless, skinless chicken meat. The second package also weighs 1 pound. However, its chicken pieces have bones, excess fat, and skin. These parts won't be eaten, giving you less than 1 pound of chicken meat. You can serve more people with the first package than with the second one.

Now suppose both packages have the same unit price. Which one is a better value? If you said the first one, you're right. It gives you more servings than the second package. Therefore, even though both packages have the same cost per *pound*, the cost per *serving* is different.

You can calculate the cost per serving when you shop. First, estimate how many servings you can get from a pound of the poultry, fish, or meat. The chart on this page shows servings per pound of poultry. Servings per pound for fish and meat are shown on pages 272 and 282.

Next, find the unit price (cost per pound) on the label. Now use the formula:

cost per pound ÷ servings per pound = cost per serving

For example, if cut-up chicken costs $1.30 per pound, the cost per serving is $1.30 ÷ 2, or 65 cents. Figure out the cost per serving for the different types of poultry, fish, or meat you might buy. Then compare to decide which is the best value.

Try It!

Figuring Cost per Serving

Suppose you find the following choices when shopping for turkey: fresh turkey breast, $2.20 per pound; ground turkey breast, $3.88 per pound; frozen turkey breast, $1.60 per pound; frozen whole turkey, $1.30 per pound.

★ What is the cost per serving of each?

★ What else would you consider when deciding what to buy?

SERVINGS PER POUND OF POULTRY	
One pound of...	Will give you...
Boneless or ground poultry	4 servings
Most poultry with bones	2 servings
Based on a serving size of 3 ounces after cooking.	

STORING FRESH AND FROZEN POULTRY

Store fresh poultry in the coldest part of the refrigerator. (This is usually under the freezer compartment or in a special meat-keeper section.) Leave the poultry in the store wrapper. Place the package on a plate or in a plastic bag. That way the juices, which may contain harmful bacteria, won't drip onto other foods. Use within one or two days. For longer storage, wrap the poultry in airtight wrapping and freeze it.

Poultry that was purchased frozen can be kept in its original wrapper. Store in the freezer up to 12 months.

Leftover cooked poultry should be stored in a covered container in the refrigerator. It will keep for three to four days. If you want to keep it longer, freeze it.

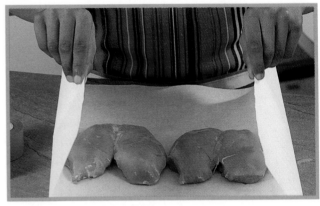

You can divide a large package of poultry into smaller portions before freezing. Wrap tightly in freezer paper or heavy foil.

CONVENIENCE POULTRY PRODUCTS

Chicken and turkey are also used to make cured products, such as cold cuts, frankfurters, and bacon. **Cured** means the product has been treated with ingredients that slow spoilage and add a distinctive flavor. Curing ingredients include salt, sugar, and chemicals such as sodium nitrate. Since curing adds sodium, cured poultry and meat should be enjoyed in moderation. Many cured poultry products are ready to eat, while others need to be cooked.

Some cured poultry products are lower in fat than traditional cured products made from beef or pork.

Many other convenience forms of poultry are available. For instance, you can find canned chicken meat and microwavable meals on store shelves. Frozen main dishes and dinners often include poultry. The deli department may have precooked chicken ready to heat and serve.

When buying convenience poultry products, read labels and compare the nutrition of different products. Follow package directions for storage and use.

 # FOOD SKILLS

Poultry is a versatile part of meal planning. It can be a main dish in itself or part of a recipe for soup or a casserole. Cooked poultry can be sliced or cubed for use in salads and sandwiches.

KEEPING POULTRY SAFE TO EAT

Proper food handling is especially important when you work with poultry. Raw poultry may contain salmonella and other types of harmful bacteria. Review the food safety guidelines in Chapter 21. Pay special attention to these points:

◆ Never let poultry sit at room temperature.

SAFE HANDLING INSTRUCTIONS

This product was prepared from inspected and passed meat and/or poultry. Some food products may contain bacteria that could cause illness if the product is mishandled or cooked improperly. For your protection, follow these safe handling instructions.

 Keep refrigerated or frozen.
Thaw in refrigerator or microwave.

 Keep raw meat and poultry separate from other foods. Wash working surfaces (including cutting boards), utensils, and hands after touching raw meat or poultry.

 Cook thoroughly.

 Keep hot foods hot. Refrigerate leftovers immediately or discard.

You may see a label similar to this one on a package of raw meat or poultry. Be sure to read and follow the guidelines for safe food handling.

◆ Thaw frozen poultry in the refrigerator, in cold water, or in the microwave oven. Review proper thawing methods as described on page 166.

◆ If you don't have time to thaw frozen poultry properly, you can cook it while still frozen. Cook it in the oven or on top of the range—not in the microwave oven or in a slow cooker. Frozen poultry takes about 1½ times as long to cook as thawed poultry.

◆ You don't need to rinse poultry before cooking it. Any bacteria present will be destroyed by properly cooking the poultry. If you wish, however, you can rinse poultry under cold running water and pat dry with paper towels.

◆ After working with raw poultry, thoroughly wash your hands, tools, work surfaces, and anything else that touches the raw poultry.

◆ To store leftovers from a whole turkey, first remove the bones. (If you wish, you can use them to make turkey soup.) Divide the meat into several small portions for faster chilling. Do the same with the stuffing. Refrigerate or freeze.

PRINCIPLES OF COOKING POULTRY

Poultry is a protein food. Remember, protein foods are delicate. When overcooked, they become tough and dry.

Properly cooked poultry is tender, moist, and flavorful. If roasted or broiled, the skin should be brown and crisp.

Undercooked poultry is not safe to eat. It hasn't been cooked long enough to kill harmful bacteria.

How can you tell if poultry is done? Use a meat thermometer. Place it in the thickest area (in the thigh for whole poultry), not touching bone. Check for these internal temperatures:

◆ Whole chicken or turkey: 180°F

◆ Poultry thighs and wings: 180°F

◆ Poultry breasts and roasts: 170°F

◆ Ground poultry: 170°F

◆ Stuffing: 165°F

If it's not possible to use a thermometer, pierce the poultry with a fork. The juices should run clear, not pink.

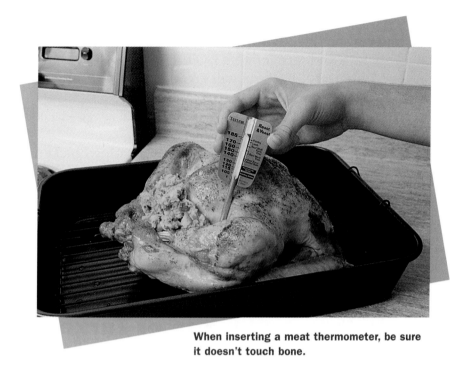

When inserting a meat thermometer, be sure it doesn't touch bone.

METHODS OF COOKING POULTRY

A number of basic cooking methods can be used for poultry. These include broiling, roasting, braising, frying, and microwaving.

Broiling Poultry

Chicken halves, quarters, or pieces can be broiled. Leave the skin on to protect the meat from drying out. To reduce fat, remove the skin just before eating.

Place the chicken skin side up on a cold broiler pan. Put it in the broiler unit so the tops of the pieces are about 4 to 6 inches from the heat. Broil until nicely browned (usually about 20 to 30 minutes). Turn the pieces over with tongs and continue broiling until done. For extra flavor, you can brush the chicken with a sauce, such as barbecue sauce, as it cooks.

Broiled poultry is a delicious, low-fat alternative to fried poultry.

Roasting Poultry

Roasting, or baking, is a popular cooking method for both chicken and turkey. Leave the skin on during roasting to protect the bird from drying out. You can remove the skin just before eating.

A whole bird can be filled with stuffing before it's roasted. Never stuff a bird the day before and refrigerate it overnight. The stuffing won't chill properly and harmful bacteria will grow. Instead, stuff the bird just before roasting. Be sure to check the stuffing for doneness with a thermometer. Many people find that it's easier—and safest—to cook stuffing separately in a baking dish.

A large whole bird takes a long time to cook. Roasting chicken or turkey pieces is often more convenient.

How to Roast Chicken or Turkey Pieces

1. Arrange pieces in a single layer in a large roasting or baking pan, skin side up. Use a rack if desired.

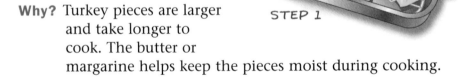

STEP 1

2. If you're roasting turkey, brush with melted butter or margarine.

   Why? Turkey pieces are larger and take longer to cook. The butter or margarine helps keep the pieces moist during cooking.

3. Sprinkle lightly with seasoning, such as ground black pepper and dried, crushed marjoram or oregano.

4. Roast uncovered at 350°F until parts test done. Cooking time varies with the size of the pieces and amount of bone.

   Tip Turn turkey pieces over after half the cooking time. Baste with pan drippings or melted butter or margarine.

Braising Poultry

Braising is a common method of cooking poultry. There are endless ways to vary the flavor depending on the ingredients you add.

Braising can be used to tenderize older poultry, such as stewing chickens. Broilers or fryers can also be braised. They cook in less time than older poultry.

You can find many recipes for braised poultry dishes in cookbooks. In general, here are the steps in braising.

◆ Brown the chicken in a small amount of oil in a skillet. To reduce fat, you can remove the skin before browning.

◆ Next, add seasonings and liquid. The liquid might be water, chicken broth, or vegetable juice. Vegetables can also be added and cooked along with the poultry.

◆ Simmer the mixture until done. Chicken pieces from a broiler or fryer will take about 1 hour to cook.

◆ If desired, serve over a grain such as rice.

Braising chicken makes it tender and blends flavors.

Frying Poultry

Poultry can be coated with crumbs or batter and pan-fried. Remember that frying adds fat and calories because the chicken absorbs fat as it fries.

If you fry chicken, follow these guidelines:

◆ Wash and dry chicken pieces carefully. If you put moist chicken in hot fat, the fat will spatter or "pop" and could burn you.

◆ Use only enough oil to cover the bottom of the skillet.

◆ Make sure the oil is hot before you add the chicken. The chicken will absorb less oil.

◆ Start with large, meaty pieces such as the breast and thigh. Place in the skillet skin side down. Once these are partially cooked, add the smaller pieces.

◆ Turn pieces after half the cooking time.

This quick recipe offers an Italian flavor that's sure to be a favorite!

◆ What food safety practices are important to follow when preparing the chicken for baking?

◆ How would you test the chicken for doneness?

Italian-Style Chicken Strips

Yield: 4 servings

¼ cup	Italian-style dry bread crumbs
½ tsp.	Italian seasoning
½ tsp.	garlic salt
¼ tsp.	ground black pepper

1 lb.	boneless chicken breasts or tenders
1 tsp.	olive oil
½ cup	prepared spaghetti sauce, heated

1. Preheat oven to 425°F.
2. Combine bread crumbs, Italian seasoning, garlic salt, and pepper in a medium bowl.
3. Cut chicken crosswise into 1/2-inch strips. Place in bowl with bread crumb mixture and stir to coat all pieces.
4. Place chicken in a single layer on a non-stick baking sheet. Drizzle oil over chicken.
5. Bake 9 minutes. Turn pieces over. Bake another 7 to 11 minutes or until thoroughly cooked.
6. Serve hot with spaghetti sauce on the side.

Nutrition Notes

Per serving: 256 calories, 7 g fat
Good source of: protein, potassium, magnesium, niacin, vitamin B₆, phosphorus

Microwaving Poultry

Poultry cooked in the microwave will be moist and juicy, but not brown or crisp. Sometimes a coating or sauce is added to give more color.

Before microwaving, be sure the poultry is completely thawed. Pierce or remove the skin to keep it from bursting. When microwaving pieces, put the meatier parts near the outside of the dish and the bonier parts toward the

Be sure to arrange poultry properly for even cooking.

center. Cover the cooking dish. If it has no cover, use an upside-down plate or waxed paper. Don't use plastic wrap.

Change the position of the poultry or rotate the pan often. This will help the poultry cook more evenly.

Standing time is needed to allow the center or thicker portions to finish cooking. At the end of the standing time, check the poultry in several thick spots with a meat thermometer. Make sure the poultry has reached the internal temperature recommended on page 262.

Microwave Hints

* When microwaving, don't coat chicken with flour—it gets gummy. If you want a coating, use bread crumbs.

* Remove fat and juices with a baster as they accumulate. They attract microwaves and lengthen the cooking time.

CHAPTER 33 REVIEW

Understanding Key Ideas

1. Describe the nutritional value of poultry.
2. What signs indicate quality in fresh or frozen poultry?
3. Why do different types of poultry give a different number of servings per pound? How can knowing the servings per pound help you find the best buys?
4. What are the advantages of removing poultry skin after broiling and before eating?
5. Summarize how to braise poultry.

Applying Knowledge and Skills

◆ **Food Safety:** Create a handout that gives food safety tips for buying, storing, and preparing poultry. Share it with your family.

◆ **Recipe Analysis:** In a cookbook, find a poultry recipe for each of the cooking methods described in the chapter. What are the key recipe steps that identify the cooking method? What tips or reminders would you add to help make each recipe successful?

Exploring Further

◆ **Creative Thinking:** Brainstorm ways to use leftover cooked chicken or turkey. Use your ideas to create a recipe booklet.

◆ **Social Studies:** Learn about three traditional poultry dishes from other cultures. What type of poultry is used in each? How is it prepared? What ingredients make each dish unique? Share your findings with the class.

FISH AND SHELLFISH

Discover...

★ *how fish and shellfish fit into a healthful eating plan.*

★ *how to select and store fish and shellfish.*

★ *how to prepare fish and shellfish.*

Key Terms

fillets
shucked
surimi
translucent
opaque

Fish and shellfish are sometimes called "nature's fast food" because they're quick and easy to prepare. They're also nutritious and flavorful.

Fish have fins and bones. Cod, catfish, and haddock are examples. Shellfish have a hard outer shell and no bones. Clams, lobsters, crabs, and oysters are shellfish.

FOOD FOR THOUGHT

What are your favorite kinds of fish and shellfish? How have you had them prepared?

NUTRITION NOTES

Fish and shellfish are part of the Meat, Poultry, Fish, Dry Beans, Eggs, and Nuts Group. They're excellent sources of complete protein. As explained in Chapter 5, your body needs protein for growth and repair.

Other nutrients in fish and shellfish vary, depending on the kind of fish and where it's caught. Fish and shellfish may be good sources of:

◆ Vitamin A and the B vitamins for growth and health.

◆ Iron for healthy red blood cells.

◆ Iodine, an essential nutrient supplied by saltwater fish and shellfish.

◆ Vitamin D, calcium, and phosphorus for healthy bones and teeth. For example, canned sardines and salmon, when eaten with the bones, are excellent sources of calcium.

Most fish and shellfish are low in fat. Generally, most of the fat is unsaturated. When fish and shellfish are baked, steamed, broiled, or poached, they remain low in fat. Frying adds fat and calories.

 ## CONSUMER POWER

Fish and shellfish give you a chance to be creative with meal planning. Often the same recipe will work with different kinds and forms of fish and shellfish. When you shop, look at the available choices to find the best quality and value.

KINDS AND FORMS OF FISH

Hundreds of different kinds of fish are available on the market. Some, such as catfish, pollock, bass, halibut, and perch, have light-colored flesh. Others, like trout and salmon, have darker flesh. Generally, you can substitute one kind of fish for another of the same color.

Fish is available fresh or frozen. Some of the most common forms of fresh and frozen fish are:

Whole. This is the entire fish as it's caught. Whole fish aren't frozen.

Drawn. The insides have been removed.

Dressed or pandressed. Scales and insides have been removed. The head, tail, and fins have been cut off.

Steaks. These are slices cut across a large, dressed fish. They may contain bones.

Fillets. Sides of fish cut away from the ribs and backbone are called **fillets** (fill-AYS). They're usually boneless, but some contain tiny bones.

In addition, many convenience forms of fish are available. You can buy canned fish, such as sardines, salmon, and tuna. Frozen fish is available with breading, seasoning, or a sauce. There are also frozen or packaged meals made with fish.

KINDS AND FORMS OF SHELLFISH

There are many different kinds of shellfish. Some of the most popular include lobster, crab, shrimp, clams, mussels, oysters, and scallops.

Lobster

Clams

Shrimp

Crab

Mussels

Scallops

Oysters

Depending on the type, shellfish are sold in different forms. You may find clams and oysters whole in the shell or **shucked**—with the shell removed. Lobster tails and crab legs may be available. Shellfish may be fresh or frozen, uncooked or already cooked. Many shellfish are sold live. You can also buy canned shellfish as well as frozen main dishes and meals.

Imitation shellfish products are made from **surimi** (soo-REE-mee). Surimi contains chopped fish plus other ingredients for flavor. It's shaped and colored to resemble shellfish, such as imitation crab legs, scallops, or lobster chunks. Surimi products are fully cooked and can be purchased refrigerated or frozen.

SIGNS OF QUALITY

When buying fresh fish, check for signs of quality and freshness.

Appearance. Look for shiny flesh or skin with good, clear color. Whole or drawn fish should have clear, bulging eyes. Avoid fish with slime or dry, discolored edges.

Touch. Press on the flesh with a finger. It should be firm and spring back to its original shape.

Aroma. Fresh fish have a mild aroma, not a "fishy" or ammonia smell.

When buying frozen fish, look for solidly frozen packages with little or no frost. Avoid frozen fish that looks discolored or dry.

Read labels carefully. Products that have been inspected carry a round seal of inspection. Some fish products are also graded for quality. Grade A fish is the highest grade.

When buying fresh shellfish, look for a good, clear color and fresh aroma. Live lobsters and crabs should be active when purchased. Clams, oysters, mussels, and scallops should have their shells closed tight.

FINDING THE BEST VALUES

You don't have to live near a fishing port to enjoy different kinds of fish and shellfish. Most supermarkets carry a wide selection. However, local varieties (if any) are likely to be more plentiful and less expensive.

To find the best values, consider cost per serving. (You may want to review the discussion on page 259.) The chart on the next page shows how many servings you can get from a pound of fish. Check the label to find the cost per pound. Then use the formula:

cost per pound ÷ servings per pound = cost per serving

SERVINGS PER POUND OF FISH	
One pound of...	Will give you...
Whole or drawn fish	1 serving
Dressed fish	2 servings
Fish steaks or fillets	3 servings
Lobster or crab in shell	1 serving
Shrimp in shell	3 servings
Cooked shellfish meat or surimi	5 servings
Based on a serving size of 3 ounces cooked fish or shellfish (without bones or shells).	

STORING FISH AND SHELLFISH

◆ Refrigerate fresh fish and shellfish in the coldest part of the refrigerator. Except for live shellfish, keep them covered tightly. Their odor is easily picked up by other foods.

◆ You can keep fresh fish in the refrigerator up to two days. Use fresh shellfish within one day. For longer storage, wrap tightly and freeze.

◆ Refrigerate live shellfish in a shallow dish covered with a damp towel. Use the shellfish as soon as possible.

◆ Keep frozen fish and shellfish solidly frozen.

◆ Refrigerate cooked fish or shellfish in a covered container for up to three or four days. Freeze for longer storage.

FOOD SKILLS

Preparation of fish and shellfish can be simple or fancy. Clam chowder can warm you up on a cold day. Broiled salmon steaks can be an elegant main dish. With fish and shellfish you can make everything from appetizers to casseroles.

USING CONVENIENCE FORMS

Many convenience forms of fish and shellfish are already cooked. Canned fish and shellfish, for instance, are ready to use in salads, sandwiches, casseroles, and other recipes.

Read the labels of frozen items carefully. Some products need cooking. Others are precooked and only need to be heated. Frozen convenience products should usually be prepared without thawing, but check the directions to be sure.

COOKING FISH

When you buy uncooked fish—fresh or frozen—cook it thoroughly before eating. Raw fish may contain harmful bacteria. Cooking destroys these bacteria.

Recipes usually call for frozen fish to be thawed before cooking. However, you can cook fish while still frozen. Just add more cooking time.

When you thaw frozen fish, do it safely. Never thaw fish in warm water or at room temperature. Harmful bacteria will grow. Instead, thaw the fish in the refrigerator or cold water. (See page 166.) You can also use a microwave oven to defrost fish. Follow the directions in the instruction book for the oven. Watch carefully so parts of the fish don't begin cooking while the rest is still thawing.

(See page 166.)

Try It!

Flaky Fish

Examine a freshly cooked fish or canned fish. Separate it into pieces with a fork.

★ What do you observe about its texture?

★ What accounts for the texture of the flesh?

Principles of Cooking Fish

Like other protein foods, fish is sensitive to heat. In addition, it has very little connective tissue. This means it's naturally tender. It needs to be cooked only a short time at moderate temperatures. Raw fish is **translucent,** or semi-clear. As it cooks, it becomes **opaque** (oh-PAKE)—that is, a solid color you can't see through.

Properly cooked fish should be opaque throughout. The flesh should flake easily when tested with a fork. If overcooked, fish becomes dry and mealy. It will also fall apart.

Notice the appearance of raw fish. As it cooks, the appearance and texture change.

How can you judge how long to cook fish? For conventional cooking, use the 10-minute rule (below).

There are many ways to cook fish. Some of the easiest include broiling, baking, and microwaving.

10-minute Rule for Cooking Fish

◆ Measure the thickest part of the fish. Include the stuffing if it's stuffed.

◆ Cook the fish 10 minutes for every 1 inch of thickness.

◆ If the fish is more than 1/2 inch thick, turn it over after half the cooking time.

Broiling Fish

Fish for broiling should be about 1 inch thick. Thinner fish will dry out before it's cooked.

How to Broil Fish

1. Brush the grid of a cold broiler pan with oil or use a cooking spray.

2. Place the fish on the broiler pan in one layer.

STEP 3

3. Brush the top of the fish lightly with oil, butter, margarine, or a sauce.

   Why? This helps keep the fish from drying out.

4. Place the broiler pan in the broiler about 4 inches from the heat source.

5. Broil until the fish flakes easily. For timing, use the 10-minute rule above.

STEP 5

Tip Thick fillets or steaks should be turned over after half the cooking time. After turning, brush lightly with oil, butter, margarine, or a sauce.

Baking Fish

Baking is one of the easiest ways to cook fish. You can add seasonings or a sauce. Whole fish may be stuffed for baking. You can also spread fillets with stuffing and then roll them up.

Microwaving Fish

The microwave oven does an excellent job of cooking fish. However, be careful to avoid overcooking. For best results, check the oven's instruction book or a microwave cookbook.

With most microwave recipes, you cover the dish to keep moisture inside. However, fish with a crumb coating usually doesn't need to be covered. The crumbs keep the fish moist.

To cook fish, microwave at 100% power for 3 to 5 minutes per pound. If you add liquid or a sauce to the fish, it may need more cooking time. Thick pieces, such as steaks, may need to be turned over after half the cooking time.

After microwaving, the fish should be slightly underdone in the center. Let stand 5 to 10 minutes to complete the cooking.

Test the fish for doneness after the standing time is completed. Make sure the fish flakes in the center as well as along the edges.

After the standing time, make sure the fish is completely cooked in the center.

Microwave Hints

* Frozen uncooked fish microwaves best if thawed first.

* You can reheat cooked fish in the microwave oven if it has a sauce. Otherwise, it will probably become tough.

* Look for convenience products, such as frozen breaded fish sticks, developed just for microwave cooking. Follow package directions.

COOKING SHELLFISH

Like fish, shellfish are tender and easily overcooked. Cooking times and tests for doneness vary. They depend on the kind of shellfish and the cooking method.

Lobsters and crabs may be baked, broiled, or simmered. When simmered, they're usually put in the water whole and alive.

Recipe File

Try this recipe with any light-fleshed fish. To vary the flavor, you can use another juice, such as lime or pineapple.

◆ Why is it important to cut the fillets into equal portions?

◆ What would you do to make sure the fish doesn't overcook?

Orange-Parsley Fish Fillets

Yield: 4 servings

1 Tbsp.	butter or margarine	¹/₄ cup	orange juice
2 Tbsp.	chopped fresh parsley	1 lb.	sole or cod fillets, thawed if frozen
¹/₄ tsp.	salt	4	orange slices (for garnish)
¹/₄ tsp.	ground black pepper		

1. In a medium microwave-safe baking dish, microwave butter or margarine on 100% power until melted.

2. Add parsley, salt, pepper, and orange juice. Stir to combine.

3. Cut fish into four equal portions. Coat both sides of fish with orange juice mixture. Place in single layer in bottom of dish. Cover dish with waxed paper.

4. Microwave on 100% power for 4 to 6 minutes, rotating dish every 2 minutes.

5. Let stand, covered, for 2 to 3 minutes. Test for doneness by making sure the thickest part of the fish flakes easily with a fork.

6. Garnish with orange slices. Serve immediately.

Nutrition Notes

Per serving: 183 calories, 5 g fat
Good source of: protein, potassium, magnesium, vitamin B$_6$, vitamin B$_{12}$, phosphorus

Clams and oysters may be baked, sautéed, or steamed. Scallops may be broiled, sautéed, or steamed. Shellfish are frequently used in stews and chowders.

To microwave shellfish, follow directions in the owner's manual or recipe book. Different kinds of shellfish require different methods.

Shellfish can be used to make elegant dishes for special occasions. You can also find simpler recipes that are quick to prepare.

CHAPTER 34 REVIEW

Understanding Key Ideas

1. What are the advantages of including fish and shellfish in your diet?
2. Could you substitute perch in a recipe that calls for salmon? Why or why not?
3. What is the difference between a drawn fish and a dressed fish? Between fish steaks and fillets?
4. Compare and contrast how to store fresh fish and fresh shellfish.
5. How can you tell when fish is properly cooked? What happens if it's overcooked?

Applying Knowledge and Skills

◆ **Shopping Skit:** Create and present a skit that explains how to choose quality fish and shellfish.

◆ **Restaurant Menu:** Imagine you own a seafood restaurant. Design an informative menu that explains the available choices. Include at least five types of fish or shellfish and three preparation methods.

Exploring Further

◆ **Supermarket Survey:** Compare the cost of fresh fish and shellfish to that of meat and poultry. What factors do you think account for the difference? Based on your findings, what strategies would you use to plan meals with fish and shellfish?

◆ **Environment:** Research issues related to the safety of the fish and shellfish supply. What groups help insure that fish and shellfish are safe to eat? Why is a clean environment of special concern when it comes to fish and shellfish?

MEAT

Discover...

★ how meat fits into a healthful eating plan.

★ how to select and store meat.

★ how to prepare meat.

Key Terms

cut
wholesale cuts
retail cuts
marbling
score
marinade

Meat is a favorite food, and a nutritious one. The term "meat" has several different meanings. For example, it's common to refer to the white meat of chicken. In this chapter, however, "meat" refers to beef, veal, pork, and lamb.

FOOD FOR THOUGHT

Meat is one of the most expensive foods you can buy. How can you include meat in your meals without spending a lot of money?

NUTRITION NOTES

Meat is part of the Meat, Poultry, Fish, Dry Beans, Eggs, and Nuts Group. It's an excellent source of:

◆ Protein for growth and repair of the body.

◆ Iron for healthy red blood cells.

◆ B vitamins for a healthy nervous system.

Some meats are also high in total fat, saturated fat, and cholesterol. However, meat can be part of a low-fat eating plan. Just remember these four basic rules. You'll learn more about following them as you read this chapter.

Eat meat in moderation. Remember that a serving is just 2 to 3 ounces of cooked meat. Eat a variety of protein foods, including dry beans and peas.

Choose lean meat. Meat varies in its fat content. Lean means less fat.

Trim fat before cooking. You may be able to remove almost half the fat this way.

Use low-fat cooking methods. Avoid adding extra fat to meat, such as shortening or margarine. Whenever possible, drain off fat during cooking.

CONSUMER POWER

Most supermarkets carry these four kinds of meat. Each comes from a different animal.

Beef comes from mature cattle over one year old. It has a rich, hearty flavor.

Veal comes from young cattle about three months old. The meat has a mild flavor.

Lamb comes from young sheep. It has a delicate but distinctive flavor.

Pork is meat from pigs or hogs. It has a mild flavor.

At the store, you can buy fresh or frozen meat. In addition, many convenience forms of meat are available. They're described on page 283.

When deciding which to buy, consider cost, nutrition, and how the meat will be used. Your choice will depend on the situation.

CUTS OF MEAT

Meat comes in different cuts. A **cut** of meat is a slice or portion from a specific part of the animal.

Meat animals are first divided into large sections called **wholesale cuts.** The drawing below shows the basic wholesale cuts of beef. Pork and lamb have somewhat different wholesale cuts.

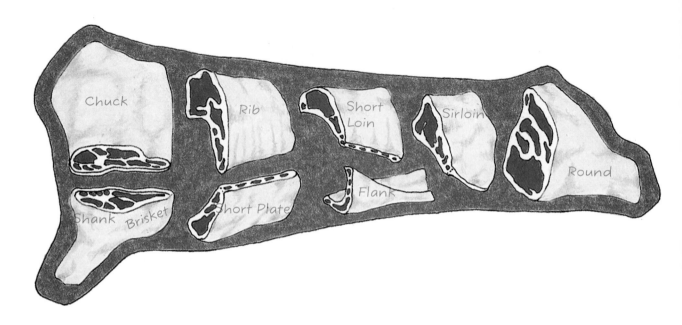

At the supermarket or butcher shop, the wholesale cuts are divided into smaller pieces called **retail cuts.** These are what you buy. For example, round steak and bottom round roast are retail cuts of beef. What wholesale cut do you think they come from?

Cuts of meat differ in tenderness, which affects your choice of cooking method. Cuts also vary in leanness and price. That's why it's important to be able to identify cuts.

You can usually identify cuts of meat by checking the label. It may look similar to the one shown above. Look for the kind of meat, wholesale cut, and retail cut.

COMPOSITION OF MEAT

Meat is made up of four kinds of tissue:

Connective tissue.
This is tough tissue that surrounds the sections of muscle.

Fat. Layers of fat are found between the muscles. In addition, flecks of fat, known as **marbling**, are found throughout the muscle.

Muscle. This is the lean, red or pinkish part of meat.

Bone. Many retail cuts include one or more bones.

BUYING FRESH MEAT

When buying beef, veal, or lamb, look for the grade stamp or label. Grading is based partly on the amount of fat in the meat. The top three grades are:

Prime. Top grade. Has the most marbling and is the most expensive.

Choice. High quality. Lower in price and has less marbling than Prime.

Select or Good. Has less fat and costs less than the two top grades. "Select" is used for beef; "Good" for veal and lamb.

Check for a "sell by" date on the label. Fresh meat should have good color and aroma. If a package has an odor, don't buy it.

Getting the Most for Your Money

Smart shopping can help you save money when you buy meat. Be sure to compare the cost per serving, not just the price on the package. For example, boneless pork at $1.20 per pound is actually more economical than spare ribs at $0.99 per pound. Can you explain why? Remember the formula:

cost per pound ÷ servings per pound = cost per serving

Look for the cost per pound on the meat label. The number of servings per pound of meat depends on the amount of bone and fat in the cut. Typical servings per pound are shown in the chart below.

SERVINGS PER POUND OF MEAT	
One pound of...	Will give you...
Lean boneless meat	 3 to 4 servings
Cuts with some bone and/or fat (such as bone-in steaks or chops)	 2 to 3 servings
Cuts with a large amount of bone and/or fat (such as ribs)	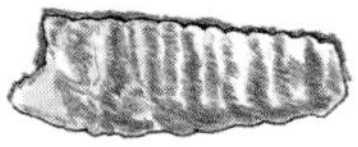 1 to 2 servings
Based on a serving size of 3 ounces after cooking.	

Here are other tips for saving money:

◆ Choose meat graded Select or Good.

◆ Combine a small amount of meat with other ingredients for low-cost main dishes, such as stew.

◆ Less tender cuts of meat usually cost less. They can be a good buy if you know how to prepare them. (You'll find out on page 286.)

Selecting Lean Meat

By choosing lean meat, you can reduce the fat in your diet. To find lean meat, first check the label. Meat graded "Select" or labeled "Lean" is lower in fat than other grades.

Also compare the amount of visible fat in different cuts. As a general rule, the following cuts have the least amount of fat:

Beef—Round or sirloin

Pork—Tenderloin

Lamb—Leg

Veal—All cuts except breast

STORING MEAT

Meat packages may have a food safety label similar to the one shown on page 261. The label gives reminders for safe storing and cooking.

Store fresh meat in the coldest part of the refrigerator, such as below the freezer or in a meat drawer. Keep meat in its original package. Put it on a plate or in a plastic bag to catch drippings. Use the meat within a few days (one to two days for ground meat). For longer storage, wrap meat properly and freeze. Refrigerate or freeze leftover cooked meat promptly.

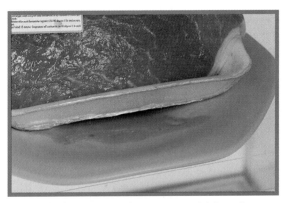

Why is it important to keep raw meat juices from dripping on other foods?

CONVENIENCE MEATS

Many convenience meat products can be found on store shelves and in the refrigerated and frozen food sections. They range from canned meats to main dishes, dinners, and microwavable foods.

Cured meats include ham, cold cuts, bacon, corned beef, and sausages. Most cured meat is in the refrigerated section. Some is canned.

When buying convenience meats, read labels carefully. Follow package directions for storage and use. Some types are ready to eat. Others require cooking.

🍳 FOOD SKILLS

Meat can be part of the menu at any meal. Sometimes it's a main dish in itself. You can also combine meat with other foods to make soups, stews, stir-fried dishes, casseroles, or sandwiches. A small amount of meat can add flavor and nutrients to a salad or vegetable dish.

THAWING MEAT SAFELY

Thaw frozen meat in the refrigerator, in cold water, or in the microwave oven. (To review these thawing methods, see page 166.) If you don't have time to thaw meat safely, you can cook it while still frozen. Just add more cooking time. Check the label of frozen convenience foods. Some must be thawed; others should be cooked while still frozen.

TRIMMING THE FAT

You can reduce fat by trimming meat before cooking. Using a sharp knife and cutting board, cut away the fat around the outside of the meat. Check for fat separating large sections of muscle. If you find any, cut the meat sections apart and trim away the fat. Remember to wash your hands and equipment thoroughly after handling raw meat.

Trimming away visible fat helps lower the fat content in the meat you eat.

HOW COOKING AFFECTS MEAT

What does cooking to do meat? It makes it tender and brings out the natural flavor. It browns the meat, giving it a pleasant color and aroma. Most important, cooking kills harmful bacteria that might cause foodborne illness. Remember, meat must be cooked thoroughly before eating.

Like other protein foods, meat is sensitive to heat. If overcooked, it becomes dry and tough. For flavorful, tender meat, cook at low or moderate temperatures just until done.

WHEN IS IT DONE?

How can you tell whether meat has cooked long enough? The only accurate way is to use a meat thermometer. You can't judge by the color of the meat.

Here are some tips for using a meat thermometer:

◆ When roasting large pieces of meat, you can use an ovenproof thermometer designed to stay in the meat during cooking. With other cuts and cooking methods, use an instant-read thermometer at the end of cooking time.

◆ Insert the thermometer as far as you can into the thickest part of the meat.

◆ Don't let the thermometer touch bone or fat. Bone and fat get hot more quickly and may give you an inaccurate temperature reading.

◆ With hamburger patties, insert the meat thermometer sideways into the patty. Be sure to check the temperature of each burger individually.

Meat that's reached an internal temperature of at least 160°F is safe to eat. If the internal temperature hasn't reached 160°F, continue cooking until it does.

How long does it take for meat to cook until done? That depends on the size and shape of the meat and the cooking temperature. Most recipe books have timetables for cooking meat.

Whether a hamburger is pink or brown in the middle doesn't matter. Always use a thermometer. Insert the thermometer from the side until the tip reaches the center of the burger.

CHOOSING A COOKING METHOD

There are many cooking methods for meat. Which you choose depends in part on the meat's tenderness.

Tender cuts include beef rib, loin, and sirloin; all cuts of pork; and ground meat. Tender cuts can be cooked by dry heat methods, such as broiling and roasting.

Less tender cuts, such as beef chuck, stew meat, and brisket, are tougher because they have more connective tissue. There are several methods you can use to tenderize them:

Try It!

Tenderizing Meat

Cut two equal pieces of round steak. Pound one piece with a meat mallet or score it with a knife. Broil both pieces for the same amount of time following the directions on pages 287-288.

* Which piece is easier to chew?

* Why does pounding or scoring meat make it more tender?

- Cook them slowly using moist heat methods, such as stewing or braising.

- Pound or score the meat. To **score** means to make cuts partway through the meat. You may be able to buy meat that's already been tenderized this way, such as cube steak.

- Soak the meat in a marinade before cooking. A **marinade** is a mixture of an acid food, such as citrus juice or vinegar, and seasonings. It adds both flavor and tenderness.

- Buy powdered meat tenderizer. Follow the directions on the package.

Roasting Meat

Only large, tender cuts of meat are roasted, such as rib, loin, and some leg roasts. Leave a thin layer of fat on the meat to keep it from drying out.

The juices that drip from meat as it roasts can be thickened to make a flavorful gravy. Remember, however, that the drippings include fat from the meat.

How to Roast Meat

1. Place the roast, fat side up, on a rack in a large roasting pan.

   Why? The rack allows the fat to drain away as it melts.

2. Insert a meat thermometer in the thickest part of the meat away from bone and fat.

STEP 2

3. Roast, uncovered and without liquid, at about 300°F until the internal temperature of the meat reaches at least 160°F.

   Tip If you prefer meat that's "well done," cook to an internal temperature of 170°F.

4. When the roast is done, remove it from the pan. Allow it to stand for 15 to 20 minutes.

   Why? The roast will carve more easily after standing. Serve immediately after carving.

Broiling Meat

Broiling can be used for tender cuts of meat such as ground beef, beef steaks, lamb chops, and ham slices. The meat should be at least 3/4 inch thick. Thinner pieces may dry out before they're done.

Check a cookbook for the appropriate cooking time. It depends on the distance of the meat from the heat and the meat's thickness.

Broiling is a popular way to cook steaks or chops. Why might you need to cut slashes around the edges?

Before broiling, make slashes through any remaining fat around the edges of the meat. This helps keep the meat from curling up as the fat melts and shrinks.

Broil the meat until the top is brown and about half the estimated cooking time is over. Turn the meat. Broil until done. If you use salt, add it after broiling, not before. Otherwise the meat may not brown properly.

Panbroiling Meat

Thin pieces of tender meat can be panbroiled. These include hamburgers, cube steaks, pork chops, bacon, and liver. The meat should be less than 1 inch thick.

Usually, you don't need to add fat. Most meat has enough fat of its own to prevent sticking. If the meat is very lean, you may need to use a nonstick pan, a light coating of cooking spray, or a very small amount of oil.

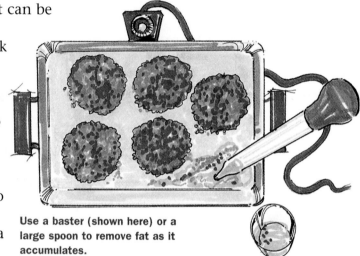

Use a baster (shown here) or a large spoon to remove fat as it accumulates.

Brown the meat slowly in a heavy skillet over medium or low heat. Don't cover or add water. Turn the meat occasionally for even cooking. As the meat cooks, pour off fat or skim it off with a spoon or baster. Season the meat after cooking.

Braising Meat

Braising is a good choice for less tender cuts of meat. First the meat is browned to seal in juices and give a flavorful crust. After browning, liquid is added. The rest of the cooking can be done on the cooktop or in the oven. You can also use a slow cooker for braising. Follow the directions in the owner's manual.

If you like, cook vegetables along with the meat. For example, carrots and potatoes can be cut in half and added about an hour before the meat will be done.

How to Braise Meat

STEP 1

1. Brown the meat well in a large, heavy pan or pot using a small amount of oil.

2. Remove the meat to a clean plate. Drain the fat from the pan.

STEP 2

> **Tip** Leave the browned, crusty bits of meat in the pan. They'll add flavor and color to the cooking liquid.

STEP 3

3. Return the meat to the pan. Add a small amount of liquid, such as water, broth, or vegetable juice.

4. Cover the pan. Cook over low heat on the cooktop or in the oven at about 325°F.

STEP 4

5. During cooking, turn the meat several times. Skim the fat off the top of the cooking liquid.

6. Cook until the internal temperature reaches at least 160°F. A fork inserted into the thickest part of the meat should come out easily.

7. If desired, thicken the cooking liquid with flour to make gravy.

Burritos began in Mexico, but are now enjoyed around the world with different fillings.

◆ What other foods would you serve with these burritos to make a complete, nutritious meal?

◆ How would you change this recipe if you wanted to make six servings?

Pork and Salsa Burritos

Yield: 4 servings

1/4 lb.	ground pork
1/4 tsp.	chili powder
1/8 tsp.	cumin
1 1/2 cups	chopped fresh spinach
1/2 cup	fat-free refried beans
1/2 cup	prepared chunky salsa
4	large (7- to 8-in.) fat-free flour tortillas, warmed
1/4 cup	low-fat shredded cheddar cheese

1. Place pork in a 1-quart microwave-safe bowl. Microwave at 100% power for 2 minutes or until browned, stirring every minute. Drain.

2. Add chili powder and cumin. Stir until combined.

3. Stir in spinach, beans, and salsa.

4. Microwave at 100% power for 2 minutes, stirring every minute.

5. Spoon 1/4 of filling onto center of each tortilla. Top each with 1 Tbsp. of cheese. Fold top and bottom of tortilla over filling; fold sides in towards center, overlapping. Serve immediately.

Nutrition Notes

Per serving: 201 calories, 5 g fat
Good source of: protein, potassium, magnesium, iron, vitamin A, vitamin C, thiamin, riboflavin, niacin, folate, phosphorus, fiber

Microwaving Meat

Meat will microwave more evenly if it's tender, boneless, and uniform in shape and size. Follow recipe directions for turning and rotating the meat during cooking. A plastic cooking bag can help large cuts, such as pork roasts, cook more evenly in the microwave oven.

A plastic oven cooking bag holds moist heat in to help meat cook evenly.

Remember to use a thermometer to test for doneness. You can buy a microwave-safe meat thermometer to leave in the meat while it microwaves. If you prefer, you can test the internal temperature with a standard meat thermometer *after* you remove the meat from the microwave oven.

Microwave Hints

* Cover meat loosely with waxed paper to keep it from spattering.

* Meat doesn't brown in the microwave oven. You may want to add color by brushing on a dark-colored sauce, such as barbecue or steak sauce.

CHAPTER 35 REVIEW

Understanding Key Ideas

1. What are the nutritional benefits and drawbacks of meat? How can the drawbacks be overcome?
2. How can identifying cuts help you get value when you choose and prepare meat?
3. Explain how to store fresh meat.
4. What are good methods of preparing tender cuts of meat? Less tender?

Applying Knowledge and Skills

◆ **Meat Booklet:** Create a small booklet comparing the leanness and tenderness of common cuts of meat. Carry the booklet with you when shopping.

◆ **Demonstration:** Demonstrate safety tips for storing fresh meat, thawing meat, cutting away fat, using a broiler, or another aspect of preparing meat.

Exploring Further

◆ **Research:** Find out how pork of today differs from that produced in the first half of the 20th century. Report to the class.

◆ **Experiment:** Make a patty of regular ground beef. Make another patty, the same size and shape, using a lower-fat ground beef. Panbroil each separately in a nonstick pan without adding fat. After cooking, compare the weight of the patties and the amount of drippings. Which type of beef would you rather buy? Does it depend on the cooking method you plan to use? Explain.

CHAPTER 36

E G G S

W hat do meat loaf, egg drop soup, custard, and muffins have in common? All include eggs as an ingredient. Eggs are a bargain—they pack a lot of nutrients into a small package at low cost. With so many ways they can be used, eggs are one of the most versatile foods you can buy.

Discover...

★ how eggs fit into a healthful eating plan.

★ how to select and store eggs.

★ how to prepare eggs.

Key Terms

quiche
meringue
omelets

FOOD FOR THOUGHT

Think of ways that eggs can be used in appetizers, main dishes, side dishes, salads, and desserts. Make a list of your ideas.

NUTRITION NOTES

Eggs are a part of the Meat, Poultry, Fish, Dry Beans, Eggs, and Nuts Group. They're an excellent source of protein, B vitamins, vitamins A and D, phosphorus, and iron. Can you recall how these nutrients contribute to good health? You may want to review the discussion in Chapter 5.

The egg yolk contains some fat and is high in cholesterol. For this reason, it's best to eat no more than four egg yolks or whole eggs per week. To reduce cholesterol, some people use egg substitutes. They're made from egg whites, which have no fat or cholesterol.

CONSUMER POWER

Eggs are most commonly sold in cartons of a dozen. They're available in different sizes, such as medium, large, and extra large. The size of the egg has no effect on quality. Most recipes are tested using large eggs.

Eggs are inspected for safety and graded for quality. Grade AA and Grade A are both high in quality.

Look for the grade shield on the egg carton. What else should you look for?

BUYING AND STORING EGGS

When buying eggs, compare unit prices for the different grades and sizes. Buy only refrigerated eggs. Open the egg carton and make sure the eggs are clean. Don't buy broken or cracked eggs.

Eggs lose quality quickly at room temperature. After buying, refrigerate them in their original carton. Don't wash eggs before storing them. Use within five weeks.

Egg substitutes come in liquid, frozen, and dried forms. Read the label for ingredients and storage directions.

Egg substitutes are made from egg whites. What advantages do they offer?

FOOD SKILLS

Eggs are versatile. They can be cooked alone in a variety of ways and served at any meal. Hard-cooked eggs often show up in salads or sandwiches and can be eaten as a snack. Popular egg dishes include **quiche** (KEESH), a main-dish pie with a filling made of eggs, milk, and various other ingredients. Eggs are also an ingredient in many recipes.

Raw eggs may contain bacteria that can cause foodborne illness. Proper cooking destroys any harmful bacteria. Don't prepare or eat any food in which eggs aren't thoroughly cooked.

USING EGGS IN RECIPES

In recipes, eggs are used to:

◆ Bind ingredients together, as in meat loaf.

◆ Thicken, as in custard or pumpkin pie.

◆ Add lightness. Beaten egg whites, which contain trapped air, can make mixtures light.

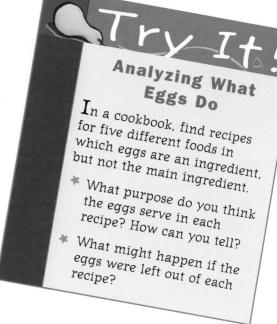

Try It!

Analyzing What Eggs Do

In a cookbook, find recipes for five different foods in which eggs are an ingredient, but not the main ingredient.

★ What purpose do you think the eggs serve in each recipe? How can you tell?

★ What might happen if the eggs were left out of each recipe?

A soufflé (soo-FLAY) is light and fluffy because of beaten egg whites. Soufflés can be made with a variety of ingredients to serve as a main dish or dessert.

Breaking Eggs

Breaking eggs is a basic cooking skill. With a little practice, you'll find it easy to do.

Never break an egg directly into other ingredients. Break it into a cup or bowl instead. If the egg looks or smells unusual, throw it away. If a piece of egg shell falls into the egg, use a clean spoon to scoop it out.

How to Break Eggs

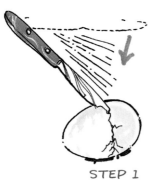

1. Tap the egg firmly but gently in the center with the edge of a knife so it cracks.

2. Hold the egg in both hands over a cup, small bowl, or dish.

3. Place your thumbs on the cracked area. Gently pull each end apart. Let the egg fall into the dish.

STEP 1

STEP 3

Separating Eggs

Some recipes call for only the yolk or white of an egg. You'll have to separate the white from the yolk. Eggs separate more easily when they're cold.

An egg separator is a low-cost kitchen tool. It gives you an easy, safe way to separate eggs.

How to Separate Eggs

1. Place a clean egg separator across the rim of a small bowl.

2. Crack the egg in the center.

3. Hold the egg over the round part of the egg separator. Gently pull the shell apart. Slip the yolk into the egg separator.

4. Let the white flow through into the bowl. Then drop the yolk into a different bowl.

STEP 4

Before you separate more eggs, pour the white you just separated into a third bowl. Set it aside. That way you'll be sure not to get any yolk in it.

Another way to separate eggs is to pass the yolk back and forth between the two shells. As this is done, the white flows out into the bowl below. However, this method isn't recommended. Bacteria from the shell could get into the yolk or white.

Do not use this method for separating eggs.

Beating Egg Whites

Many recipes depend on beaten egg whites for their light texture. When you beat egg whites, air is trapped in tiny bubbles. The mixture of egg white and air is light and fluffy.

To prepare beaten egg whites, first separate the whites from the yolks. If any yolks fall into the white, save that egg white for another use. The yolk contains fat, which would keep the whites from beating properly.

Beat the egg whites using a mixer or rotary beater at high speed. Egg whites at room temperature give the best volume.

As you beat the egg whites, they change in appearance and texture. Recipes will tell you to beat egg whites to one of three stages: foamy, soft peaks, or stiff peaks. It's all a matter of how long you keep beating the egg whites.

Foamy whites. Air begins to mix into the whites. Bubbles and foam form. The whites are still transparent.

Soft peaks. If you on keep beating, the mixture becomes white, shiny, and thick. When you lift the beaters out, the whites stand up in peaks that bend over.

Stiff peaks. If you beat still longer, the peaks will stand straight up.

Don't beat egg whites past the stiff peaks stage. Overbeaten whites are dry and break into pieces. They can't be used.

Handle beaten egg whites gently so the air bubbles don't break. The whites are usually folded into other ingredients. Review the technique for folding as shown in Chapter 15.

Some dessert recipes call for **meringue** (mur-ANG). This is made by beating egg whites and sugar until stiff peaks form. The mixture is then baked.

Meringue is often used as a pie topping.

COOKING EGGS

Like other protein foods, eggs are sensitive to heat. Cook them at low or medium temperatures only until done. If overcooked, eggs turn tough and rubbery.

For food safety, cook eggs until both the whites and yolks are firm. Eggs with runny yolks are undercooked. Harmful bacteria may still be present. For egg dishes such as casseroles and quiche, use a thermometer to check for an internal temperature of 160°F.

Frying Eggs

Frying is a quick way to prepare eggs. Break the eggs into a hot, greased skillet. Try to keep the yolks whole. Cook the eggs at a low temperature until the yolks are firm. To finish cooking the yolks, put a cover on the skillet or carefully turn the eggs over with a turner.

When frying eggs, use cooking spray or a very small amount of oil. That way you'll add only a little fat to the eggs.

Scrambling Eggs and Preparing Omelets

Scrambled eggs and simple **omelets** (AHM-lets) are very similar. Both make a filling main dish for any meal. They're made from the same basic ingredients—beaten eggs plus milk or water.

The main difference is the way they're cooked. When making scrambled eggs, you gently move the egg mixture around in the skillet. The eggs mound up and are light and fluffy. An omelet is more like a large egg pancake. After cooking, an omelet is usually folded in half with a filling in the middle. Compare the directions for scrambling eggs on page 298 with the omelet recipe on page 299.

There are dozens of ways to vary scrambled eggs and omelets by adding extra ingredients. Try adding herbs to scrambled eggs before cooking. Chopped cooked vegetables can be added to omelets or scrambled eggs.

How to Scramble Eggs

1. Heat 1 Tbsp. butter or margarine in a skillet.

    Tip The fat should be just hot enough so a drop of water sizzles.

STEP 2

2. For one serving, mix two eggs in a bowl with 2 Tbsp. fat-free milk or water and a dash of pepper.

3. Pour the egg mixture into a hot skillet. Don't stir.

STEP 3

4. As the eggs begin to set, gently draw a turner or spoon completely across the bottom of the skillet.

    Why? Large, soft curds will begin to form. The uncooked portion will flow to the bottom.

5. Repeat as needed until eggs are firm.

STEP 4

Tip Avoid constant stirring—the mixture will get mushy.

Baked Eggs

For something different, try baking eggs in the oven. Break one or two eggs into a greased custard cup or small baking dish. Add a splash of milk, if desired. Bake at 325°F until firm.

Omelets can contain a wide variety of fillings, making them great for breakfast, lunch, or dinner!

◆ Why should eggs be cooked on low or medium heat?

◆ What are some other ingredients that could be added to an omelet?

Golden Omelet

Yield: 2 servings

3	eggs
1 Tbsp.	water
1 tsp.	butter or margarine
2 Tbsp.	chopped ham

2 Tbsp.	shredded low-fat cheddar cheese
1 tsp.	chopped green onion

1. Beat eggs and water until combined.
2. Heat a small (7- to 8-inch) skillet over medium heat until a drop of water sizzles when added to the pan. Add butter or margarine and turn pan so it coats all of surface.
3. Pour egg mixture into skillet. Cook over medium-low heat until eggs begin to set.
4. Lift the edge of the cooked mixture with a spatula, allowing uncooked portion to flow underneath. Continue cooking until omelet is set, but still moist on the surface.
5. Place ham, cheese, and onion on one half of the omelet. Fold the other half over the ham mixture.
6. Continue cooking 1 minute, or until cheese is melted.
7. Slide omelet onto plate. Cut in half and serve immediately.

Nutrition Notes

Per serving: 159 calories, 11 g fat
Good source of: protein, vitamin A, riboflavin, vitamin B_{12}, phosphorus

Cooking Eggs in the Shell

Do you like hard-cooked eggs? They're made by cooking eggs, shell and all, in hot water. Place the eggs in a saucepan and cover with cold water. Bring the water to a boil, turn off the heat, and cover the pan.

The hot water provides enough heat to cook the eggs. Experiment with different standing times to find out how long it takes the yolk to become firm.

After cooking the eggs, run cold water over them. That stops the cooking process and helps prevent a green ring around the yolk. Store hard-cooked eggs in the refrigerator.

Hard-cooked eggs may take 15 to 18 minutes to become firm.

Poaching Eggs

Poached eggs are cooked in simmering water or in a special poaching pan. The shell is removed before the eggs are cooked. Poached eggs are usually served on toast.

When poached eggs are done, use a slotted spoon to remove them from the water.

Microwaving Eggs

Before cooking eggs in the microwave oven, check a microwave cookbook. The microwave oven works well for some methods of cooking eggs, such as scrambling. Other methods don't work as well. Some can even be dangerous.

Why is this an important step when microwaving eggs?

Heat and steam pressure can build up inside whole eggs and yolks. They may explode while they're cooking or after you take them out of the microwave oven. Never use the microwave oven to cook eggs in the shell or to reheat whole cooked eggs. When microwaving whole egg yolks, pierce the yolks with a toothpick to let steam escape.

Microwave Hints

* In the microwave oven, egg yolks cook faster than whites. Microwave just until the yolk is cooked. During standing time, the white will finish cooking.

* Avoid overcooking—it causes rubbery eggs.

CHAPTER 36 REVIEW

Understanding Key Ideas

1. Explain how eating a limited number of eggs promotes good nutrition.
2. How should you choose and store eggs for quality and safety?
3. What should you do when adding eggs to other recipe ingredients? Why?
4. Distinguish between the three stages of beaten egg whites that a recipe may call for.
5. Compare and contrast scrambled eggs and omelets.

Applying Knowledge and Skills

◆ **Egg Safety:** Create a pamphlet that gives food safety tips for buying, storing, and preparing eggs.

◆ **Foods Lab I:** With a partner, demonstrate how to separate and beat egg whites. While one of you beats, the other should identify when the egg whites have reached the next stage. Then trade places.

◆ **Foods Lab II:** Practice making fried, scrambled, baked, or hard-cooked eggs. Evaluate the results. What would you do differently next time? Why?

Exploring Further

◆ **Math:** Compare the nutrients and cost per serving of eggs with those of several other protein foods. Do you agree that eggs are a nutrition bargain? Why or why not?

◆ **Research:** Use library or Internet resources to learn at least five interesting facts about eggs that you didn't know before. Share what you learn with the class.

SALADS

Discover...

★ *how salads fit into a healthful eating plan.*

★ *how to select and store salad ingredients.*

★ *how to prepare salads.*

Key Terms
base
body
croutons

Salads can add flavor, variety, and nutrients to your daily food choices. Almost any type of food can be used to make an attractive, interesting, and delicious salad. Salads can be used in many ways. A large, filling salad can serve as a main dish. A fruit salad can be a dessert. A salad can also be a snack, an appetizer, or an accompaniment to the main dish.

FOOD FOR THOUGHT

Describe a salad that you could use as a main dish. What ingredients would you include? What food groups do they represent?

NUTRITION NOTES

Salads can give a nutritional boost to a meal. Many salad ingredients are low in fat and high in other nutrients.

◆ Vitamins and minerals can be supplied by including greens, vegetables, fruits, cooked grains, cheese, and eggs.

◆ Fiber and complex carbohydrates can be added with fruits, whole grains, cooked dry beans, and vegetables.

◆ Good sources of protein include cooked beans, lean meat, poultry, fish, cheese, and eggs.

Some foods, such as eggs and many cheeses, are high in fat or cholesterol. Use them sparingly. Choose salad dressings that are low in fat and sodium.

 ## CONSUMER POWER

Good salads start with good ingredients. Chapters 28 through 36 tell how to select and store many salad ingredients such as fruits, vegetables, cheese, pasta, and meat. Two foods that play a part in many salads are salad greens and dressings.

BUYING AND STORING SALAD GREENS

You can choose from a wide variety of salad greens. They vary in color, shape, flavor, and texture. In general, greens that are darker in color have more nutrients. A pleasing combination of greens can make a salad more interesting.

When buying greens, follow the guidelines on page 242 for buying fresh vegetables. Store the greens in the refrigerator in a plastic bag or container.

Leaf lettuce

Iceberg lettuce

Curly endive

Butterhead lettuce

Escarole

Romaine

Fresh spinach

BUYING AND STORING SALAD DRESSINGS

A dressing adds flavor to a salad and can help hold the mixture together. You can buy many varieties of prepared dressings. Look for ones that are low in fat, sodium, and calories.

You can also make your own dressing. Keep in mind that there are many no-fat ways to add flavor to a salad. Try mixing plain fat-free yogurt with seasonings such as mustard. On a tossed green salad, you might use lemon juice or an herb-flavored vinegar, such as tarragon vinegar.

To store salad dressings, follow label instructions. Many dressings, including homemade ones, need refrigeration.

FOOD SKILLS

With a little imagination, you can make meals more interesting with creative salads. There are many ways to put together a salad. The ingredients can be:

◆ Mixed or tossed together.

◆ Arranged in an attractive pattern.

◆ Molded in a decorative container.

Many, though not all, salads have three parts: base, body, and dressing. The **base** is a decorative foundation on which the other ingredients are placed. An example is a leaf of lettuce placed under a fruit salad. The **body** is the main part of the salad. The dressing can be mixed into the salad, drizzled on top, or served alongside.

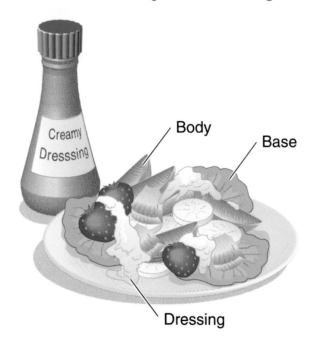

PREPARING SALAD INGREDIENTS

Preparing a salad begins with preparing the ingredients. You can even create a mini salad bar in your refrigerator by keeping several containers of fresh, ready-to-use salad foods on hand.

To prepare salad greens, wash them carefully in plain cool water. Drain thoroughly. Before washing iceberg lettuce, remove the core.

How to Core and Wash Lettuce

STEP 1

1. Hold the head with both hands, bottom side down. Hit the bottom hard against a flat surface.

   Why? This will loosen the core.

2. Remove the core with your fingers.

STEP 2

STEP 3

3. Run cold water into the hole.

4. Let the lettuce drain, hole side down.

STEP 4

MAKING A TOSSED GREEN SALAD

A tossed green salad can be made in one large bowl or individual servings. You can vary a tossed green salad every time you make one. Think of all the different vegetables and dressings you could use. If you like, add toppings, such as sunflower seeds, raisins, or **croutons**—seasoned, toasted bread cubes—for extra flavor and texture.

How to Make a Tossed Green Salad

STEP 1

1. Wash fresh vegetables and fruits carefully. Drain thoroughly.

    Why? If water is left on the foods, it will thin the dressing.

2. Tear greens into bite-size pieces.

    Why? Cutting greens with a knife may cause the edges to brown.

STEP 2

STEP 3

3. Cut other ingredients. For example, you may grate carrots, slice cucumbers, dice green peppers, and separate sliced onions into rings.

    Tip Remember to use a cutting board.

STEP 4

4. Toss the ingredients together gently. If the salad won't be served right away, cover and refrigerate it so it stays fresh and crisp.

STEP 5

5. Add the dressing just before serving, or serve it separately.

You may want to let people add their own dressing to their serving of tossed salad. That way they can add as much or as little dressing as they like. If you prefer to toss the dressing along with the salad, wait until just before serving. Dressing can make greens wilt if added too far ahead of time.

MIXED SALADS

A variety of ingredients can be combined with a light dressing to make a mixed salad. Potato salad, pasta salad, and coleslaw are common examples. Here are more ideas:

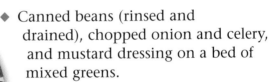

◆ Apple, carrot, and jicama strips tossed with a citrus dressing.

Try It!

Dressy or Droopy

Put two dry lettuce leaves in separate storage containers. Coat one with salad dressing. Refrigerate both overnight. Compare them the next day.

★ How do the two lettuce leaves differ?

★ If you need to make a salad some time before it will be served, how can you keep it fresh and crisp?

◆ Canned beans (rinsed and drained), chopped onion and celery, and mustard dressing on a bed of mixed greens.

◆ Sliced strawberries, melon, peaches, and bananas with lemon-poppyseed dressing.

◆ Canned tuna or chicken, diced celery, grapes, walnuts, and plain low-fat yogurt.

Many nutritious ingredients can be included in a mixed salad. What combinations can you think of?

ARRANGED SALADS

Arranged salads give you a chance to use your creativity. You can invent your own arranged salad without even using a recipe. Choose ingredients with a pleasing variety of colors and shapes. Make sure the flavors work well together, too.

An arranged salad makes an elegant presentation at any meal.

Arranged salads often have a base of leafy greens. The body of the salad is arranged in an attractive pattern on the base. For instance, you might arrange fresh vegetable sticks in a fan shape around a mound of cottage cheese.

Recipe File

Instead of being topped with dressing, this elegant salad has a base of raspberry sauce.

◆ As what part of the meal might you serve this salad? What else would you include in the menu?

◆ What other fruits could you use for the sauce? For the body of the salad?

Ruby Glow Salad
Yield: 4 servings

2 cups	frozen raspberries, thawed		1 can (16 oz.)	sliced peaches in light syrup, drained
2 Tbsp.	sugar		1 medium	banana, peeled and sliced
2 tsp.	lemon juice			fresh mint leaves (for garnish)
1 can (16 oz.)	pear halves in light syrup, drained			

1. Measure about ¼ cup raspberries and set aside.
2. Puree remaining raspberries, sugar, and lemon juice in blender or food processor.
3. Push sauce through a strainer with a rubber spatula into a medium bowl. Discard seeds. Using a clean spoon, taste sauce; add more sugar or lemon juice if needed.
4. Spoon about 2 to 3 Tbsp. sauce in the center of each salad plate.
5. Slice pear halves lengthwise. Arrange pears, peaches, and bananas in an attractive pattern on top of sauce.
6. Garnish with reserved raspberries and mint leaves. Serve immediately.

Nutrition Notes
Per serving: 240 calories, 0 g fat
Good source of: potassium, vitamin C, vitamin B$_6$, fiber

MOLDED SALADS

A molded salad is made in a decorative container. When removed from the container, the salad is firm enough to hold its shape.

Molded salads are often made with gelatin. You can buy gelatin in different flavors or unflavored. By combining gelatin with other ingredients, you can make dozens of interesting salads.

When preparing gelatin, be sure to follow the package directions or recipe closely. Pay special attention to the temperature of the liquids used. Wait to add other ingredients until the gelatin reaches the right stage of thickness. Certain ingredients, including fresh pineapple, shouldn't be used because they'll keep the gelatin from thickening.

Unmolding a salad is easier if you dip the mold briefly in hot water first. Then put the serving plate on top of the mold. Carefully turn the plate and mold over together. Then gently lift the mold off. You may need to shake it slightly to loosen it.

Diced fruits or vegetables can add flavor, texture, and nutrients to a molded gelatin salad.

CHAPTER **37** REVIEW

Understanding Key Ideas

1. Explain why salads can boost the nutrition of your eating plan.
2. What are the benefits of being familiar with different types of salad greens?
3. What are some healthful ways to "dress" a salad?
4. How should salad greens be stored? How should they be prepared for use?
5. What's the difference between the base and body of a salad? Give an example of each.

Applying Knowledge and Skills

◆ **Planning a Salad:** Plan a main meal salad. Identify the ingredients you'd include. Tell how each one fits into the Food Guide Pyramid. How would you prepare the salad? What preparation, if any, could be done ahead of time? If possible, carry out and evaluate your plan.

◆ **Foods Lab:** Try making your own low-fat dressings. You might use dressing mixes, herbs, and flavored vinegars. Conduct a taste test of your recipes on different types of salad.

Exploring Further

◆ **Creativity:** Invent a salad that you'd enjoy for dessert and another that you'd like for breakfast. Share your ideas with the class.

◆ **Science:** Using library or Internet resources, learn why gelatin won't set when fresh pineapple is added. Report to the class.

SOUPS

Soups come in many varieties. There are clear, light soups and creamy ones made with milk. Heartier soups are full of cooked vegetables, meat, poultry, or fish. Some thick soups made with vegetables, fish, or seafood are called *chowder*.

Discover...

★ how soups fit into a healthful eating plan.

★ how to select and store convenience forms of soup.

★ how to prepare simple soups.

Key Terms

chowder
broth
bouillon
stock

FOOD FOR THOUGHT

What type of soup might you use for an appetizer or snack? What type might you use for a main dish?

NUTRITION NOTES

When soups are made with nutritious ingredients, they're an excellent source of the nutrients you need for good health. The liquid in soup—called **broth**—contains water-soluble vitamins and minerals. (These are often lost with other foods because the cooking water is thrown away.) Vegetables or fruits in soup boost the vitamins and minerals. Meat, poultry, or fish adds protein. Dry beans can supply both protein and fiber.

What nutrients will a soup made from these ingredients provide?

Soups made with meat or poultry may contain fat. Chilling soup in the refrigerator allows the fat to come to the surface and harden. Simply remove the hardened fat and you'll have a nutritious, low-fat soup. Another way to make soups more healthful is to use herbs for flavoring instead of salt.

CONSUMER POWER

In Chapters 27-36, you learned how to buy and store many foods that can be used to make soup. When you don't have time to make soup from scratch, you can choose from a wide variety of convenience forms:

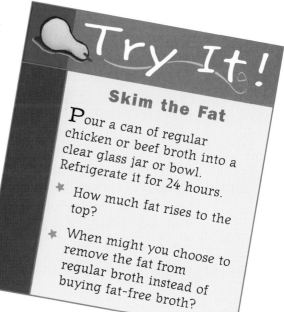

Try It!

Skim the Fat

Pour a can of regular chicken or beef broth into a clear glass jar or bowl. Refrigerate it for 24 hours.

* How much fat rises to the top?

* When might you choose to remove the fat from regular broth instead of buying fat-free broth?

Canned and frozen soup. These only need to be heated and served. Check the labels. Water or milk must be added to some.

Bouillon cubes or granules. Bouillon (boo-YOWN) is clear, flavorful broth. The convenience version is made by adding the cubes or granules to hot water.

Dried soup mixes. These come in packages and are usually just mixed with hot water.

Follow the general guidelines in Chapter 12 for buying these products. Read labels carefully. Many convenience soups, like other convenience foods, are high in sodium. Look for low-sodium varieties.

Store canned soups and packaged mixes in a cool, dry place. Keep frozen soups in the freezer until you're ready to prepare them. Cooked soups can be kept in a covered container in the refrigerator for two or three days. Freeze for longer storage.

FOOD SKILLS

Have you ever made soup from scratch? Bony pieces of meat or poultry are cooked in water with a few seasonings. Long, slow cooking will give a flavorful broth that's often called **stock.** Add a few vegetables, the meat from the bones, and perhaps some pasta. The result—a tasty, filling meal.

MANAGING WITH SOUP

You can practice good management when you make soup. Manage time by making a large batch of soup and freezing remaining portions to use as needed. Soups are also a good way to use up foods that might go to waste. Many leftovers are perfect additions to soup. Even vegetables that have lost some of their freshness are fine for soup.

Long, slow cooking isn't the only way to make soup. There are many quick and easy possibilities.

You can save time by making a large batch of soup and freezing meal-size or individual portions.

USING CONVENIENCE SOUPS

Convenience soups are easy to prepare—just follow package directions. But you don't have to stop there. You can use your own creativity to liven up canned soups or mixes.

One way is to combine several different kinds of canned soups. Choose flavors that go together—perhaps a vegetable soup with chicken soup, or two different vegetable soups. Add the amount of liquid specified on each can.

You can also give convenience soups more flavor and nutrients by adding your own ingredients. You might mix in leftover cooked meat, poultry, fish, vegetables, or pasta. Herbs and other seasonings can lend a special flavor. Try topping soup with chopped chives, snipped parsley, or croutons.

Create new flavors by mixing two kinds of soup together. What else might you add to this soup?

SIMPLE CREAM SOUP

Cream soups can be easy to make. They often have a white sauce base. Refer to the directions for making white sauce on page 210. Vary the amount of flour and margarine or butter to get the thickness you want. Add cooked vegetables such as corn, chopped broccoli, or diced carrots. Season to taste.

QUICK AND HEARTY SOUP

You can make an easy homemade soup using canned broth or vegetable juice as a base. Add an assortment of vegetables or other ingredients. To save time, you can use frozen vegetable combinations.

How to Make a Homemade Soup

STEP 1

1. Chop or dice fresh vegetables that give flavor to soup, such as onion, garlic, celery, and sweet pepper. Sauté them in a small amount of oil.

2. Add broth or vegetable juice and thawed frozen vegetables. If desired, add cooked dry beans, meat, poultry, or fish. Season with herbs and spices such as thyme, basil, and pepper.

STEP 2

3. Bring the mixture to a boil. Lower the heat and cover the saucepan.

4. Simmer 10 to 15 minutes or until vegetables are cooked, stirring occasionally.

STEP 4

Would you like a thicker soup? Use one of the following techniques to thicken it.

◆ Puree cooked potatoes or cooked dry beans in a blender or food processor. Add them to the soup.

◆ Add a grain, such as pasta or barley, to the soup. As the grain cooks, it will absorb liquid. The directions on the grain package can help you decide how much to add.

This delicate soup is sometimes called "Egg Flower Soup." The cooked egg resembles flowers floating in the broth.

◆ Why do you think the egg is poured through a strainer as it's added to the soup?

◆ What other foods besides green onions could be used to garnish this soup?

Egg Drop Soup

Yield: 4 servings

4 cups	reduced-sodium chicken broth
1 Tbsp.	cornstarch
3 Tbsp.	water
½ cup	canned mixed peas and carrots, drained

1	egg
1 tsp.	water
2	green onions, chopped

1. Heat broth in a 2-quart saucepan over medium heat until it simmers.
2. Combine cornstarch and 3 Tbsp. water in a small bowl. Stir into broth. Simmer until mixture is slightly thickened.
3. Stir in peas and carrots.
4. Beat egg and 1 tsp. water in a small bowl.
5. Do this step with the help of a partner. While one of you stirs the soup, the other carefully pours the egg mixture through a strainer into the soup. Stir constantly until egg is set, 30 seconds to 1 minute.
6. Ladle into bowls. Garnish with chopped onion. Serve hot.

Nutrition Notes

Per serving: 78 calories, 3 g fat
Good source of: vitamin A, niacin, phosphorus

MICROWAVING SOUPS

You can use the microwave oven to make homemade soups in less time than by conventional cooking. Check a microwave cookbook for directions.

If you make homemade soup and freeze it, you can defrost and reheat it in the microwave for a quick meal. Most convenience soups can also be heated in the microwave oven. Check the package for directions.

Use a large container for cooking soups in the microwave to allow room for boiling and stirring. For example, use a 1½ quart container for 1 quart of soup.

Microwave Hints

* If you have a temperature probe, use it to bring soup to 170°F.

* Microwaved soup will bubble around the edges before it's done. For even heating, stir soup once or twice during cooking.

CHAPTER 38 REVIEW

Understanding Key Ideas

1. How can soups contribute nutrients to your eating plan?
2. Describe how to store dried soup mix and soup made from the mix.
3. What is stock? How is it made?
4. How can you thicken a broth-based soup?
5. How might you vary a recipe for cream soup?

Applying Knowledge and Skills

◆ **Meal Planning:** Plan a meal using soup as the main course. Consider nutrition, appeal, and time management. If possible, carry out and evaluate your plan.

◆ **Foods Lab:** Make your own soup based on broth or white sauce. Also prepare a similar convenience product. Compare their appearance, flavor, texture, and preparation time. When might you use each method?

Exploring Further

◆ **Creativity:** Beginning with a convenience form of soup, add your own ingredients to enhance the flavor, texture, or nutritional value. Evaluate the results.

◆ **Product Comparison:** Compare regular, low-fat, and low-sodium convenience soups. Read the labels. How do the ingredients vary? Taste-test the soups. Are they equally appealing? If not, how might you enhance the flavor without adding fat or salt?

CHAPTER 39

MAIN DISH MIXTURES

Discover...
* how main dish mixtures fit into healthful eating.
* the role of convenience products.
* how to prepare main dish mixtures.

Key Terms
casserole
wok

What's a main dish mixture? It's a main dish that combines foods from several food groups. The variety of ingredients makes it almost a meal in itself. One example is a pizza topped with chicken strips, vegetables, and cheese. How many food groups are represented in it?

Main dish mixtures have several advantages. Many of them are economical because they use only a small amount of meat, poultry, or fish. In addition, many are quick and easy to prepare.

FOOD FOR THOUGHT

In what ways would a main dish mixture simplify meal preparation?

NUTRITION NOTES

Depending on the ingredients, main dish mixtures can supply a wide range of nutrients. They're generally high in vitamins, minerals, protein, and complex carbohydrates. If whole grains are used, they also provide fiber.

These dishes can also be high in fat and sodium if the foods aren't chosen wisely. To lower the fat, choose ingredients such as lean meat, cooked dry beans, low-fat cheeses, and fat-free milk.

To complete the meal, add other foods to fill in your food group servings for the day. For example, you might have a tossed salad and fruit juice with the pizza described earlier.

CONSUMER POWER

Your shopping skills can help you choose ingredients for main dish mixtures. Refer to Chapters 27 through 36 for information on how to buy and store specific foods.

People often use a combination of fresh ingredients and convenience foods to create main dish mixtures quickly. Many convenience foods discussed in other chapters, such as canned fish or dried soup mix, can be used in main dish mixtures. In addition, look for products such as packaged mixes and ready-to-use stir-fry vegetables. These can be combined with fish, poultry, or meat for a quick main dish.

Frozen vegetables
Fresh meat
Instant rice

You can also buy already prepared main dishes. Look for them on store shelves and in the frozen, refrigerated, and deli sections. Most simply need reheating. Having some ready-to-heat main dishes in the cabinet or freezer can be handy for times when plans change suddenly.

Use your consumer and decision-making skills when considering whether to buy convenience foods. Remember that convenience foods often cost more than foods you prepare yourself. Many are high in fat and sodium.

You can make your own "convenience foods" to use in main dish mixtures. How? Refrigerate or freeze leftovers such as cooked vegetables, dry beans, grains, meat, poultry, or fish. You can also prepare extra batches of these foods when you have time and freeze them to use later.

FOOD SKILLS

If you've read Chapters 37 and 38, you've already learned about preparing some types of main dish mixtures. A large, filling salad can be a main dish, as can a hearty soup. Stew is similar to soup, but less liquid is used. The recipe below is based on a Native American stew.

Many main dish mixtures are cooked in a skillet on the range. For example, you could simmer a combination of browned, drained ground turkey, instant rice, tomato sauce, vegetables, and seasonings. This type of dish is sometimes called a skillet meal.

Recipe File

Posole (poh-SO-leh) is the name given to many hominy stews. It's also another name for hominy itself.

◆ If you were to prepare this recipe using dry or frozen hominy, how would you need to change the directions?

◆ Find at least two other recipes for posole. How are the recipes alike? How are they different?

Easy Posole Stew

Yield: 4 servings

2 tsp.	oil
1/4 cup	chopped onion
1/4 cup	chopped red or green pepper
1 clove	garlic, minced
2 cups	low-sodium chicken broth
2 cups	canned hominy, drained and rinsed
1/2 tsp.	oregano cooked rice or bread bowls (optional) fresh cilantro leaves (for garnish)

1. Heat oil in a 2-quart saucepan. Sauté onion, pepper, and garlic in oil until tender, about 5 minutes.
2. Add broth, hominy, and oregano. Bring to a boil.
3. Reduce heat to low. Simmer, uncovered, 15 to 20 minutes.
4. Serve hot. If desired, serve over cooked rice or in bread bowls and garnish with cilantro leaves.

Nutrition Notes

Per serving: 350 calories, 7 g fat
Good source of: protein, potassium, magnesium, iron, zinc, vitamin C, thiamin, riboflavin, niacin, vitamin B₆, phosphorus, fiber

CASEROLES

In Chapter 14, you learned that a casserole is a type of baking dish. **Casserole** can also mean a mixture of foods baked in a casserole dish. The ingredients are precooked or ready-to-eat. The final baking heats them and blends their flavors.

A main dish casserole often includes the following types of foods:

Protein food. You can use cooked meat, poultry, fish, or dry beans; cheese; or tofu. Cut into small pieces, if needed.

Vegetables. Vegetables add variety, flavor, texture, and nutrients to the casserole. Starchy vegetables, such as potatoes, can also help thicken it.

Grain product. A grain product such as cooked pasta, rice, or grits helps thicken the casserole. It also adds flavor, texture, and nutrients.

Liquid. The liquid helps hold the other ingredients together and adds flavor and nutrients. Try using fat-free milk, vegetable juice, broth, canned soup, or white sauce.

Other ingredients. For flavor and texture, add small amounts of foods such as celery, green pepper, parsley, onions, nuts, or seeds. Chop or dice these ingredients as needed. Also try different combinations of herbs or other seasonings.

Topping. Sometimes a topping is added, such as buttered bread crumbs, grated cheese, or biscuits. The topping keeps the casserole from drying out and adds flavor and texture.

In a conventional oven, casseroles are usually baked at about 350°F. The baking time varies, depending on the foods used. If a topping isn't used, cover the casserole during baking. Check about 10 minutes before the time is up. If the mixture is too thin, remove the cover so some of the liquid evaporates.

Ingredients for this lima bean casserole are precooked. Final baking is done in the oven.

You can make sure a casserole is thoroughly heated by inserting a thermometer into the center at the end of baking time. The internal temperature should be 160°F.

STIR-FRIES

You may recall that stir-frying is a method of cooking food quickly in a small amount of oil. The food is stirred as it cooks. You can stir-fry in a large skillet, an electric skillet, or a wok. A **wok** is a large pan with a rounded bottom. Some woks have a separate metal ring to hold the pan on the heating unit. Electric woks are also available.

A wok has sloping sides that make it easy to stir food as it cooks.

A stir-fry usually includes lots of vegetables in any combination. For protein, include fish, poultry, meat, or tofu. You can also add flavorings such as ginger, garlic, thyme, soy sauce, or prepared mustard. Often the stir-fried mixture is served with hot cooked rice.

The key to successful stir-frying is preparing the ingredients before you start cooking. The actual cooking takes just a few minutes.

To prepare the ingredients, cut foods into small uniform pieces so they cook quickly and evenly. Keep each ingredient separate. Line up the ingredients in the order they'll be cooked. Foods that take longer to cook, such as meat, will go in the pan first. Liquids are added near the end.

How to Prepare a Stir-Fry

1. Cut vegetables into small, uniform pieces (about 3 cups total). On a separate cutting board, cut meat, poultry, or fish into thin strips (about 1 cup).

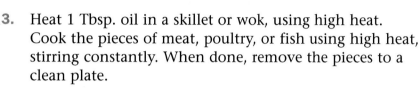

STEP 1

2. Measure 1 Tbsp. cornstarch into a small bowl. Gradually add a small amount of cold water, stirring constantly. Set this mixture aside.

3. Heat 1 Tbsp. oil in a skillet or wok, using high heat. Cook the pieces of meat, poultry, or fish using high heat, stirring constantly. When done, remove the pieces to a clean plate.

   Tip If you're using already-cooked meat, poultry, or fish, skip this step.

STEP 3

4. Begin cooking the vegetable pieces. Cook and stir over high heat until the vegetables begin to wilt.

   Tip Start with the tougher vegetables, like carrots. They take longer to cook. Add tender vegetables, like tomatoes, toward the end of this step.

5. Add 1 cup liquid, such as broth or vegetable juice, along with any seasonings. Cover the pan and allow the vegetables to steam until tender-crisp.

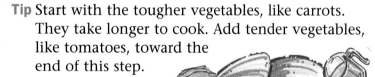

STEP 5

6. Add the cooked meat, poultry, or fish.

7. Pour the cornstarch mixture slowly into the pan, stirring constantly. Cook and stir over medium heat only until the mixture thickens and becomes clear.

   Why? If overcooked, cornstarch loses its thickening power.

STEP 7

8. Serve over hot cooked rice, if desired. Makes 4 to 6 servings.

PIZZA

Pizza is simple to put together. All you need is a crust or base, sauce, and your choice of toppings.

The crust is usually made of yeast dough, rolled or patted thin. To save time, you can buy a ready-to-use pizza crust. It's generally found in the refrigerated section of the store. Follow the package directions for preparing the crust. Some types are already rolled out into a circle. Others are folded and needed to be pressed into a pan. You can use a flat, round pizza pan or a shallow, rectangular baking pan.

You could also use other foods as a base for the pizza. Try French bread sliced lengthwise or English muffin halves.

Homemade pizza is a delicious main dish that's quick and easy to make.

Next, spread a seasoned sauce evenly over the crust. You can make your own or use a prepared sauce. Then add your choice of toppings. You might try fresh vegetables such as green or red peppers, mushrooms, onions, zucchini, or steamed broccoli or cauliflower. You can also add cooked meat, poultry, or fish, diced or thinly sliced.

Sprinkle grated or shredded cheese over the other toppings, if desired. You can use mozzarella, Swiss, or Parmesan, or combine two or more cheeses for variety. Consider using low-fat cheese.

Finish the pizza by baking in a conventional oven until lightly brown. This generally takes about 20 minutes at 425°F.

MICROWAVING MAIN DISH MIXTURES

The microwave oven can save time and energy in preparing main dish mixtures. You can use it to thaw or precook ingredients such as meat or vegetables.

The microwave can also handle final heating of many casseroles. Spread the mixture evenly in the pan. Stir or turn the dish halfway through the cooking time and again at the end. Cover the casserole to hold in moisture.

Microwave Hints

★ Defrost frozen casseroles in the microwave oven to save time.

★ You can sauté chopped vegetables in the microwave oven. For 1 cup vegetables, use 1 Tbsp. oil. Microwave in a covered container at 100% power for 3 to 4 minutes.

Understanding Key Ideas

1. How can main dish mixtures help you with meal management?
2. Summarize the nutrition of main dish mixtures.
3. What are the benefits and drawbacks of using convenience products in main dish mixtures?
4. Explain the sequence in which foods should be added to the wok when stir-frying.
5. How is assembling a pizza different from putting together a casserole?

Applying Knowledge and Skills

◆ **Recipe Analysis:** Choose a casserole recipe. What role does each ingredient play in making the casserole successful? What food group does each ingredient represent? What ingredients might you add or substitute and why?

◆ **Demonstration:** Demonstrate and explain how to prepare a successful stir-fried main dish.

Exploring Further

◆ **Critical Thinking:** How do you think combining foods in a main dish mixture affects the taste and texture of each ingredient? Would the effect be the same if all the ingredients were prepared and served separately? Explain.

◆ **Creativity:** Create three original pizza recipes—one for breakfast, lunch, and dinner. Include foods from several food groups in each recipe without repeating any ingredients. Prepare and taste-test your pizzas with family and friends.

SNACKS

Discover...

★ how snacks fit into a healthful eating plan.

★ how to choose snacks wisely.

★ how to prepare nutritious snacks.

Key Term
spreads

FOOD FOR THOUGHT

When do you usually have a snack? Why do you like to snack at those times?

NUTRITION NOTES

Snacks fit well into a healthy—and fast-paced—lifestyle. They're quick to prepare and eat, yet can provide energy and nutrients to help keep you going all day.

When it comes to snack foods, you have a wide variety of choices. Too often, people forget that snacks need to be chosen with the same care as meals. They're part of your daily food choices, just as meals are.

How can you choose snacks wisely? Just remember that snacks, like meals, should be based on the five food groups in the Food Guide Pyramid. Snacks are a great way to add food group servings to your day's eating plan. How are you doing on the 6 to 11 servings of grain products you need each day? If you're coming up short, try munching on some crunchy cereal mix. Need another serving of fruit? Grab a fresh pear and go!

Foods such as whole grains, fruits, vegetables, and yogurt make excellent snacks. They're full of flavor and important nutrients, yet can be low in fat, sugar, and sodium.

What about snacks such as chips, candy bars, and soft drinks? They're usually high in calories, fat, sugar, or sodium. At the same time, they have little or no protein, vitamins, minerals, or fiber. Enjoy them as an occasional treat, not an everyday choice.

Here are more tips for smart snacking:

◆ If you snack all day long, it's easy to lose track of what you're eating. You might eat too much or too little, or miss out on important nutrients.

◆ Enjoy snacks two to three hours before mealtime. That gives you enough time to develop an appetite for the nutritious foods served at the meal.

◆ Frequent snacking can lead to tooth decay. Brush your teeth after snacks whenever possible.

◆ Consider individual needs when planning snacks. A growing teen who's active in sports may need extra calories for fuel. Someone with smaller energy needs can choose snacks that are nutritious but low in calories.

◆ Snack because you're hungry—not because you're bored, nervous, or upset. Snacking won't solve those types of problems. Try taking a walk or talking to a friend instead.

CONSUMER POWER

You can buy snack foods almost anywhere—not just at the supermarket, but at sports events, movie theaters, shopping malls, and from vending machines. Remember to use your nutrition knowledge and consumer skills wherever you go. Many choices look tempting, but how will they fit into your total eating plan?

One way to beat the pitfalls of "impulse snacking" is to plan ahead. You can find many nutritious, low-fat snack foods at the grocery store. Keep some on hand at home. When you have the urge for something sweet or crunchy, you'll have nutritious foods to choose from.

✓ fresh fruit and vegetables
✓ unsalted pretzels
✓ low-fat yogurt and cheese
✓ bread sticks
✓ rice cakes
✓ whole-grain crackers
✓ peanut butter
✓ popcorn

Put smart snack food choices on your shopping list.

You can also bring your own snacks from home to eat at school or when you go out with friends. You'll probably save money, too.

When you shop for snack foods, read labels carefully. For example, crackers might be promoted as "whole grain" and "all natural," yet be high in fat and sodium. Compare the Nutrition Facts panel of different varieties.

Try It!

Planning Healthful Snacks

Make your own snack food shopping list. Think of nutritious foods, not too high in fat and sodium, that you'd enjoy snacking on.

★ How could you make these foods more convenient to use for snacks?

★ What are the advantages of planning ahead for snacking?

 ## FOOD SKILLS

Many snacks come ready to eat. You may just open a carton of yogurt or peel a banana. Other tasty snacks require only a few simple steps. Here are some to try.

SPREADS

Spreads are seasoned mixtures of meat, poultry, fish, beans, or cheese. They can be spread on breads, rolls, crackers, fruits, or vegetables.

Bean spread is a good choice. It's high in protein and low in fat. Try it on crackers topped with salsa, in pita pockets, or in place of refried beans in tacos and tostadas.

How to Make Bean Spread

1. Drain a 15½-oz. can of red kidney beans or other beans.

> **Tip** If desired, save the liquid for making soup or sauce.

2. Mash the beans in a medium bowl or use a blender.

3. Add a small chopped onion, a minced garlic clove, 1/4 tsp. each dried crushed rosemary and thyme, and a dash of hot pepper sauce.

4. Mix well. Refrigerate in a covered container overnight to blend the flavors.

STEP 1

STEP 4

POPCORN

Popcorn is an ideal snack. It's a good source of fiber. It combines the sweet flavor of corn with a crunchy texture.

You can buy already-popped corn or packaged, ready-to-pop corn for microwaving. However, read labels carefully. Some products are high in calories, fat, and sodium. For the least fat, make your own popcorn using a hot-air popper or a special microwave popper.

To liven up plain popcorn, try seasoning it with herbs or spices. You might also mix dry roasted peanuts with plain popcorn. This gives a delicious peanut flavor.

What seasonings would you like to try on popcorn?

FRUIT AND VEGETABLE SNACKS

Fresh fruits and vegetables make great snacks. Keep both on hand so they're always available when hunger strikes.

For a flavorful dip to eat with vegetables, mix low-fat cottage cheese or plain yogurt with seasonings. You might use minced onion, garlic powder, chopped parsley, dill weed, chopped chives, or chili powder.

Try this fruit dip: Blend 1/2 cup mashed fresh fruit (such as strawberries) with 1 cup vanilla low-fat yogurt. Add 1 Tbsp. honey and mix well. Serve with fruit chunks or small whole fruits.

To make fruit kabobs, place chunks of fruit and low-fat cheese on skewers. Dip the fruit in lemon juice first so it doesn't turn brown. (You may want to review page 236.)

Fruit kabobs are colorful as well as tasty.

Here's a snack that tastes great, is easy to make, and is fun to serve!

◆ How might you adapt this recipe to make a portable snack?

◆ What other foods could you roll up in a tortilla to make "mountains"?

Banana Mountains

Yield: 4 servings

2	fat-free flour tortillas
4 Tbsp.	peanut butter
4 Tbsp.	marshmallow creme
2 medium	bananas

1. Place tortillas on a cutting board. Spread each with 2 Tbsp. peanut butter, then 2 Tbsp. marshmallow creme.
2. Peel bananas. Place each banana on the edge of a tortilla. Roll tortillas as tightly as possible.
3. Trim off the ends of each rolled tortilla (about 1/8 inch).
4. Slice each rolled tortilla into 3 equal-length pieces, cutting straight across.
5. Slice each of the pieces in half, cutting at an angle.
6. On a serving plate, stand each piece on its flat edge to make a "mountain." Arrange the pieces to look like "mountain ranges."

Nutrition Notes

Per serving: 238 calories, 9 g fat
Good source of: protein, magnesium, vitamin E, niacin, vitamin B_6

HOT SNACKS

In just a few minutes, you can make delicious hot snacks. You might enjoy these:

Mini-pizzas. Split English muffins or bagels in half. Top with prepared pizza sauce, chopped vegetables, and shredded cheese. Broil until cheese melts.

Tortilla treats. Spread a corn tortilla with a very thin coating of margarine. Sprinkle with 1 Tbsp. Parmesan cheese and 1 tsp. sesame seeds. Cut the tortilla into triangles. Bake in the oven at 350°F until cheese melts and the tortilla triangles are crisp.

These tortilla treats are garnished with tomatoes and parsley.

Roasted pumpkin or sunflower seeds. Rinse all the pumpkin fibers from the seeds. For sunflower seeds, remove the hulls. Sprinkle 1/2 tsp. salt in the bottom of a microwave-safe baking dish. Place the damp seeds on top of the salt in the baking dish and microwave at 100% power for about 6 minutes. Stir twice during cooking time. Seeds should be crispy when ready to eat.

MORE SNACK IDEAS

◆ Make a small salad. Refer to Chapter 37 for ideas.

◆ Have a cup of soup along with some crackers or breadsticks.

◆ Make a mini-sandwich. See the sandwich ideas in Chapter 26.

◆ Have a small serving of leftovers, such as a slice of pizza.

◆ Make a nutritious blender shake. You'll learn how in the next chapter.

◆ Mix cereal with pretzels, nuts, seeds, and dried fruit.

Snacks can be light or hearty, depending on your needs.

- Add fresh or canned fruit to plain yogurt or cottage cheese.

- Make your own frozen yogurt pops. Mix 8 oz. plain low-fat yogurt with a thawed 6-oz. can of your favorite frozen juice concentrate. Add chopped fruit if you wish. Pour into paper cups. Place a wooden ice pop stick or plastic spoon in the middle. Freeze. To eat, simply peel away the cup.

CHAPTER **40** REVIEW

Understanding Key Ideas

1. What nutrition benefits can snacks offer?
2. Give tips for fitting snacks into a healthful eating plan.
3. What strategy can help you avoid making poor snack choices when away from home?
4. How can you make popcorn with little or no fat?
5. Describe three ways to use yogurt as a nutritious snack.

Applying Knowledge and Skills

- **Suggesting Alternatives:** Identify several popular snacks that offer few nutrients. What is the appeal of each? (Examples: sweet, creamy, crunchy.) Suggest nutrient-dense alternatives with similar appeal.

- **Foods Lab:** Prepare one of the snack recipes described in this chapter. Evaluate it for flavor, texture, and appearance.

Exploring Further

- **Critical Thinking:** Analyze three television advertisements for popular snacks. What images do these ads use? Why? How might they influence viewers? What questions might a thoughtful consumer have after viewing these commercials?

- **Social Studies:** Investigate snacking habits in another culture. What snack foods are typically eaten and when? How do attitudes toward snacking in that culture compare to attitudes in this one? Share your findings with the class.

CHAPTER 41

BEVERAGES

Discover...

★ how beverages fit into a healthful eating plan.

★ how to select and store nutritious beverages.

★ how to prepare blender shakes and fruit punches.

Key Terms
caffeine
fruit punch
mulled

Beverages are part of any meal, but they can also be enjoyed as a snack or refreshment. This chapter will help you choose and prepare flavorful, healthful beverages.

FOOD FOR THOUGHT

How often do you choose a soft drink as a beverage? What other options do you have?

NUTRITION NOTES

Beverages help fulfill your body's need for water. In fact, plain water is the best beverage when it comes to quenching your thirst. For good health, drink at least six to eight glasses of water each day.

If you choose beverages wisely, they can also help meet your body's need for other nutrients.

◆ Miik supplies protein, calcium, phosphorus, and vitamins D and A. (For information on buying, storing, and using milk, see Chapter 27.) Beverages such as cocoa and milk shakes can also provide these nutrients because they're made from milk. Just remember that they have more sugar, fat, and calories as well.

◆ Fruit and vegetable juices generally provide the same vitamins and minerals as those found in the fruit or vegetable. For example, orange juice is high in vitamin C and potassium.

Coffee, tea, and soft drinks such as cola supply few or no vitamins and minerals. Instead, they may supply too much of what you don't need, such as sugar and sodium. Many of these beverages also contain **caffeine** (kaff-EEN), a chemical that stimulates the nervous system. Too much caffeine can make some people anxious or unable to sleep.

Beverage Choices

Which beverages are good sources of nutrients?

Yogurt Smoothie
180 calories
Vitamin C, calcium, protein, phosphorus, vitamin D, B vitamins

Cola
100 calories

Tea
0 calories

Orange Juice
110 calories
Vitamin C, B vitamins

Tomato Juice
40 calories
Vitamin C, vitamin A, B vitamins

Grape Drink
120 calories
Vitamin C

Cocoa
190 calories
Calcium, phosphorus and other minerals, vitamin D, protein, B vitamins, vitamin A

Too often, soft drinks are chosen instead of nutritious beverages such as milk. That can be a problem—especially for children and teens, who need plenty of calcium while their bones are still growing. What beverages do you choose most often? What improvements can you make in your beverage choices?

 ## CONSUMER POWER

The shopping skills and nutrition information you've already learned will help you choose beverages. Here are more tips to help you be a wise consumer.

JUICES AND FRUIT DRINKS

Many different kinds of fruit are used to make juice. You can also buy vegetable juices, such as tomato.

Only products that are pure juice can be called "juice" on the label. What if the label uses another term, such as fruit drink or punch? These products typically contain from 5% to 50% juice. The rest is water and sugar or another sweetener. Some are fortified with vitamin C.

You'll find juices and fruit drinks on the store shelves as well as in the refrigerated section. They may be packaged in bottles, cartons, or cans. Also look for frozen juice concentrate and powdered mixes. Before using these products, you must reconstitute them by adding water as directed on the label.

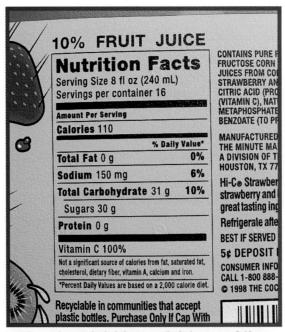

Is this product a fruit juice or a fruit beverage? How can you tell?

BUYING BEVERAGES

When shopping for beverages, read labels carefully. What nutrients does the product provide? How much sugar, sodium, and caffeine does it contain?

Unless you read carefully, it may not be easy to tell the difference between pure fruit juice and other fruit beverages. A product that says "100% natural" may not be 100% juice. Remember, the label must list any added ingredients.

How can you tell how much sugar has been added? The Nutrition Facts panel tells you the total amount of sugar. This figure includes the natural sugars in the fruits or vegetables. To find added sugars, check the ingredients list. Honey, corn syrup, fructose, and other ingredients that end in "ose" are all forms of sugar. Remember that ingredients are listed by weight, from most to least.

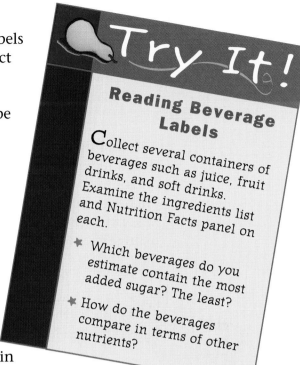

Try It!

Reading Beverage Labels

Collect several containers of beverages such as juice, fruit drinks, and soft drinks. Examine the ingredients list and Nutrition Facts panel on each.

* Which beverages do you estimate contain the most added sugar? The least?
* How do the beverages compare in terms of other nutrients?

STORING BEVERAGES

Like other foods, beverages need to be stored properly to maintain their nutrients and fresh flavor.

◆ Juice from the refrigerated case should be kept cold. Most other unopened products can be stored in a cool, dry area.

◆ Refrigerate opened containers of juice. Use within a few days.

◆ Keep fruit juice concentrates frozen until you're ready to use them. After they're reconstituted, refrigerate them.

FOOD SKILLS

With a few simple steps, you can make a variety of tasty beverages for snacks or special occasions.

FRUIT PUNCH

It's fun to create your own fruit juice combinations. Choose juices that will blend well in color and flavor. A mixture of fruit juices is sometimes called **fruit punch**. Here's an idea for a bubbly fruit punch you can serve at a party.

How to Make Fruit Punch

1. Ahead of time, thaw a 6-ounce can of frozen lemonade concentrate. Mix with 2 qt. cranberry juice cocktail in a large pitcher or punch bowl. Chill to allow flavors to blend. Also chill a 1-qt. bottle of plain seltzer water.

STEP 1

2. Just before serving, slowly add the chilled seltzer water to the fruit punch.

STEP 2

3. For a garnish, float lemon or orange slices in the punch.

STEP 3

BLENDER SHAKES

You can use a blender or food processor to make nutritious low-fat shakes. Try creating your own combinations of fresh fruit, fruit juice, fat-free or low-fat milk, and yogurt. Here are some ideas to get you started.

Banana Shake. Cut an overripe banana into chunks and freeze solid. Combine the frozen banana chunks with 2/3 cup fat-free milk in a blender or food processor. Blend on high speed until smooth.

Lemon-Strawberry Smoothie. Blend 1/2 cup lemon yogurt, 1/2 cup fat-free milk, 1/4 cup sliced strawberries, and 1 tsp. sugar.

Sunshine Shake. Blend 3/4 cup chilled pineapple or orange juice, 1/4 cup plain fat-free or low-fat yogurt, 2 tsp. honey, and 3 crushed ice cubes.

What nutrients would this Sunshine Shake provide?

HOT BEVERAGES

Fruit juice or punch can also be served hot. If spices such as cinnamon or cloves are added, the hot mixture is called a **mulled** beverage. "Rosy Cider," the recipe below, is an example.

When making a mulled beverage, simmer the mixture at least 10 minutes to blend the flavors. Serve the beverage piping hot in mugs. For a garnish, you can use a stick of cinnamon or a slice of orange or lemon.

Cocoa is a popular hot beverage. Making hot beverages with milk requires special care. Follow the guidelines for cooking with milk in Chapter 27. You'll find a cocoa recipe on page 212.

You can vary cocoa by adding flavorings such as cinnamon or peppermint.

Recipe File

A hot beverage on a cold day is a great way to warm up. The cider can also be chilled for a refreshing treat on a hot summer day.

◆ What is the advantage of using cinnamon sticks and whole cloves instead of ground spices?

◆ Why do you think this recipe says to let the hot mixture stand for 10 minutes?

Rosy Cider   Yield: 4 servings

2½ cups pasteurized apple cider	10 whole cloves
1½ cups cranberry juice	dash allspice
2 sticks cinnamon	

1. In a 1-qt. microwave-safe bowl, combine apple cider, cranberry juice, cinnamon sticks, cloves, and allspice.
2. Microwave at 100% power for 6 to 8 minutes or until mixture starts to simmer.
3. Let stand 10 minutes.
4. Remove cinnamon and cloves with a slotted spoon. Serve hot in mugs or cups.

Nutrition Notes

Per serving: 113 calories, 0 g fat
Good source of: vitamin C

MICROWAVING BEVERAGES

Some beverages, especially those made with milk, need careful attention when they're microwaved. They can develop a film on the surface of the liquid. This acts as a cover and lets steam build up under the surface. The hot liquid may spurt out of the container and cause burns. Stir before and after microwaving to prevent this problem. Also stir after microwaving to mix hotter and cooler parts of the liquid.

When should microwaved beverages be stirred? Why?

Microwave Hints

* Microwave beverages at 100% power unless the recipe specifies a different power level.

* You can reheat hot beverages that have cooled to room temperature. One serving takes about 1½ minutes at 100% power. Two servings take about 3 minutes.

Understanding Key Ideas

1. Explain how beverage choices can help or hinder the healthfulness of an eating plan.
2. Is a drink labeled "fruit juice" nutritionally equal to one labeled "fruit drink"? Explain.
3. When should fruit juice be refrigerated?
4. What ingredients might you use in a flavorful, nutritious shake?
5. Explain how to make a mulled beverage.

Applying Knowledge and Skills

◆ **Meal Planning:** Plan a day of meals and snacks. What beverages will you choose to go with these? Why? What nutrients do the beverages provide?

◆ **Foods Lab:** Experiment with creating your own recipe for a fruit punch, blender shake, or hot mulled beverage. Share the finished recipe with the class.

Exploring Further

◆ **Nutrient Comparison:** Research the sugar, vitamin, and mineral content of several popular beverages. Make a bar graph or picture graph comparing the nutrients in each product.

◆ **Critical Thinking:** Many people choose diet soft drinks in an effort to be health-conscious. What are the benefits of this strategy? What are the drawbacks?

Beverages   339

PRINCIPLES OF BAKING

"**W**hy does bread have a different texture from cake?" "Is baking powder the same thing as baking soda?" "Why did my muffins stick to the pan?" This chapter will help you learn the answers to questions like these. Understanding the principles of baking will help you prepare any baked product—from apple pie to zucchini bread—more successfully.

FOOD FOR THOUGHT

Do you think baking is an art, a science, or both? Why?

THE CHEMISTRY OF BAKING

A recipe for a baked product is like a chemical formula. In fact, chemical reactions that take place during mixing and baking give the product its final appearance, texture, and flavor.

WHAT INGREDIENTS DO

Recipes for baked products such as breads, cakes, and cookies can vary a great deal. However, most use the same basic types of ingredients. Each ingredient has a specific purpose. They all work together to make a product with the desired texture and flavor.

Flour provides proteins and starch that make up the structure of baked products.

Liquids help flour form the structure of baked products. They also make possible many of the chemical changes that take place in the mixture. Water, milk, fruit or vegetable juice, yogurt, and sour cream are some of the liquids used in baked products.

Leavening agents, such as baking powder, make products rise. They do this by causing air or gas to be trapped in the mixture. Without leavening agents, products would be flat with a dense texture.

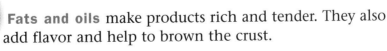

Fats and oils make products rich and tender. They also add flavor and help to brown the crust.

Sweeteners, such as sugar, give flavor. They also help the crust to brown.

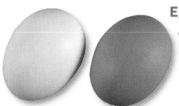

Eggs make baked products tender, add flavor and richness, and can help bind mixtures together so they don't separate. Beaten egg whites may be used as a leavening agent.

Flavorings include chocolate, spices, herbs, and extracts such as vanilla and almond.

If you look at a recipe for muffins or other baked goods, you'll see most or all of these types of ingredients. If you use a convenience mix, some of the ingredients are already included in the mix. You add what's missing, such as liquid.

You've already learned how to buy and store some ingredients, such as milk and eggs. In Chapter 43 you'll find consumer information for other baking ingredients.

DOUGH, BATTER, AND GLUTEN

The ingredients are combined and mixed in a specific way, depending on the type of baked product. Proper mixing helps give the desired texture.

The mixture of ingredients is called dough or batter, depending on how thick it is.

Dough is thick enough to be shaped by hand or cut into shapes. Biscuits, cookies, pie crust, and some breads are made from dough.

Batter is thin enough to be poured or dropped from a spoon. Pancakes, muffins, and cakes are made from batter.

One of the reasons for mixing ingredients is to distribute them evenly. Another is to develop gluten. **Gluten** is an elastic substance formed by the protein in flour. It forms the structure of the product. The more the dough is mixed, the stronger the gluten becomes. Some baked products, such as yeast bread, must have strong gluten. Others, such as cakes, don't need strong gluten.

HOW LEAVENING AGENTS WORK

As mentioned earlier, a **leavening agent** adds air or another gas to the product, helping it rise. Recipes use one or more of these four basic leavening agents:

Trapped air. Air is trapped in a mixture when you sift flour, cream fat and sugar together, or beat egg whites.

Steam. When steam is used as a leavening agent, the product must be baked at a high temperature. The high heat causes water in the mixture to turn to steam and the product rises. Éclairs and cream puffs are examples.

Chemical leavening. There are two common chemical leavening agents—baking soda and baking powder. Be sure to use the one called for in the recipe. They're not the same.

- Baking soda forms carbon dioxide gas when it's combined with an acid. It's used in recipes that contain naturally acidic foods, such as buttermilk, yogurt, or citrus juice.

- Baking powder is a combination of baking soda and a dry acid. It forms carbon dioxide when mixed with any liquid. The recipe doesn't need an acidic ingredient.

Yeast. Yeast is a microscopic plant that gives off gas as it grows. It reproduces quickly if it has warmth, food (such as sugar), and moisture. Yeast gives the baked product a distinctive flavor. It's the reason baked yeast bread smells and tastes so good.

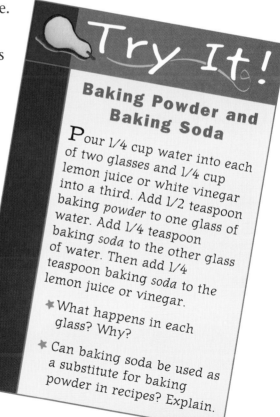

Try It!

Baking Powder and Baking Soda

Pour 1/4 cup water into each of two glasses and 1/4 cup lemon juice or white vinegar into a third. Add 1/2 teaspoon baking powder to one glass of water. Add 1/4 teaspoon baking soda to the other glass of water. Then add 1/4 teaspoon baking soda to the lemon juice or vinegar.

★ What happens in each glass? Why?

★ Can baking soda be used as a substitute for baking powder in recipes? Explain.

Leavening agents work together with gluten. As the batter or dough is mixed, the gluten strengthens to form an elastic mesh. The air or gas from the leavening agent forms tiny cells or pockets within the mesh. When the batter or dough is baked, heat causes the air or gas to expand. The gluten stretches and the product rises. As baking continues, the heat causes the proteins and starch in the flour to set (become firm). As they set, they give the product its final shape.

SUCCESSFUL BAKING

The chemical reactions that take place during baking are sensitive. Baking success depends on accurately following the recipe.

Use the exact ingredients called for. A different ingredient, such as honey in place of sugar, will give a different flavor and texture to the finished product. The results may not be what you expect.

> What happened? All I did was use oil instead of shortening.

> I never thought a little extra lemon juice would make that much difference!

Measure accurately. Even a few extra drops of an ingredient can make a difference.

> I just threw everything in the bowl and mixed it up real good.

Follow the mixing directions in the recipe. Don't take shortcuts.

Use the correct type and size of pan. If you use a pan that's too small, the mixture will overflow as it rises. If you use a pan that's too large, the product will be thin and may not brown on top.

> I couldn't find the angel food cake pan, so I used this big pizza pan.

> I thought if I turned the heat up the cookies would bake faster.

Use the correct oven temperature. Too high a temperature causes overbrowning, poor volume, and a tough texture. Too low a temperature causes a pale color, soggy texture, uneven grain, and a sunken center.

PREPARING PANS FOR BAKING

Pans must be properly prepared for baking. Otherwise the baked product may be difficult to remove. Follow the directions in the recipe. Some recipes call for greased pans, others for ungreased pans.

When greasing pans, use unsalted shortening or a cooking spray. The salt in butter or margarine could cause the crust to overbrown and stick to the pan.

Some recipes call for greased and floured pans. The flour makes the product easier to remove. It also absorbs the fat and keeps it from soaking into the crust.

How to Grease and Flour a Pan

STEP 1

1. Using waxed paper or a paper towel, spread shortening in a thin, even layer over the bottom and sides of the pan.

   Tip Be sure corners and the areas where the bottom and sides meet are well greased.

   STEP 2

2. Sprinkle about 1 Tbsp. all-purpose flour into the pan.

3. Hold the pan in both hands. Gently turn it at different angles to spread the flour evenly over the bottom and sides. Tap the pan gently to help spread the flour.

STEP 3

4. When the flour is spread evenly over the pan, hold the pan over a large piece of waxed paper. Turn the pan upside down and tap gently to remove excess flour.

STEP 4

SETTING THE OVEN TEMPERATURE

The correct oven temperature may depend on the type of pan you use. Some pan materials retain more heat than others. Unless they state otherwise, recipes are usually based on using shiny metal pans. If you use dull metal pans, lower the oven temperature about 10°F. If you use glass pans, lower the oven temperature about 25°F.

For best results, preheat the oven. About 10 minutes before you're ready to put the pan in, turn the oven control to the desired temperature. Preheating ensures that the oven will be at the correct temperature. The mixture will start to bake right away and will rise properly.

PLACING PANS IN THE OVEN

Before placing pans in the oven, wipe off the pan sides and bottom. Food particles on the pan will burn.

Use these guidelines to place pans in the oven. Proper placement allows air to circulate freely for even baking.

One pan. Place the pan in the center of the oven.

Two pans. Place each pan on a separate rack in corners diagonally opposite each other.

Three pans. Place two pans on one rack in diagonally opposite corners. Place the third pan on another rack in a different corner.

Four pans. Place two pans on one rack in diagonally opposite corners. Place the other two pans on another rack in the other diagonal corners.

Be sure the pans don't touch each other or the sides, top, bottom, or door of the oven. If pans touch each other or any part of the oven walls or door, they create a hot spot. A hot spot is a concentration of heat. The product will overbrown in that area. Leave at least 1 inch of space between each pan and between the pans and oven walls.

REMOVING BAKED PRODUCTS FROM PANS

The recipe should tell you when to remove the baked product from the pan. Some baked products should be taken out of the pans as soon as they're removed from the oven. Others must first cool for a few minutes. After products are taken out of the pan, they're usually placed on a wire rack to cool completely.

CHAPTER 42 REVIEW

Understanding Key Ideas

1. Compare and contrast baking soda and baking powder.
2. What's the difference between batter and dough? Give examples of products made from each.
3. How do leavening agents and gluten make baked goods rise?
4. If you don't preheat the oven before baking, what may be the effect on the product? Why?
5. What may result if pans are not properly placed in an oven? Why?

Applying Knowledge and Skills

◆ **Recipe Analysis:** Find a recipe for each of the following: muffins, biscuits, whole wheat bread, cookies, angel food cake. Identify the basic category of each ingredient in each recipe. How are the ingredients for each recipe similar and different? What conclusions can you draw?

Exploring Further

◆ **Critical Thinking:** Your friend tells you, "My grandmother has baked for years. I've never seen her measure anything, and her baked goods turn out great. Why should I bother to measure accurately?" How would you reply?

◆ **Math:** Calculate the volume of a 9-inch square baking pan, 2 inches deep, and a 9-inch (diameter) round baking pan, 1½ inches deep. Predict what would happen if you used the round pan when the recipe called for the square pan. What if you used the square pan when the recipe called for the round pan?

Principles of Baking   347

BAKING BREADS

Homemade breads, fresh from the oven, have a delicious aroma and flavor. Some recipes use yeast to make the bread rise. Whole wheat and rye loaves, for example, are yeast breads. Other breads use baking powder or baking soda instead of yeast. They're called quick breads. That's because they take only minutes to prepare, not hours as yeast breads can. Quick breads include pancakes, waffles, muffins, biscuits, and some loaf breads and coffee cakes.

Discover...

* the differences between quick and yeast breads.

* how breads fit into a healthful eating plan.

* how to select and store baking ingredients and convenience forms.

* how to prepare homemade breads.

Key Terms

self-rising flour
muffin method
biscuit method
knead

FOOD FOR THOUGHT

What breads have you eaten this week? Were they quick breads or yeast breads?

NUTRITION NOTES

Quick and yeast breads provide complex carbohydrates along with some B vitamins and iron. If made with whole grain flour, they give you fiber, too. Using milk in breads adds calcium. Nuts, fruits, and vegetables in the recipe add flavor and nutrients.

The amount of sugar, fat, cholesterol, and calories in breads depends on the recipe. For example, a muffin made with fat-free milk and vegetable oil will be lower in saturated fat and cholesterol than one made with whole milk and butter.

CONSUMER POWER

You can bake breads from scratch or with convenience products. In either case, use your consumer skills to select the products you want and store them properly.

BUYING AND STORING BAKING INGREDIENTS

As you learned in Chapter 42, each ingredient in baked products has a specific job to do. Here's more information about buying and storing some of those ingredients.

Flour

Many types of flour are available, such as:

◆ All-purpose flour—enriched white flour made from wheat.

◆ Whole wheat flour—made from the entire wheat kernel.

◆ **Self-rising flour**—has leavening and salt added.

Use the type of flour called for in the recipe. If the recipe doesn't specify a type, use all-purpose flour.

Store flour in a cool, dry place. After opening the bag, put the flour in a tightly covered container.

Once a bag of flour has been opened, the flour should be stored in an airtight container.

Sweeteners

Here are some of the most common sweeteners used in baking. All should be stored in tightly closed containers in a cool, dry place.

◆ Granulated sugar is white table sugar.

◆ Brown sugar is granulated sugar with molasses added. Dark brown sugar has a stronger flavor than light brown.

◆ Powdered, or confectioner's, sugar has a fine texture.

◆ Honey is a liquid sweetener with a distinct flavor. Use it only when the recipe calls for it.

You can also buy artificial sweeteners. Use these only in recipes that have been specifically developed for them.

Sweeteners differ in flavor, texture, and amount of moisture.

Baking Breads   349

Leavening Agents

Quick bread recipes call for either baking powder or baking soda. Check packages of baking powder for a "use by" date. After that date, the products won't give good results.

Store baking soda and baking powder in a cool, dry place. Baking powder must always be kept dry, so cover it tightly.

The most common type of yeast is called active dry yeast. It's sold in a package and doesn't need refrigeration. You can buy regular or quick-acting. Use yeast by the date on the package.

Fats and Oils

The fats and oils most commonly used in baking are butter, margarine, vegetable oil, lard, and shortening. Each one gives a slightly different flavor and texture. Lard is highest in saturated fat, while vegetable oil is lowest.

Solid fats and liquid fats can't be used in place of one another in baking. The results won't be the same.

Butter, margarine, and lard should be stored in the refrigerator. Shortening should be stored in a cool, dry place. Vegetable oils will stay usable longer if stored in the refrigerator. Most have been treated to prevent them from turning cloudy when cold. Olive oil, however, isn't treated and is often stored in a cool, dry place.

Try It!

Fat or Oil?

What happens if you substitute liquid fat (oil) for solid fat? Cut 3 Tbsp. chilled butter into 1/2 cup flour. Mix in 1 Tbsp. water. Then add 3 Tbsp. oil or melted butter to another 1/2 cup flour. Mix in 1 Tbsp. water.

★ Compare the textures of the two mixtures. How do they differ?

★ Compare several recipes for pie crust. Do they use fat or oil? Do you think substituting one for the other would affect the texture of the finished crust? Explain.

CONVENIENCE FORMS

If you don't have time to bake breads from scratch, you can use convenience forms. For example, refrigerated biscuits are ready to bake. With boxed quick bread mixes, you mix in the liquid and bake according to package directions.

Refrigerated or frozen yeast dough gives you homemade taste in less time than making your own dough. Refrigerated dough is ready to bake. Frozen dough is usually placed in a greased pan to thaw and rise before baking.

Of course, you can also buy ready-made breads, fresh or frozen. However, preparing your own can be creative and satisfying. What are some other reasons for choosing to bake your own breads?

Convenience quick breads can help you eat a nutritious breakfast, even if you don't have much time.

STORING BREADS

Wrap home-prepared breads tightly. For best flavor, store them at room temperature. However, in hot, humid weather, you may need to refrigerate yeast bread to keep mold from growing. In either case, use home-prepared breads within a few days. For longer storage, freeze them. Store convenience products according to package directions.

FOOD SKILLS

The leavening agent is not the only difference between quick breads and yeast breads. The preparation method also differs.

Before baking, yeast bread dough is set aside in a warm place for at least an hour. This gives the yeast time to grow, which makes the dough rise. Quick breads, however, are baked as soon as they're mixed.

The mixing method varies, too. Most quick breads are mixed in one of two basic ways. One is called the muffin method, and the other is the biscuit method. Once you know these two basic mixing methods, you'll find it easy to follow all kinds of quick bread recipes.

MAKING MUFFINS

The **muffin method** of mixing gets its name because it's used for muffins. The same method is also used for pancakes, waffles, cornbread, and loaves like banana bread.

First the dry ingredients are mixed together in a bowl. Then the liquid ingredients are combined and added to the dry ingredients. The recipe for Surprise Muffins on page 356 gives specific directions.

The batter is mixed just long enough to moisten the dry ingredients. The batter should be lumpy, not smooth. Too much mixing can cause an irregular shape, a tough crust, and tunnels.

Over-mixed muffin

Lumpy batter gives you a muffin that's well-shaped and evenly textured.

To check muffins and quick bread loaves for doneness:

◆ Check the appearance. The crust should be golden brown, slightly rough, and shiny.

◆ The sides of the quick bread should have pulled away slightly from the sides of the pan.

◆ When the top is tapped gently, it should feel firm.

Check the recipe to see whether the product should cool in the pan. Some quick breads are best when served warm. Before removing muffins and loaves from the pan, first loosen them by running a spatula around the product.

MAKING BISCUITS

Biscuits are mixed in a different way. The **biscuit method** of mixing gives biscuits their flaky texture.

How to Mix Biscuit Dough

1. Sift the dry ingredients together in a mixing bowl.

2. Add the shortening to the dry ingredients. Cut it in using a pastry blender, two table knives, or a fork. Stop when the mixture looks like large crumbs.

3. Add the milk. Mix with a fork to make a soft dough.

STEP 3

Tip   The dough should come away from the sides of the bowl.

STEP 2

After the biscuit dough is mixed, it's kneaded. To **knead** means to work or press the dough with your hands. Kneading helps gluten, the elastic structure of the dough, to form.

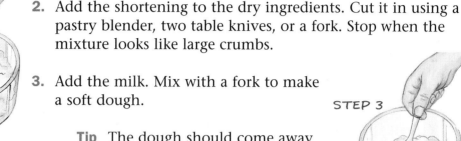

How to Knead Biscuit Dough

1. Turn the dough out onto a clean, lightly floured surface.

2. Gently fold the dough in half.

3. Push down on the dough with the heels of both hands.

4. Give the dough a quarter turn. Continue to knead by repeating the folding and pushing process.

STEP 2

STEP 3

STEP 4

Biscuit dough should be kneaded for only about 30 seconds. If you knead too long, the biscuits will be tough.

Next, roll and cut the biscuits.

How to Roll and Cut Biscuits

STEP 1

1. Using light, gentle strokes, roll the dough out into a circle 1/2 inch thick.

2. Dip the cutter in flour. Cut the biscuits, pushing straight down.

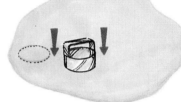

STEP 2

Why? Flour keeps the dough from sticking to the cutter. Cutting straight down will give you evenly shaped biscuits.

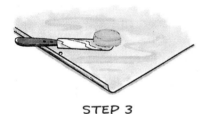

STEP 3

3. Use a spatula or turner to move the biscuits to the baking sheet. Leave about 1 inch space between the biscuits.

4. Push the leftover dough together. Don't knead it.

Why? Kneading the dough again would make the gluten too strong. The biscuits would be tough.

5. Roll and cut more biscuits.

Bake the biscuits in a preheated oven for the time given in the recipe. To test them for doneness:

◆ Check the color. The biscuits should be lightly browned on top. The sides will be a lighter, creamy color.

◆ Check the shape and height. The sides should be straight. The biscuits should be doubled in size.

Serve the biscuits while still warm or let them cool on a wire rack before storing.

Making Yeast Breads

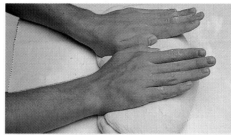

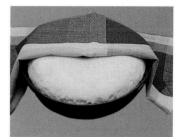

1. Yeast comes alive. Dry yeast is added to warm water. When the mixture bubbles, it's ready to use.

2. Kneading. After other ingredients are mixed in, the dough is kneaded for a few minutes. Kneading helps form gluten, making the dough stretchy.

3. Rising. Dough is covered with a cloth and set in a warm place to rise. It will double in size as gas bubbles form and grow.

4. Shaping. Dough is punched down, then shaped into rolls or loaves.

5. Rising. Rolls or loaves are allowed to rise again.

6. Baking. Heat firms the gluten, setting the shape of the loaf. The gas bubbles made by the yeast escape, leaving tiny holes in the bread. The crust turns golden brown.

Baking Breads **355**

Try these muffins for breakfast, a snack, or dessert!

◆ How can you tell if muffin batter has been overmixed?

◆ What other ingredients could be used as a "surprise" in the center of these muffins?

Surprise Muffins

Yield: 12 muffins

2	bananas (or 1 mango or papaya)		½ tsp.	salt
1¾ cups	all-purpose flour		¾ cup	fat-free milk
⅓ cup	sugar		¼ cup	vegetable oil
1 Tbsp.	baking powder		1	egg

1. Peel fruit and cut into 1-inch chunks. (You'll need 12 pieces.) Set aside.
2. Preheat oven to 400°F. Lightly grease twelve (2-inch) muffin cups or use paper liners.
3. In a medium bowl, combine flour, sugar, baking powder, and salt.
4. In a small bowl, stir together milk, oil, and egg.
5. Add liquid ingredients all at once to dry ingredients. Stir until the dry ingredients are just moistened, about 15 strokes. Do not overmix. Batter will be lumpy.
6. Spoon 1 Tbsp. batter into each muffin cup. Place 1 piece of fruit in each muffin cup. Spoon remaining batter evenly over fruit.
7. Bake 22 to 24 minutes or until golden brown.
8. Cool 5 minutes on wire rack. Remove muffins from pan.

Nutrition Notes

Per muffin: 156 calories, 5 g fat
Good source of: vitamin E, thiamin

MICROWAVING BREADS

You can make muffins and other quick breads in the microwave oven. Usually a round or ring-shaped pan is used. Follow the directions in a microwave cookbook.

Quick breads made in the microwave have a heavier and coarser texture. In addition, they don't brown. To make up for the lack of color, you can add a topping, such as chopped nuts, toasted coconut, or a sugar and cinnamon mixture. After microwaving biscuits, you can brush them with melted butter or margarine and broil in a conventional oven.

Yeast breads are seldom baked in a microwave oven. They would not turn out the same as with conventional baking. However, the microwave oven can be helpful for some steps in a yeast bread recipe. You might use it to warm ingredients to the right temperature or to thaw frozen bread dough. Check the owner's manual or a microwave recipe book for instructions.

Microwave Hints

* If you don't have a microwave-safe muffin pan, arrange custard cups in a circle on a plate.

* To reheat quick breads, microwave uncovered at 100% power. One muffin takes about 10 seconds if at room temperature or 15 seconds if frozen. Don't overheat or the bread will be tough.

CHAPTER 43 REVIEW

Understanding Key Ideas

1. Why can quick breads be prepared in less time than yeast breads?
2. What can breads contribute to a healthful eating plan?
3. Why is it important to look carefully at the labels of baking ingredients when shopping?
4. Which types of fats should be refrigerated? How should others be stored?
5. Contrast the muffin method and the biscuit method of mixing.
6. Describe what is done to yeast bread dough after mixing and before baking.

Applying Knowledge and Skills

◆ **Convenience Comparison:** Prepare a convenience bread and a similar product made from a recipe. Compare cost, nutrition, appearance, flavor, and texture.

When might you choose each product? Why?

◆ **Kneading Experiment:** Prepare a biscuit recipe. Before kneading, divide the dough into three portions. Knead one portion exactly as the recipe directs. Roll out the second portion without kneading. Knead the third portion longer than the recipe directs. Bake the biscuits and compare the results. What can you conclude about kneading, gluten, and the texture of biscuits?

Exploring Further

◆ **Sourdough Bread:** Learn how and why the method for making sourdough bread differs from that for other types of yeast bread. Report to the class.

COOKIES, CAKES, AND PIES

Many kinds of cookies, cakes, and pies originated centuries ago. Every country and culture has its own special baked sweets, which are often a traditional part of celebrations.

Discover...

★ how cookies, cakes, and pies fit into a healthful eating plan.

★ convenience forms of cookies, cakes, and pies.

★ how to prepare and store different kinds of cookies, cakes, and pies.

Key Terms

shortened cakes
foam cakes
pastry

FOOD FOR THOUGHT

How many different kinds of cookies can you think of? What about cakes and pies? What are some of your favorites?

NUTRITION NOTES

Cookies, cakes, and pies are delicious treats. They're usually high in calories, fat, and sugar, but can be part of a healthful eating plan. Just enjoy them in moderation—once in a while or on special occasions.

Some baked treats have ingredients that add vitamins, minerals, and fiber. Examples include carrot or oatmeal cookies, banana or date cake, and pumpkin or strawberry pie.

Some cookies, including fig bars and gingersnaps, are low in fat. Angel food cake has almost no fat. You can also save fat and calories by choosing pies with only one crust instead of two.

CONSUMER POWER

Cookies, cakes, and pies can be made from the same basic ingredients as other baked goods. Review the buying and storing information on pages 349-350. Remember to use the specific type of product called for in the recipe. For example, some cake recipes require cake flour.

BUYING CONVENIENCE FORMS

There are many products to help you prepare cakes, cookies, and pies more quickly and easily.

◆ Packaged cookie and cake mixes are usually dry. They require the addition of liquids and often other ingredients, such as oil or eggs.

◆ Refrigerated cookie dough is ready for baking.

◆ Convenience pie crusts can be found in several forms: packaged mixes, dough sticks, ready-to-use rolled pastry, and ready-to-fill frozen pastry shells.

◆ Pie fillings may be canned or made from packaged mixes.

When buying, read the labels on these products carefully. Are low-fat varieties available? How do calories and nutrition compare? If you have time, could you bake from scratch and save money?

STORING COOKIES, CAKES, AND PIES

Check the labels of convenience products for storage instructions. Proper storage will also let home-baked treats keep their quality longer.

Store crisp cookies and soft cookies in separate containers. For crisp cookies, use a loose-fitting cover. Soft cookies should have a tight-fitting cover to keep them moist. Most cookies can also be frozen.

Using the right type of container will help cookies keep their texture.

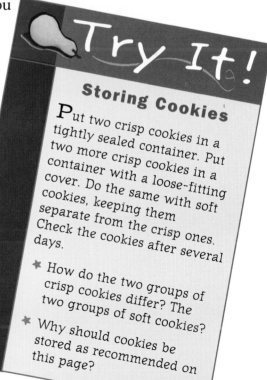

Try It!

Storing Cookies

Put two crisp cookies in a tightly sealed container. Put two more crisp cookies in a container with a loose-fitting cover. Do the same with soft cookies, keeping them separate from the crisp ones. Check the cookies after several days.

★ How do the two groups of crisp cookies differ? The two groups of soft cookies?

★ Why should cookies be stored as recommended on this page?

Cookies, Cakes, and Pies   359

Cakes with cream fillings are perishable. Store them in the refrigerator. Other cakes can be stored in tightly closed containers at room temperature for a few days. Cakes can be frozen for longer storage.

Refrigerate custard and cream pies immediately after baking. If they stand at room temperature, harmful bacteria can grow rapidly. Store fruit pies in the refrigerator and heat them to serve warm.

 # FOOD SKILLS

Baking cookies, cakes, and pies lets you be creative. Many people gain satisfaction from baking treats for special occasions and to give as gifts.

COOKIES

Most cookies are a variation of six basic types. The main difference in these types is the way they're shaped.

Bar cookies are baked in a square or rectangular pan, just like a cake. After baking, the cookies are cut into bars or squares. Brownies are a popular bar cookie.

Drop cookies are made by dropping teaspoonfuls of batter onto a baking sheet. Chocolate chip cookies are usually made by this method.

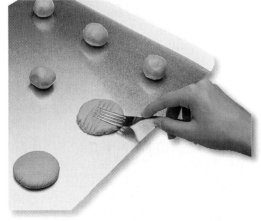

Molded cookies are made from a stiff dough and shaped by hand. One common method is to roll the dough into balls about the size of walnuts. The balls are spaced on a baking sheet and flattened with a fork or the bottom of a glass. Some peanut butter cookies are molded this way.

Pressed cookies are made by pushing the dough through a cookie press onto a baking sheet. The cookie press comes with several design plates to give the cookies different shapes. The dough must be stiff enough to keep the shape of the design. Spritz cookies are an example.

Rolled cookies are made by rolling out a stiff dough to the thickness specified in the recipe. Then cookie cutters are used to cut shapes. Sometimes the cookies are decorated with colored sugar or frosting.

Refrigerator cookies are sliced from a long roll of chilled dough and baked on a cookie sheet.

Tips for Making Cookies

Cookies should be well shaped and delicately browned with a pleasing flavor and texture. Here are some tips for good-looking, good-tasting cookies.

◆ Sometimes dough sticks to the fork, rolling pin, or cookie cutters. Try dipping utensils in flour or sprinkling some flour on the rolling pin. Use just a little flour. Too much will make the cookies tough and dry.

- Make all cookies in a batch the same shape and thickness. If some are thin and some thick, the thin ones will be done before the thick ones.

- Prepare the pan according to recipe directions. Check the recipe for how to space cookies on the sheet. Some types of cookies spread as they bake.

- Allow hot cookie sheets to cool before using them again. If you put cookie dough on a hot baking sheet, the dough will melt and spread. If you have two cookie sheets, one can cool while the other is in the oven.

- An extra minute or two of heat can overbrown cookies. Watch them carefully.

- Test bar and drop cookies for doneness by pressing lightly with your finger. The imprint of your finger should show slightly.

- Follow recipe directions for cooling cookies. Some can cool in the pan. Others are removed while hot and cooled on a wire rack. Use a wide spatula or turner to remove them.

Warm cookies are fragile, so handle them gently.

These bar cookies are easy and fun to make—and taste great, too!

◆ How do bar cookies differ from the other five basic types of cookies?

◆ How should these cookies be stored?

Jammin' Bars

Yield: 25 cookies, $1\frac{1}{2}$ x $1\frac{1}{2}$ inch each

1 cup	packed brown sugar
$\frac{1}{3}$ cup	butter or margarine, softened
1	egg

$\frac{1}{2}$ tsp.	vanilla extract
$1\frac{1}{2}$ cups	all-purpose flour
1 cup	uncooked quick oats
$\frac{1}{4}$ tsp.	salt
$\frac{3}{4}$ cup	peach or apricot jam or preserves

1. Preheat oven to 375°F. Lightly grease an 8 x 8 x 2-inch baking pan.
2. In a medium bowl, cream brown sugar and butter until light and fluffy.
3. Add egg and vanilla. Beat until blended.
4. Stir in flour, oats, and salt until combined.
5. Reserve $\frac{3}{4}$ cup of batter. Press remaining batter evenly into prepared pan.
6. Spread jam or preserves over batter. Drop tablespoonfuls of reserved batter over jam.
7. Bake 25 to 27 minutes or until lightly browned.
8. Cool on wire rack. Slice into $1\frac{1}{2}$ x $1\frac{1}{2}$-inch squares.

Nutrition Notes

Per cookie: 135 calories, 3 g fat
Good source of: carbohydrates

CAKES

There are two basic types of cakes: shortened and foam.

◆ Cakes that contain fat—such as shortening, margarine, or oil—are called **shortened cakes**. For leavening, they use baking powder or baking soda. Shortened cakes can be baked in round, square, rectangular, or specially shaped pans. Two or more layers may be put together with frosting.

◆ Angel food cake and sponge cake are examples of **foam cakes**. For leavening, they use the air beaten into egg whites. They don't include fat or oil. Most foam cakes are baked in a tube pan—a deep, round pan with a tube in the center. The tube helps the heat get to the center quickly so the cake bakes evenly. The pan is left ungreased so the cake can cling to the sides. That helps it rise.

Tips for Baking Cakes

A properly made cake should have a smooth, slightly rounded top. The inside should be finely textured without tunnels or air bubbles. When you taste it, the cake should be moist, tender, and pleasantly flavored.

Proper mixing is one key to a successful cake. The mixing method will vary depending on the type of cake and the recipe. Follow directions carefully. Review the other baking principles discussed in Chapter 42.

To test a cake for doneness, check the top. It should be evenly browned. When you tap the top gently, it should spring back. Look at the area where the top meets the sides of the pan. A shortened cake should be pulled away from the sides of the pan. A foam cake will continue to cling to the sides of the pan.

If the top springs back, the cake is done.

After Baking

Shortened cakes are removed from the pan after baking and cooled on a wire rack.

How to Remove a Cake from the Pan

1. Run a spatula around the sides of the pan between the cake and the pan.

2. Place a wire rack over the top of the cake. Hold the cake and the rack securely with pot holders.

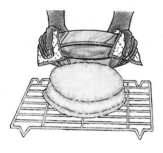

STEP 2

3. Turn the cake and rack upside down. Place the wire rack on a level surface, such as a table or counter.

STEP 3

4. Lift off the cake pan. It should come off easily.

STEP 4

5. The cake is now upside down. Place another wire rack on the cake. Grasp both wire racks with both hands. Quickly turn them so the cake layer is right side up.

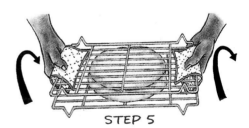

STEP 5

6. Remove the top wire rack. Allow the cake to cool on the bottom wire rack.

STEP 6

Foam cakes, such as angel food cakes, are cooled in the pan. The pan is turned upside down so the cake won't fall.

Once the cake has completely cooled, it can be decorated with frosting or powdered sugar. You can also top cake with fresh fruit.

Most tube pans rest on metal legs when upside down. You can also slip the tube over the neck of an empty bottle.

PIES

A pie is a combination of a crust and a flavorful filling.

◆ A two-crust pie has a bottom and top crust with a filling in between. Usually a fruit filling, such as apple, is used.

◆ A one-crust pie has a bottom crust only. Sometimes the crust is baked first. Then a ready-to-eat filling, such as chocolate pudding, is poured into the baked crust. One-crust pies often have toppings such as whipped cream or a meringue (a mixture of sugar and stiffly beaten egg whites).

◆ A deep-dish pie is a fruit pie with only a top crust. Fruit filling is placed in a baking dish, covered with a crust, and baked. The pie is often served hot.

No matter what type of pie you're making, it should have an even, tender crust that's nicely browned. The crust should have a delicate, crisp texture. Pastry crusts should be flaky. The filling should be thick, but not sticky. The whole pie should have a rich, delicate flavor.

Crusts

The most common pie crust is made from pastry. **Pastry** is a mixture of flour, fat, cold water, and salt. When mixed properly, the pastry forms flaky layers as it bakes.

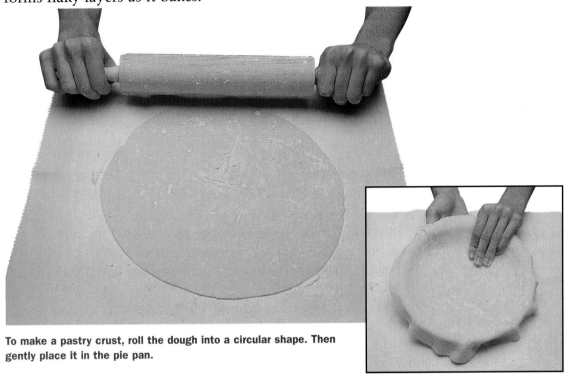

To make a pastry crust, roll the dough into a circular shape. Then gently place it in the pie pan.

If you're making a one-crust pie that doesn't have to be baked, you can use a crumb crust. It can be made from finely crushed graham crackers, gingersnaps, vanilla wafers, or chocolate cookies. The crumbs are mixed with melted butter or margarine and sugar. The mixture is pressed into a pie pan, baked, and cooled. Then the filling is added. You can also buy a ready-to-bake crumb crust.

Fillings

Pie fillings can be made from scratch or prepared from convenience products.

◆ Fruit is the most popular filling for pie. You can use fresh, frozen, or canned fruit. Follow recipe directions for sweetening and thickening. Canned fruit pie filling is ready to use.

◆ Cream pies have a pudding-type filling. The mixture is poured into a baked pie shell. Packaged mixes for puddings and pie fillings sometimes have to be cooked first. Others are instant mixes.

◆ The filling in custard pies contains eggs and milk. They're baked with the crust.

◆ Chiffon pies are made with gelatin and flavored with fruit. Beaten egg whites make the pie lighter.

MICROWAVE METHODS

Some types of cookies, cakes, and pies can be prepared in the microwave oven. Remember that microwaving differs from conventional baking. Recipes developed for microwave use should give good results if you follow directions carefully.

Bar cookies and shortened cakes adapt well to microwaving. Some can be mixed and microwaved in the same dish. For best results, use a microwave-safe round pan or ring mold. If you use a pan with corners, the batter in the corners will cook faster. These parts may get hard and dry.

To microwave a one-crust pie, precook the crust before adding the filling. Otherwise the crust won't be done. Two-crust pies should be baked in a conventional oven.

With a dark-colored batter, the lack of browning isn't noticeable. For a fancy design, try sprinkling powdered sugar through a paper doily.

Microwaved products won't brown. To make up for the lack of browning, you might choose recipes that are a dark color, such as chocolate cookies or spice cake. You can also top foods with chopped nuts, frosting, or a sprinkling of cinnamon and sugar. Try adding yellow food coloring to the water when mixing pie crust. You can also microwave the crust, then broil in a conventional oven until lightly browned.

Microwave Hints

* It's easier to check bar cookies for doneness if you use a clear glass baking dish. Microwave until they look set on the bottom.

* For cakes and pies, use the tests for doneness given in the recipe. Standing time may be needed to complete the cooking.

CHAPTER 44 REVIEW

Understanding Key Ideas

1. What points should you remember when including cookies, cakes, and pies in your eating plan?
2. What products could help you save time when making a pie?
3. What types of cookies, cakes, and pies should be refrigerated? How should others be stored?
4. How can extra flour be helpful and harmful when making cookies?
5. How do shortened cakes and foam cakes differ in ingredients?
6. Which is a better filling for a graham cracker crumb crust: a custard or instant pudding? Why?

Applying Knowledge and Skills

◆ **Recipe Analysis:** Choose a cookie, cake, or pie recipe. Which category described in the chapter (such as molded cookie or shortened cake) does this recipe represent? How can you tell? Discuss the nutrients that the ingredients contribute. If possible, prepare the recipe and evaluate the results.

Exploring Further

◆ **Social Studies:** Learn about the types of cookies, cakes, or pies linked with a specific celebration in another culture. Report to the class.

◆ **Consumer Research:** Research the nutrition, cost, and preparation time for three different types of convenience pie crust products. How do they compare to making pie crust from a recipe?

GLOSSARY

This glossary defines all vocabulary terms listed at the beginning of each chapter, plus selected additional terms explained in the text. Within the definitions, *italics* indicate words that have their own glossary entries.

A

aerobic (uh-ROE-bik). Helping the body use and take in more oxygen than it normally does. Used to describe certain types of exercise, such as running. (Ch. 4)

amino acids (uh-MEE-no). Chemical "building blocks" that combine to make different *proteins*. (Ch. 5)

au gratin (oh GRAH-tun). Topped with cheese or buttered bread crumbs. (Ch. 10)

B

bacteria (bak-TEER-ee-uh). Tiny living things that can be seen only with a microscope. (Ch. 21)

bake. To cook food in *dry heat* in an oven. Also called *roast*. (Ch. 18)

basal metabolic rate (BAY-suhl meh-tuh-BALL-ik). The speed at which your body uses energy for basic processes. (Ch. 6)

base. The decorative foundation of a salad on which other *ingredients* are placed. (Ch. 37)

baste. To brush or pour liquid over food as it cooks. (Ch. 15)

beat. To stir very quickly. May be done with a spoon, wire whisk, rotary beater, or electric mixer. (Ch. 15)

biscuit method. A mixing method in which a solid fat is combined with the dry *ingredients*, then liquid is added. (Ch. 43)

blend. To mix *ingredients* together thoroughly until they're completely uniform. (Ch. 15)

body. Main part of a salad. (Ch. 37)

boil. To heat a liquid until bubbles rise to the surface and break; or to cook food in boiling liquid. (Ch. 15)

bouillon (boo-YOHN). Clear, flavorful *broth*. (Ch. 38)

braise. To *brown* food in a small amount of hot fat, then cook it slowly in *moist heat*. (Ch. 18)

bran. The outer covering of a grain kernel. (Ch. 29)

broil. To cook food by direct heat from above. (Ch. 18)

broth. The liquid in soup. (Ch. 38)

brown. To cook food briefly until the surface turns brown. (Ch. 15)

C

caffeine (kaff-EEN). A chemical that stimulates the nervous system; found in some beverages. (Ch. 41)

calorie. A unit of measure for energy supplied by food or used by the body. (Ch. 6)

carbohydrates (kar-bo-HIGH-drates). *Nutrients* made up of carbon, hydrogen, and oxygen; your body's main source of energy. (Ch. 5)

career. The work you choose to do for a long period or in one field. (Ch. 3)

casserole. A mixture of foods baked together; also, the type of dish the mixture is baked in. (Ch. 14, Ch. 39)

cholesterol (kuh-LESS-tuh-rol). Fat-like substance that helps the body carry out its many processes. (Ch. 5)

chop. To cut food into small irregular pieces. (Ch. 15)

chowder. Thick soup made with vegetables, fish, or seafood. (Ch. 38)

colander (KOLL-uhn-der). A bowl-shaped utensil with many small holes; used to *drain* foods. (Ch. 14)

complete proteins. *Proteins* that contain all the essential *amino acids* in the right amounts. (Ch. 5)

complex carbohydrates. Starches; one of two types of *carbohydrates*. (Ch. 5)

convection oven. Oven in which a fan circulates heated air at high speed. (Ch. 13)

conventional oven. Oven in which heated air flows naturally around the food and cooks it. (Ch. 13)

cooking power. The amount of electricity a *microwave oven* uses to create *microwaves*. Measured in watts. (Ch. 19)

cream. To *beat* shortening and sugar until soft, smooth, and creamy. (Ch. 15)

cross-contamination. Letting harmful *bacteria* spread from raw foods to other foods. (Ch. 21)

croutons (KROO-tawnz). Seasoned, toasted bread cubes. (Ch. 37)

cube. To cut food into same-size pieces about 1/2 inch or more on each side. (Ch. 15)

curd. The solid part of milk after it has been thickened. Used to make cheese. (Ch. 28)

curdle. To become separated into many small lumps and a watery liquid. Milk may curdle if improperly cooked. (Ch. 27)

cured. Treated with *ingredients* that slow spoilage and add a distinctive flavor. (Ch. 33)

customary system. Most commonly used system of measurement in the United States. (Ch. 16)

cut. A slice or portion of meat from a specific part of an animal. (Ch. 35)

cut in. To mix shortening and flour using a pastry blender or two knives and a cutting motion. (Ch. 15)

D

danger zone. The temperature range in which *bacteria* multiply fastest: between 40°F and 140°F. (Ch. 21)

deep-fat fry. To cook food by completely covering it in hot fat. (Ch. 18)

diabetes (die-uh-BEE-tuss). A condition in which the body can't control blood sugar properly. (Ch. 11)

dice. To cut food into same-size pieces about 1/4 inch on each side. (Ch. 15)

diet. The total balance of foods that you eat over a period of time. (Ch. 7)

disposables. Products that are used once or a few times and then thrown away. (Ch. 23)

dovetailing. Working ahead on some tasks while others are still going on. (Ch. 22)

drain. To remove excess liquid from a food. (Ch. 15)

dry heat methods. Ways to cook foods uncovered without adding liquid or fat. They include *broiling, panbroiling,* and *baking* or *roasting*. (Ch. 18)

E

eating disorders. Illnesses that involve harmful attitudes about the body, self, and food, as well as actions that are dangerous to health. (Ch. 11)

enriched. A term used to describe foods with added *nutrients*. (Ch. 12)

enriched grain products. Grain products made by removing the *bran* and *germ* from the grain kernel, then adding iron and B vitamins to partly make up for lost *nutrients*. (Ch. 29)

entry-level job. A job which does not require experience or a college degree. (Ch. 3)

equivalent (ee-KWIV-uh-lunt). A measurement that is equal in value to another measurement. (Ch. 16)

evaluate. To judge how well you reached your goal. (Ch. 2)

F

fat-soluble vitamins. Vitamins A, D, E, and K, which can mix only with fat. (Ch. 5)

fiber. Plant materials that your body can't digest completely. (Ch. 5)

fillets (fill-AYS). Sides of fish cut away from the ribs and backbone. (Ch. 34)

flammable. Burns easily. (Ch. 20)

flatware. Items such as forks and spoons. (Ch. 25)

foam cakes. Cakes that are made with beaten egg whites and without fat or oil. (Ch. 44)

fold in. To combine two foods, such as beaten egg whites and batter, with a very gentle motion. (Ch. 15)

food allergy. A condition in which eating a particular food triggers a reaction in the body's immune system. (Ch. 11)

foodborne illness. Illness caused by food that's not safe to eat. (Ch. 21)

food guides. Simple guidelines to help you make healthy food choices, such as the Dietary Guidelines for Americans. (Ch. 7)

food intolerance. Inability to digest certain foods. (Ch. 11)

food safety. Taking steps to prevent *foodborne illness.* (Ch. 21)

fortified. A term used to describe foods with added *nutrients.* (Ch. 12)

fruit punch. A mixture of fruit juices. (Ch. 41)

fry. To cook in hot fat or oil. (Ch. 18)

G H

garnish. To decorate a food or dish with a small, colorful food such as parsley or a lemon slice. (Ch. 15)

generic (juh-NEHR-ik). Term used to describe plain label products that are less expensive than brand name products. (Ch. 12)

germ. The innermost sprouting section of a grain kernel from which a new plant can grow. (Ch. 29)

gluten (GLOO-tuhn). An elastic substance formed by the *protein* in flour. (Ch. 42)

grate. To rub food on a grater to make very fine particles. (Ch. 15)

homogenized (huh-MAH-jen-ized). Term that describes milk processed so that the cream does not separate. Fat is broken into tiny drops and mixed permanently with the milk. (Ch. 27)

hydrogenated oil (hy-DRAH-juh-nay-ted). Oil that has been turned into a more solid fat. In the process, it becomes more *saturated.* (Ch. 5)

I J K

impulse buying. Buying an item you don't need just because it seems appealing at the moment. (Ch. 12)

incomplete proteins. *Proteins* that lack one or more of the essential *amino acids* needed by the body. (Ch. 5)

ingredients. Foods in a *recipe.* Also, what a purchased food product is made of. (Ch. 15)

knead (NEED). To work or press dough with your hands. (Ch. 43)

L

leavening agent (LEH-vuh-ning). Substance that helps a baked product rise. Examples include baking powder, baking soda and yeast. (Ch. 42)

legumes (leh-GYOUMZ). Seeds that grow in a pod. Dry beans and dry peas are legumes. (Ch. 32)

long-term goal. Something you plan to accomplish in the far future. (Ch. 1)

M

management. Using *resources* wisely to meet goals. (Ch. 2)

marbling. Flecks of fat within the muscle tissue of meat. (Ch. 35)

marinade. Liquid in which meat may be soaked before cooking to add flavor and tenderness. Usually a mixture of an acid food, such as citrus juice or vinegar, and seasonings. (Ch. 35)

meal management. Using your *management* skills to help you prepare good meals. (Ch. 24)

meal pattern. The number of meals and snacks you eat throughout the day and when you eat them. (Ch. 9)

menu. A list of foods that you plan to serve at a meal. (Ch. 24)

meringue (mur-ANG). A mixture of egg whites and sugar beaten until stiff peaks form, then baked. (Ch. 36)

metric system. Standard system of measurement in most of the world. (Ch. 16)

microwave oven. Oven in which tiny waves of energy produce heat inside the food. (Ch. 13)

microwaves. Tiny waves of energy produced by a *microwave oven*. (Ch. 19)

mince. To *chop* food until the pieces are as small as possible. (Ch. 15)

moist heat methods. Ways of cooking foods using a hot liquid, steam, or both. (Ch. 18)

muffin method. A mixing method in which the liquid and dry *ingredients* are mixed in separate bowls, then combined and mixed briefly. (Ch. 43)

mulled. Term describing a beverage, such as fruit juice or punch, that is spiced and served hot. (Ch. 41)

N O

nutrient density. A way of comparing the amount of energy, or *calories*, supplied by a food with the *nutrients* it provides. (Ch. 6)

nutrients. Chemicals in food that the body needs to work properly. (Ch. 4)

omelet (AHM-let). A dish made by cooking beaten eggs in a pancake-like shape. Usually folded in half with a filling. (Ch. 36)

opaque (oh-PAKE). Not clear; solid color that you can't see through. Fish turns opaque as it cooks. (Ch. 34)

osteoporosis (AH-stee-oh-pour-OH-sis). A condition in which one's bones, having lost calcium, become so weak they can break very easily. (Ch. 5)

P Q

panbroil. To cook food in a skillet without added fat. (Ch. 18)

panfry. To cook food in a skillet in a small amount of fat. (Ch. 18)

pare. To cut a very thin layer of peel from fruits or vegetables. (Ch. 15)

pasta. General term for spaghetti, macaroni, noodles, and similar products. (Ch. 29)

pasteurized (PASS-tyoor-ized). Term for milk that has been heat-treated to kill harmful *bacteria*. (Ch. 27)

pastry. A mixture of flour, fat, cold water, and salt, often used for pie crust. (Ch. 44)

peak season. A certain time of year when the supply of a particular fruit or vegetable is greatest, quality is highest, and prices are generally lowest. (Ch. 30)

perishable. Spoils easily. (Ch. 21)

phytochemicals (FIE-toe-KEH-mih-kulz). Natural chemicals, found in fruits and vegetables, that may help prevent diseases. (Ch. 5)

place setting. The arrangement of tableware for each individual who will be served a meal. (Ch. 25)

poison control center. A place you can call on the telephone that has a staff specially trained to deal with poison emergencies. (Ch. 20)

poultry. Birds raised for food, such as chickens and turkeys. (Ch. 33)

pre-preparation. Getting food or equipment ready to use in a *recipe*. (Ch. 22)

processing. Steps that are taken to prepare and package food for sale. (Ch. 12)

proteins (PRO-teens). A type of *nutrient* that the body uses to build new cells and repair injured ones. (Ch. 5)

puree (pure-RAY *or* pure-EE). To put food through a blender, food processor, food mill, or strainer so it becomes a smooth, thick mass. (Ch. 15)

Pyramid serving. The amount of a food that is considered one serving when using the Food Guide Pyramid. (Ch. 8)

quiche (KEESH). A main-dish pie with a filling made of eggs, milk, and various other *ingredients*. (Ch. 36)

R

recipe. A guide to help you prepare a certain food. (Ch. 15)

reconstitute. To replace water that has been removed from a food. (Ch. 27)

resource. Something you can use to help meet your goals. (Ch. 2)

retail cuts. The *cuts* of meat that you can buy in the store; come from dividing *wholesale cuts* into smaller pieces. (Ch. 35)

ripe. Having developed full flavor and sweetness; ready to eat. (Ch. 30)

roast. To cook food in *dry heat* in an oven. Also called *bake*. (Ch. 18)

S

saturated fats. Fats that tend to raise the amount of *cholesterol* in the blood. Found in all animal foods and in the tropical oils (coconut, palm, and palm kernel). (Ch. 5)

sautéing (saw-TAY-ing). Quickly *panfrying* a food, such as chopped onions, until softened. (Ch. 18)

scalloped. Baked in a creamy sauce topped with crumbs. (Ch. 10)

score. To make cuts partway through a piece of meat in order to tenderize it. (Ch. 35)

self-confidence. Your belief in your ability to succeed. (Ch. 1)

self-rising flour. Flour that already has a *leavening agent* and salt in it when you buy it. (Ch. 43)

shortened cakes. Cakes that contain fat, such as shortening, margarine, or oil. (Ch. 44)

short-term goal. A task that can be accomplished in the near future. It may help you reach a *long-term goal*. (Ch. 1)

shred. To cut food into long, thin pieces. (Ch. 15)

shucked. With the shell removed. Some shellfish, such as clams, can be bought already shucked. (Ch. 34)

sift. To put a dry *ingredient*, such as flour, through a fine sieve or sifter in order to separate the particles. (Ch. 17)

simmer. To heat a liquid just until bubbles form slowly, but do not reach the surface; or to cook food in simmering liquid. (Ch. 15)

simple carbohydrates. Sugars; one of two types of *carbohydrates*. (Ch. 5)

slice. To cut food into thin, flat pieces. (Ch. 15)

spread. A seasoned mixture of meat, *poultry*, fish, beans, or cheese that can be spread on another food, such as crackers. (Ch. 40)

standing time. The short period of time that food is allowed to stand after microwaving. This allows the food to finish cooking and heat to penetrate all areas of the food. (Ch. 19)

steam. To cook food over, not in, *boiling* liquid. (Ch. 18)

stemware. Beverage glasses that have a stem between the base and the bowl. (Ch. 25)

stir-fry. To cook food quickly in a small amount of hot oil while stirring constantly. (Ch. 18)

stock. Flavorful *broth*, usually made from bony pieces of meat or *poultry* combined with seasonings and cooked slowly in water. Used as a base for soup. (Ch. 38)

stress. Emotional and physical tension caused by events in your life and the way you react to them. (Ch. 4)

surimi (soo-REE-mee). Product made from chopped fish and flavoring; used to make imitation shellfish. (Ch. 34)

T

tender-crisp. Tender but still firm; describes properly cooked vegetables. (Ch. 31)

tofu (TOE-foo). A custard-like product made from soybeans. (Ch. 32)

toss. To tumble a mixture, such as salad, very lightly. (Ch. 15)

translucent. Semi-clear. Raw fish is translucent. (Ch. 34)

tumblers. Beverage glasses without stems. (Ch. 25)

U V

unit price. Cost per ounce, pound, item, or other unit. (Ch. 12)

unsaturated fats. Fats that tend to help lower the amount of *cholesterol* in the blood. Found mainly in vegetable oils, except the tropical oils (coconut, palm, and palm kernel). (Ch. 5)

vacuum bottle. Insulated bottle that keeps foods at their original temperature. (Ch. 26)

vegan. Someone who eats only foods from plant sources. (Ch. 9)

W X Y Z

water-soluble vitamins. The B vitamins and vitamin C, which can mix only with water. (Ch. 5)

wellness. Taking steps toward your own good health—physical, emotional, and mental. (Ch. 4)

whey. The liquid that is separated from the *curd* after milk has been thickened. (Ch. 28)

whip. To add air and increase volume by *beating* food rapidly. (Ch. 15)

whole grain products. Products in which all parts of the grain kernel are used. (Ch. 29)

wholesale cuts. Large sections of a meat animal; later divided into *retail cuts*. (Ch. 35)

wok. A large pan with a rounded bottom; used to *stir-fry*. (Ch. 39)

work plan. A list of what you have to do to prepare food. (Ch. 22)

yield. The amount or number of servings that a *recipe* makes. (Ch. 15)

CREDITS

American Egg Board, 294 (t)

Ann's Portrait Designs/Ann Garvin, 6(r), 7(b), 56 (t), 62, 64 (t), 65 (t), 66 (t), 67 (t), 68 (t), 69, 77, 79 (b), 88, 93, 106, 109 (b), 110 (b) 111 (tl, bl, r), 112, 113 (b), 114 (tr, mr, bl, bm), 116, 118, 119,120, 121, 122, 123, 126, 127 (tr), 129, 130, 131 (b), 133, 134, 135, 137, 138, 139, 140, 141, 155 (t), 169 (b), 175 (b), 177, 178, 183, 187, 193 (b), 194 (tl, tr), 195 (br), 201 (t), 203, 205, 208 (t), 217 (t), 218 (t), 220, 224, 244, 250, 263 (t), 265, 266, 273, 275, 287 (t), 290, 307, 309, 317, 319, 320, 323, 325, 328 (b), 330 (t), 331, 339, 349 (b), 352, 354 (b), 355, 360, 361, 362, 364, 366, 367, 368 (b)

Arnold & Brown, 186, 296 (b)

Artesville, 42 (bl), 54, 63, 70, 241, 242, 302, 329
> Burke/Triolo, 39 (tr/mr-2), 40 (ml/r), 41 (tl/r), 42 (br), 43, 78, 84, 90, 108, 214, 222, 292, 332

Berry, Keith M., 73

Burns, Angela, 132 (b), 199, 269, 270 (t-5, b), 274 (b), 280 (t), 282, 345, 354 (a), 365

California Dry Bean Advisory Board, 249 (tm, tr, ml, bl)

Circle Design, (infographic/food group design), 39, 64, 65, 66, 67, 68, 117, 136, 167, 196-197, 234, 333, 355
> Carol Spengel, 131 (t), 243 (t), 246, 251 (t), 253, 296 (t, m), 297, 300 (t, m), 305, 349 (t), 353

Courtney's, 81

Denton High School/Denton, TX, 177, 178, throughout

Eating Disorders Awareness & Prevention, Inc., Seattle, 86

Envision
> Mattei, George. 193 (t)
> Needham, Steven, 71

FoodPix, 10, 40 (tr), 42 (tr), 102 (ml), 204, 225 (t), 228, 240, 256, 268, 270 (ml, mm), 279, 310 (t), 316, 340, 358, 368 (t)
> Burke/Triolo, 218 (b), 278
> Kemmelkamp, Ron, 233 (bl)
> Lestart, Brian, 348
> Vereen, Jackson, 263 (b)
> Pohuski, Michael, 270 (mr)

FPG International, LLC
> Johnson, Richard, 181
> Malyszko, Mike, 60

Frazier, David R./Photolibrary, Inc., 13, 14(br), 15 (m), 22 (br), 23 (br), 45, 184

Grand Illusions/Rick Burdett, 196-197

Greenberg, Marshall R., 11 (b), 48, 79 (t), 87, 94, 95, 96, 104, 105 (tl-2), 117, 125, 136 (b), 145, 162, 163, 168, 173, 182 (t), 188, 189 (tl), 190 (m), 206, 207, 223, 233 (br), 257, 258 (b), 261, 264, 285, 304, 326, 346

Henson, Linda, 180(m)

International Stock
> Cotton, Julian, 21 (br)
> Hollenbeck Photography, 33

Liaison Agency, Inc.
> Kozyra, James, 322
> Peterson, Sid, 185
> Wilson, James D., 36

Masterfile/Lloyd Sutton, 180(b)

Maytag, 102 (br)

McIntosh Ink, Inc./Jon McIntosh, 12, 27, 37, 74, 82 (b), 91, 99, 128, (br), 148 (t), 153, 155 (b), 158, 161, 165, 166, 167, 198

Midwest Stock/Eric Berndt, 249 (mr, br)

Mishima Photography, 38 (t), 39 (blocks), 49, 97, 113 (t), 114 (br), 182 (ml), 190 (l, r), 194 (br), 202, 111 (3-l), 114 (br), 128 (t), 142, 143, 146, 147, 148 (b), 149, 151, 152(tr), 175 (t), 215 (b), 216, 225 (b), 226 (t), 249 (tl), 258 (t), 280 (b), 334

National Fish & Seafood Council, 277

Nebraska Dry Bean Commission, 243 (b), 251 (b)

Phelps, Brent, 127 (m) 169 (t), 195 (tr), 208 (b), 226 (b), 227 (m), 281, 293 (t), 300 (br), 303, 330 (b)

Photo Researchers/Science Source/Leonard Lessin, 34

Purcell, Elizabeth, 295 (t)

Santa Monica High School, throughout

Seabright, William & Associates, 232, 234, 236, 238(t)

Shanahan, Judith, 51, 103, 156, 157 (b), 209, 210, 211, 213, 217 (b), 230, 235, 238 (b), 252, 288, 289, 294 (b), 295 (b, 298, 306, 313, 321, 327, 336 (t), 344, 359

Stockbyte, 42 (m), 363

StockFood America
    Eising, 59
    Maxmillian Stock, 237
    Schieren, 39 (ml), 233 (t)

The Stock Market
    Clifford, Geoffrey/Equinox, 25
    Erickson, Jim, 23 (t)
    Feingersh, Jon, 41 (br)

Henley, John, 38 (b)
Imaggio/Kalich, 32
Langley, David, 24 (b)
Levine, Rob, 15 (tr), 19
McCarthy, Tom & DeeAnn, 35, 44, 75
Olson, John, 22 (tl)
Palaez, Jose, 29 (t), 30,
Stewart, Tom, 28, 55
Stoecklin, David, 53
Ury, Brandy M., 29 (b)
Welzeaba, John, 85
Zaruba, Jeff, 20

Stoecker, Jeff, 61

Superstock, 58

Table Manners, throughout

Underwriters Laboratory, Inc., 107

USDA, 61

Von's Market, 23 (m), 92, 99, 100

White, Dana/Dana White Productions, 4, 5, 6(l), 7 (t), 11 (t), 14 (m), 15 (br), 16, 17, 18, 21 (tr &m), 23 (m), 24 (t), 26, 46, 52, 56 (b), 57, 64 (b), 65 (b), 66 (b), 67 (b), 68 (b), 72, 80, 81, 82 (t), 83, 86, 92, 98, 99, 100, 101, 105 (br), 109 (l, r), 110 (tl), 114 (tl), 115, 124, 127 (br), 132 (t), 136 (t), 144, 150, 152 (bl), 154, 157 (t), 159, 160, 164, 170, 172, 174, 176, 179, 189 (br), 191, 192, 197 (tr), 200, 201 (b), 215 (t), 247, 248, 260, 274 (t), 283, 284, 287 (b), 293 (b), 310 (b), 312, 314, 324, 328 (t), 333, 336 (b), 337, 338, 341, 342, 351

Text Design: Seabright & Associates

Cover: DesignNet/FoodPix

Chapter Opening/Design Element Art: Mary Lynn Blasutta

INDEX